CONVERSIONS

by George P. Elliott

AMONG THE DANGS

FROM THE BERKELEY HILLS

AN HOUR OF LAST THINGS

IN THE WORLD

DAVID KNUDSEN

PARKTILDEN VILLAGE

A PIECE OF LETTUCE

CONVERSIONS

CONVERSIONS

Literature and the Modernist Deviation

GEORGE P. ELLIOTT

E. P. DUTTON & CO., INC. | NEW YORK | 1971

FIRST EDITION

Published simultaneously in Canada
by Clarke, Irwin & Company Limited, Toronto and Vancouver

Library of Congress Catalog Card Number: 74-158579
SBN 0-525-08575-0

Certain of the essays in this volume made their first appearance, in somewhat different form, in the following publications:

"Noah Greenberg," *Commentary* (July 1966)

"Two Good Novels and an Oversized God," *Rediscoveries,* edited by David Madden (New York: Crown Publishers, 1971)

"Science and the Profession of Literature," *The Public Interest* (Summer 1966 and Spring 1969) and *The Atlantic Monthly* (September 1971)

"Teaching Writing," *College English* (November 1969)

"The Novelist as Meddler," *Virginia Quarterly Review* (Winter 1964)

"The Person of the Maker," *Experience in the Novel,* edited by Roy Harvey Pearce (New York: Columbia University Press, 1968)

"Discovering the Dangs," *Afterwords,* edited by Thomas McCormack (New York: Harper & Row, 1969)

"Confessions of a Repentant Symposiast," *The Nation* (September 15, 1969)

"Against Pornography," *Harper's Magazine* (March 1965)

"Revolution Instead," *The Public Interest* (Summer 1970)

"Never *Nothing,*" *Harper's Magazine* (September 1970)

To W. D. Snodgrass
who helped many of these ideas find their forms

Contents

I

Kicking Some Modern Habits

Two centuries ago with the Enlightenment, there began a great age which boasted of its modernity and for which the name Modern seems to me as fitting as any other, for during this period Now and the New came to be worshiped as they had never been worshiped before. Modernism substituted science for religion, technology for magic, democracy for monarchy, change for tradition, and progress for salvation. It challenged all authorities, accepting only the few that could withstand the assaults of rational criticism; as a consequence, rebellion became more orthodox than obedience. God was the essence of what Modernism opposed: He is eternal; He is outside of nature and beyond understanding; He is a king who ought to be obeyed, for His commands are always right. To deal with the vexing problem of art, Modernism employed aesthetics. That is, instead of seeing art as a form of magic and an artist as a wizard arranging physical things so as to affect the souls of others, aesthetics said that a true "object" of art was so pure it had neither moral power nor social function—in effect, was not a necessity but an adornment of life.

If the Modern Age was coming to an end in the 1960s, then the recent and continuing disintegration of music, painting, and sculpture can be thought of as part of the death throes of the old age; similarly, the worldwide disturbances among the intelligent young would be symptomatic of the birth pangs of the new age. In optimistic moods, I see the young these days as kicking some Modern habits—though when I try to understand what habits they may be getting hooked on instead, my feelings are considerably more mixed. In any case, whatever other qualities this unnamed, unshaped age we are entering may have, I hope that it will realize it needs art in order to live.

By denying any life-or-death potency to art, the Modern Age made all true artists, even the few it applauded, feel rejected or neglected, cut off from the body politic. However, because the age prided itself on its liberality, it left artists free to counterattack. Many of the great ones set their lives and best work against their age (as artists in previous epochs had almost never done) and also elevated The Artist as superior to other types of men. When, latterly, Modern society began to accept artists' damning judgment of it along with their idolatrous estimate of themselves, as it was pretty much doing by the 1960s, it was finished.

Nothing could seem less necessary to Byzantines than our Modernist exhortation to *make it new*. For them, an artist's job is to make it, really make it; let the newness take care of itself. To do his work well, the artist needs all the help he can get: conventions, rules, traditions.

The Byzantines wanted, valued, had to have the works that an artist made, but the maker himself they viewed as a cross between an artisan and a geometer. They did not honor The Artist; they hired craftsmen to make articles of use, some lowly, some exalted. Their great churches were the products not of An Artist but of many artworkers, nearly all anonymous. If I am sure of anything, I am sure it is good for the souls of those who make works of art to be paid, not adored, for their products. I also believe that society, for its own health, should use works of art rather than study those who make them.

Though the name and some of the biography of the man who

designed St. Sophia in Constantinople are known and though it is generally agreed that that church is one of the great buildings of the world, I have seen him mentioned as one of the great artists only by Byzantinologists, and I doubt that anyone I know, including the very learned, would recognize the name Anthemius. Justinian chose him to design it because he was the greatest mathematician of the time, and Procopius describes his craft not as architecture but as engineering. He was not An Artist. The building does not express anything personal whatever.

Modernism produced no greater work than *Remembrance of Things Past,* and so long as the book is known Proust's name and personality will also be known and inquired into, as the type of Artist. Yet a marvel of the book is to make us understand, with sympathy and clarity, that Marcel's way and also his world were so wrong that nothing could rescue the man whole; he gave up being himself and became An Artist. Among other things, the profoundest Modern told us, *Don't be like me if you can help it.* Let us honor Proust for his terrible honesty, and then try something different—perhaps something old.

High in the vaulted apse of a church, many smooth-faced bits of colored mineral have been fixed in such a way as to make an image that looks like a stiff young woman staring at you: not a particular woman, not even a possible woman, yet more like a woman than like anything else. What the mosaic projects is an artist's idea of a holy virgin, an idea nearly all the components of which were given him by others (including her name, the Mother of God), and his purpose in making the mosaic is to cause you, by contemplating that idea, to save your soul. The Byzantines believed: *Without feeling this idea and others like it you will perish.*

The first thing I learned about Byzantium was that the Enlightenment considered it one of the maddest blights of the Dark Ages: Christianity the enemy of civilization. At the time I learned this, I was young and eager to lapse from Protestantism, and my intellect thought itself very enlightened: I tried to read Gibbon's *Decline and Fall of the Roman Empire.* However, being already cocksure that Byzantium—which is to say, the Byzantium of the

Enlightenment's imagining—was preposterous, I had little impulse to know much more about it. Moreover, I took no joy in Gibbon's slow, condescending, self-congratulatory prose; I prefer sneer hit-and-run, not heavily hovering as his is. I gave up on him, and forgot about Byzantium.

The next thing I learned about it, years later, was Yeats's two visionary poems. I did not understand "Byzantium," though I thought it a marvel, and "Sailing to Byzantium" inspired in me an intense, obscure awe of a sort that would make a Christian rejoice and a Gibbon wince. But not only was my intellect by then less enlightened than it had been; I was darkening all through, staining.

Later still, having seen a Byzantine-inspired mosaic put together by a woman in California, I went to the Byzantine churches in Venice and Ravenna. Thereafter, I touristed among history books a good deal and collected a trunkful of facts which, isolated, jumbled, are interesting in a believe-it-or-not sort of way but which are of no importance beside what happened to me in those churches. There, I first glimpsed the Byzantium of the Byzantines themselves.

Sometimes mosaicists set tesserae at such angles that if you are too close you see pretty parts and if you are too far you see a bold but lifeless cartoon, whereas if you stand at the right place the separate rays of light converge in you and become a live image in you. So I have read, and it seems to me, when I am in those sacred buildings, that I am penetrated by what those mosaicists figured forth. The reality of Byzantium is what they imagined.

The Byzantines gave ultimate value to Idea. It ruled them, and they ruled by it. Idea never changes; what alters is our always imperfect apprehension of it. The physical world is the body of God, Who is Idea. God's incarnation as a person is for the Byzantines the center that holds all life together, gives it meaning.

Moderns, so far as I can make out, give ultimate value to Energy. They like to transform it, release it, concentrate it. They look for and find it in lifeless matter, live creatures, art, society, their own psyches. The aggressive questions they encourage imply that the asker is going to act upon the world: "How can things be rearranged to suit us better? What can I do to change things?" These are potent questions, they inspire in me fear and trembling, but they are not the one I ask in the dark of night.

That question I also hear rising about me on every side, disguised in a thousand ways—disguised because people hardly even know what this question is, so alien is it to the Modern language of problem setting and problem solving. Kafka knew the question and asked it over and over. In *The Castle*, which is the great allegory of a soul, K, who finds himself exiled in Modernity, Kafka was true to his experience of no answer: the novel was unfinishable, it leaves you unfulfilled. The form in which an Englishman three centuries ago told a tale of that question was this: "What shall I do to be saved?" The anguish with which Bunyan's Christian cried was pure as K's, but it could be, and finally was, relieved with an answer: progress for that pilgrim was the way toward a satisfying answer. In the Modern world, the question echoes, jumbles, fades; progress for the Enlightened is headed in another direction. A person who asks "What shall I do to be saved?" wishes both to act and to be acted upon; Modernism provides no home for him, no way.

America is not just Modern, democratic, materialist, any more than Byzantium was just Christian, hierarchical, idealist. Indeed, these two huge, devious, vigorous, rich empires that would sooner buy off an antagonist than conquer him outright have some things in common—the mobility of individuals and the variety of social groups in both empires; their passion for professional sports; their really staggering self-righteous hypocrisies; their unsteady, unclear, polluted, but enduring sense of mission. Each at its best in its own way, there was no one else better around.

But the elements in them that inspired marvel in others had no more in common than St. Sophia and the first moon trip. Though I video-watched those Americans in their plastic suits step on the moon, I did not imagine myself there with them; the sight did not penetrate me, any more than an "object of art" penetrates one who appreciates it aesthetically. But St. Sophia, when I went into it and looked, came into me.

A metaphor for our worst is entropy. All energy is distributed uniformly, attraction and repulsion cancel out, there can be no movement. Its social form is that egalitarianism which is total democracy and the avowed goal of socialism: justice as equality.

A metaphor for the Byzantine worst is catatonia. Idea controls matter absolutely, all things are ranked as they are supposed to be, there is no cause for movement. Its social form is that pyramidal bureaucracy which is the perfection of absolutist authority: justice as subordination.

For artists, all kinds of prolonged stasis are inimical, but the first of these two varieties is even worse than the second, because it needs artists less. The purest entropic art is aleatory or lawless music, sounds selected by chance and played in random sequence; whatever the excellence of such music, no artist is needed to make it, only computers and Moogs. Hierarchical art is frozen, law locked, but, at least in mosaic, it can nevertheless incarnate great spiritual vitality which can come only from (or through) an artist.

You stand in a church moving your gaze over a mosaic high on the vault across from you. It has been there a month, a century, twelve hundred years; no matter how long. It has changed, and seemingly can change, no more than can the laws of geometry in obedience to which it was composed, or the idea which explains the color of the background, or God the Father Whom the image represents. Yet, without moving, it acts upon and within you. As the light alters in intensity and quality, the picture continues to act on you, motionlessly various. To look at it is to participate in an action, is a rite of incarnation, is a way of taking communion. The mosaicist is as essential to the mosaic as the dancer to the dance.

I, a storyteller, a craftsman working in an art that needs and uses moving time, would have hated to be prisoned in the rigidities of Byzantinism. All the same, I prefer that stone system which could be used against itself to the mud nonsystem which I feel to be the threat of Modern progress toward homogenization. The best an artist can do with congealed mud, with plastic, is not good enough.

I grew up in Modernism, and now, a straddler who does not know what the new world is going to be like, I imagine one which needs art to be and commissions artmakers to make it: *We want, we have use for, what only you can give us.* Needed, used, art has a chance of striving again for elegance, delight, celebration, beauty, as it has pretty much ceased to do in recent years but as it always does when not turned aside from its natural courses.

2

Noah Greenberg

Noah Greenberg, at the age of forty-six, suddenly died of a heart attack. In my experience, everyone who knew him liked him. He was short on malice, and he stood in no one's way. Everyone who knew his work with the New York Pro Musica admired it. He did not do his work in order to gain fame and all that, but being a man of large appetite, he enjoyed the fame and all that when they came along because of the work he did—he did more than any other American to propagate a taste for Renaissance and medieval music. As an artist he was full of that confidence which comes from work well done and more good work yet to do, and he strove for excellence. He was a good-sized, substantial man with a husky voice and open laugh; he was warm, given to praise rather than blame, patient in the long haul but irritable now and then, delicate of understanding, respectful of you and obliging your respect of him, which is to say that he practiced courtesy; and occasionally, in a slight pulling back of the head or a coolness in the voice, he was capable, this former able-bodied seaman and union organizer, of a touch of that aristocratic hauteur which one sometimes glimpses, in our bourgeois democracy, among the *grands seigneurs* of art and mind. For such reasons, and because I too am about that age and have no history of heart trouble, but especially because I loved him, his death has set me thinking again about some last things.

Twenty-two centuries ago a Hebrew in an age of oppression wrote the miraculous story of a prophet named Daniel as though it were the history of events that had taken place three centuries earlier when the Jews were in Babylonian bondage. What actually happened to Daniel, if there was a Daniel, cannot now be known, just as it cannot be known how much of the story the man who wrote it invented and how much retold. Not that either of these matters: the actual is real only when it is imagined. All of the actual can be imagined only by God, but men can imagine some of it. The ancient Jews, being moral in bent rather than aesthetic or scientific or metaphysical, thought there was no better way to understand God's mind than by imagining what had happened to them: their holy book is mostly stories told as histories. Who told the story of Daniel never did matter except to the teller himself, only that it was told well. Likewise, neither believing Jews nor their principal heretics, Christians, care that the story is beautiful as much as that it is told in such a way as to afford a true glimpse into God's mind.

In the middle of the twelfth century, some young people in Beauvais made a play out of the story of Daniel and put it on at Christmastime in one of the churches. It was so well liked that it was put on every Christmas season for the next century. Who had the idea in the first place, who wrote the words, who composed or chose the music, who designed the costumes and banners, who told the performers what to do and where and when to do it, whether they were used to seeing plays like this one and if so how they modified what they were used to seeing, how the production changed over the century it endured, how much they invented and how much borrowed and adapted—all this we know little or nothing about because they did not think such matters important enough to chronicle. In good part they put on the play for much the same reason the first storyteller told the story, that their people might, knowing what happened to Daniel, know God's will; but also in part they did it for the greater glory of God. Like the makers of the great cathedrals, they made their play as marvelous as they could in order to glorify God the more.

In the mid-1950s, it occurred to Noah Greenberg, as apparently it had occurred to no one for seven centuries, that he and the Pro Musica group he had brought together a few years earlier might put on *The Play of Daniel* again. He did not do it in order to bring the people of New York into a better connection with the God of Jews and Christians. He had been born and raised a Jew, but in his youth had accepted the rationalistic Jewish-Christian heresy, socialism, and especially Trotsky's faction of the schism. He lived by this belief till he was thirty or so. (He was perhaps never an exclusive True Believer. Once at a summer retreat for radicals, a friend found Noah halfway to one of the endless lectures and discussion meetings. He was swinging a gate. "Come on! We're late! What are you doing? Hurry!" "Listen," said Noah giving the gate another swing, "listen to that C sharp." Then he went along.) But if he did not put on the play for a religious reason, everyone who knew him is sure that neither did he think of doing it for money or for his own aggrandizement. What mattered most was for the job to be done well, whoever did it; he had to do it, for his own satisfaction to be sure, but also because if he didn't nobody else would. His name will be attached to this event for as long as the event is known, which will be, at least latently, for as long as our libraries last. But this is none of his doing; it is because we venerate facts, record them, and preserve the records.

As we accelerate change and subvert tradition, thereby stripping ourselves of strong protection against time; as we threaten ourselves with extinction, thereby providing time with a whip of fear, our fear that we may put an end not just to ourselves who shall die in any case but to time, which we did not make and must have, which we cannot imagine unmaking but may unmake nonetheless; as we cease to do things for the purpose of connecting with God, thereby insulting the timeless in time; as we set ourselves deadlines which to meet is to survive, little false deaths, little false immortalities, we tend to make facts of things and then to preserve them. But we do more than preserve; we recover, too, and more than facts. The Byzantines were great perpetuators, but we of all men are the greatest recoverers and preservers; and as more of our own art becomes chancy, empty of meaning, and repellent, and as the forms of our social life blot and blur, we especially recover and preserve beautiful art.

What was left of *The Play of Daniel*, guarded by scholars, was one manuscript: a text of medieval Latin words and a simple musical notation, one note for each syllable. From various sources, a modern producer could gleam odds and ends of information which would permit him to guess intelligently at how to go about putting the play on—to guess which instruments to use, how, where, how many; how the singing was to be done, to what tempo, at what pitch, in what rhythm, how loud; from a few words of description here and there and especially from the rubrics on the manuscript of *Daniel*, the mode of staging; from some illustrations in paintings and drawings, the costume designs; how the original congregation, who did not understand Latin, could know what was supposed to be going on in each scene; how many actor-singers to use, what kind of voices. Not all the tunes and texts of *Daniel* were completely written out, for the scribe assumed his reader's knowledge of the most familiar; scholars helped Noah piece these out as best they could.

In other words, the given from which Noah set about to re-create the play was less in quantity, and no more essential in kind, than Milton's given (a story and an old form) when he set about writing *Paradise Lost*. Picasso in the Trocadero museum looking at African masks for the first time; Giorgio Strehler in Milano after the Second World War staging with his Piccolo Teatro Goldoni's *The Servant of Two Masters* as he imagined a commedia dell'arte troupe would have done it; the group of Florentines gathered in the house of Count Bardi, in the last years of the sixteenth century, inventing grand opera by trying to imagine Greek tragedy; Michelangelo in the Belvedere gardens studying Apollo, recently hoisted into the light of day after having been buried for many many centuries; why should an artist give a thought to expressing the spirit of his age? It's hard enough to make something beautiful, even with a great old model to go by, without taking on the spirit of the age too.

A few years ago Noah played host one day to the musicians of the Japanese Imperial Court, who were in New York giving concerts of ancient music, *gagaku,* the performance of which survives solely in this one group. After the politenesses had been exchanged, the Japanese begged permission to ask one question. A bit dismayed at the thought of what these total musicians might ask (they could play jazz and Beethoven quartets with equal expertness), Noah of course granted permission. Through the interpreter they asked, with great intensity, leaning forward for the answer, "Do you feel decadent?" As Noah recounted this anecdote, he obviously thought it both silly and too damned bad that such a question should be gnawing at people whose lives were devoted, under whatever auspices, no matter what the age might be up to, to making superb beauty, most especially since, if they did not continue to make and remake it, it would vanish, never to be reconstructed.

It was the music that first drew Noah to the play. He had been rummaging for medieval music for his Pro Musica group to perform, and he came on the bare notes of this play. By then, he had developed a way for his singers to realize such notation in sound, to make it into music; but these notes for these words made a music which he knew, from performing excerpts from the play in concert form, to be insufficient by itself. Just how insufficient, you can hear by listening to the Pro Musica record of the play, reading the text along with it. Good as it is, you need more. He needed more. There was no one for him to turn to to give him much more, as there would have been for *Otello* or the Gregorian Mass for Easter Sunday. He had to make it himself, without knowing ahead of time what it was he was going to make.

The music. When I hear it isolated from the rest of the play, I know it is the most important part of the whole, but when I am there as the play is in being, all the other parts seem essential too, the costumes, the performers' motions, the processions, the contrasts. Besides, one thing is not more essential than another; an essential is absolute, however big, however small. I saw the play four times (each time slightly altered, in most respects for the better), and I went to some rehearsals. Even so, I cannot now, listening to the record, really imagine what I remember of the performance. The thought that it might never be again makes me feel, when I listen to the recording, as a Greek might have felt looking at the fallen torso of a god he had known alive in a temple —a beautiful torso, to be sure, and the biggest, most important part of the whole statue, but armless, legless, castrated, the paint washed off, the great head noseless and lying to one side.

Noah went to the scholars: American, French, British; art historians, medievalists, musicologists, theatre historians. Only from them and from their books and manuscripts could he learn what was to be known about medieval music-drama. It was from talking with Meyer Schapiro, for example, that he got two ideas about staging *Daniel:* first, the actors' costumes should be bold and full of strong contrasts and their movements should sweep from pose to pose; and second, a text in English should be recited before each scene so that the audience might understand what was being represented. He executed the first of these with the assistance of the stage director, Nikos Psacharopoulos, and he got W. H. Auden to write the narrative—of all living poets the most competent for such a job, Auden wrote alliterative staves suggesting Middle English poetry. He found in Lincoln Kirstein, who had had long experience with the New York City Ballet, an artistic director to whom he gave quite a free hand in finding and overseeing costume designs and designers. He arranged the music himself, under advisement from scholars, and directed who should sing what and who play what on which instruments and when. The other directors and artists had ideas he would not have had and of course they were necessary to execute his and their own ideas. Nevertheless, to the limits of the possible and the courteous —and perhaps a time or two beyond these limits—he was the final arbiter of every idea and of the realization of every idea proposed for the making of the play, whoever first advanced it, himself included.

He went to work in the knowledge that his production could

not be the same as the original one. For example, the boys in the boys' choir he used, from the Episcopal Church of the Transfiguration, sing like nineteenth-century British angels; but he speculated that the boys in twelfth-century France might have sung less in the Anglican style than in controlled shrill cries, as he had heard Spanish boys sing. Even if full records existed of the original performance, it could not be duplicated: Balanchine had said he was unable to re-create one of his old ballets from studying a movie of it. Moreover, Noah knew that, even if the production were a duplication of the original, it would have to have a profoundly different effect on its audience. Our kings do not rule; our belief in miracles is tenuous at best; no American who reads the Bible as historically literal would be likely to go to a performance of a play in Catholic Latin; the music, the costumes, the processions, the props, the instruments, heraldic emblems, Latin spoken anywhere but in the liturgy and not much there, the bold simple contrasts, all these, which were more or less familiar to the original audience, are to us strange enough to run the risk of being quaint and therefore irrelevantly charming or so peculiar as to distance us too far from the play. Noah compromised. He used electric lighting, but also candles. In some respects, his use of instruments is perhaps less medieval than baroque. We expect little more than mortarboards and black gowns from a procession, and the Pro Musica *Daniel* seems gorgeous to us; whereas familiarity with banners, bright robes, and emblems had heightened the medieval expectations of a procession, and the original *Daniel* was, conceivably, far more gorgeous than his. Compromise well employed is a matter of proportion.

Going to the scholars, making and buying costumes, props, and stage equipment, renting a place to rehearse, paying the performers at Musicians Union scale during rehearsals, meeting his own family expenses, all cost. He went to the foundations and to the rich, especially to Lincoln Kirstein, the most important patron of living art in our national history. (After eight years of continuously successful performance, with costumes and props made and paid for, in a nearly rent-free church, charging standard off-Broadway admission prices, the company broke even only if all the tickets were sold for all the performances.)

Obviously the suitable place to put on a medieval religious play is in a medieval church. In Manhattan, the Metropolitan Museum's synthetic building, The Cloisters, consists of chapels and rooms transplanted from medieval churches and monasteries. Those stone rooms are right for the small sounds of the instruments—such as psaltery, minstrel's harp, straight trumpet, vielle, recorders, rebec—and the singers' not large voices.

There, in the Romanesque Hall, on January 2, 1958, to a small invited audience, *The Play of Daniel* was performed for the first time in six centuries. Who but musical and scholarly amateurs, and some friends, would care about such an event? Excellence, not popularity, was what Noah was after. But it turned out that those who attended this and the performances on the following days, spread the word fast and hot. Success came anyway—the success that often comes yapping on the heels of excellence but that Noah never allowed close enough to trip him up.

In 1960 the State Department sent the company to Europe, where *Daniel* was performed thirty-seven times, in churches and shrines in France, England, and Italy, and everywhere acclaimed —although a Communist newspaper in Italy reproved the singers for mispronouncing some Medieval Church Latin, especially for not rolling the initial R's hard enough.

For a while after *Daniel*'s success, Noah thought of staging Skelton's morality play *Magnificence*. But he could not find enough responsive enthusiasm in others to go ahead. He could have brought together and arranged contemporaneous music suitable for the play, and he probably could have bulled a production through. But, resolved to work only with people who genuinely wanted to make what he wanted to make, he dropped the project. He turned to two short, twelfth-century church plays which survived only in a manuscript in the Orleans Municipal Library, and he put them together, along with some other thirteenth-century music, especially the song for the opening procession, to form *The Play of Herod*. This was first put on in the Fuentidueña Chapel of The Cloisters in December 1963. *Herod* is less dramatic than *Daniel* but more lyrical, and even more beautiful. Rachel's lament over the slain innocents is surely one of the great dramatic arias; yet, broken off from the performance and played on a record, this lament sounds diminished, less moving; it is part of a whole essential to the part.

For the next production, he had planned an evening of Italian Renaissance court drama, two musical entertainments to be performed with jugglers, acrobats, and actors as well as singers, in the commedia dell'arte manner as he imagined it. He was alive with questions of where and who and how, when he dropped dead.

Somehow, the notion has got around that a work of art that is highly time-resistant is for that reason superior to one that perishes instantly—"Not marble, nor the gilded monuments/ Of princes, shall outlive this powerful rhyme." But if anything of Shakespeare's outlives the pyramids, the Taj Mahal, and the English language, it is less likely to be the sonnets, whose publication he attended to, than the plays, which he did not so much as proofread. *Lear* is only as it is performed and experienced, but its words, so long as they exist physically, will probably see to it that it will be reincarnated, even in translation, again and again in time to come. For beauty is only as it is known and felt. During the score upon score of centuries when nobody was in the Lascaux caves looking, those paintings were not works of beauty but pigment on rock.

Not only have we mixed up durability with excellence, we have split the performing arts off from the creative, which in some fussy way we think of as immortal; and though the performers are the ones we applaud loudest and pay highest, we have assigned a lower status to them and even to those who create solely for performance. But when you think of Noah Greenberg or George Balanchine or Marcel Marceau, this practical, sensible separation and ranking seems false, or falsely labeled. To assess how much of the production of *Daniel* was creative and how much performing is as profitless as to assess how much Noah contributed to the whole performance, how much A contributed, how much B, C, D, and so on, or to assess its relation to the spirit of its age and of our age. Such games have no application to the play, but they do have the power, if allowed, to interfere with experiencing it.

Timing is of the essence of good performance; musicians are said to keep time; and there is no dodging the fact that a performed work of art must be made fresh each time, and that it must have a responsive audience, in order to be. But, just because what live performers do is so risky and fragile, because their mistakes cannot be recalled, our joy when they come through is enormous: time has been used against itself, and Now is so filled that what was and what is to be have fallen away for a while. In our gratitude to performers who have done this, we forget notions about how the best art should be time-impervious, "creative," and give them a warm, special love. They have filled Now for us; we were essential to the doing; we did it too. Because a performance is about to die, we are quick to its life with an intensity we do not commonly feel for a temple, a poem, or a mask; these, because they were made once, we do not think of as needing to be made again and again—as though beauty were in the thing, not in the thing known.

Is the gold and ivory *Athena Parthenos* that Phidias made superior to Aeschylus's original production of *The Oresteia*, which could exist only once? But the statue was destroyed, and at least the words of the play survive. . . . What a lot of nonsense such speculations dwindle into. In the kingdom of true art, to paraphrase Blake, there is no competition.

Noah was, as one who makes through performances must be, lucky, above all lucky in those he worked with. There was a patron for him to go to, as there almost certainly would not have been thirty years earlier. There were scholars he could find to tell him what he had to know, as there would not have been a century earlier (the text of *Daniel* was first published in 1861 in a French collection of medieval liturgical plays). There were good designers. There were the Pro Musica musicians, who had a special loyalty to him; for example, the countertenor Russell Oberlin had studied at Juilliard but did not know, till Noah found him and took him to it, of the existence of this ancient music which especially needed a voice of his timbre and range.

And in his capacity as theatrical producer, Noah was lucky that he had to use singers without training as actors rather than, as a musical comedy producer often must, actors ill trained to sing. He was gifted and dedicated, he worked well with others—he could not work without them—and he produced two superb dramatic performances, the two best I know of by Americans. But I doubt that he could have done it with nearly any of the actors available to him here and now: for *Daniel* and *Herod*, his singers acted better than most American actors would have. Our actors have been trained in an inward, psychological style. They do not, most of them, put their trust in gestures as a mime must, or in the body's motions as a dancer must, or in sounds as composer and musician must, or in words as the playwright must do and as he wants the actors to. They put their trust each primarily in himself, his own feelings, his own sincerity. They must of course ask the external questions "What do these words mean?" and "What does this character mean by these words on this occasion?" But they prefer the internal question, "What do I mean?" It is an acting style that has proved itself adequate within the narrow confines of psychological realistic drama dealing with alienation, perversion, and the lusts. Not even Noah could have gotten actors, as he got his singers, to put much of their trust in things totally outside themselves, and especially in one another, each in all the others.

Socialists are moved to political action by a dream of community, but, by 1950 or so when Noah dropped out of the movement, it was difficult for Americans to trust that way to the dream, to trust any political way to it. Art offers a dream of communion—which is not the same as community but like it, near it, and realizable—and people working together to make a performance also make a small, fragile community. I would guess that a dream of community was what united the disparate halves of Noah's professional life. Among twelfth-century Frenchmen the dream of community was vivid. Their way to it was religious and his was secular, but their religion included art: of all those who knew that the words and notes of *Daniel* survived, it was Noah Greenberg, lover of beauty, who seized the great good luck of remaking it for the first time. He was as faithful to what was known of the original performance as he could be, not out of antiquarian zeal, not out of a museum keeper's scrupulosity, not only, though in large part, because he thought that that style was the best, the most beautiful. He did it also, perhaps, because he felt something like what those medieval French Catholic young people were aspiring to when they first made the play, and he wanted to share the feeling, the aspiration. Like them in making this performance he put his trust in others: in them to begin with, in their notes primarily but also in what he imagined of their performance; then in his assistants to help him imagine; finally in his performers to realize what he had imagined. And I imagine that he invested his trust in all those others, and especially in those notes, in the faith they had power to join some people together for a little while now and again.

3

Two Good Novels and an Oversized God

In 1940, Ramon Sender's *A Man's Place* was published in the United States. The publisher, Duell, Sloan, and Pearce, was respectable; Sender had a substantial reputation as a novelist, both here and abroad; the translation, by Oliver La Farge, was admirable; the book got a good many favorable reviews. And it has scarcely been heard of since. (For example, the copy in the Cornell University library was checked out ten times during the first four months, three times in 1952, and not again till 1968.) In 1954, Jean Giono's *The Horseman on the Roof* was published here. Again, reputable publisher (Knopf), respected author, excellent translation (by Jonathan Griffin), and decent reviews. And again, near silence. So far as American literary discussion has been going, it is as though these two novels had never been. I am referring not to the routine annihilators whom no book could, or at least does, deflect from their casual chant *The novel is dead*, but to those who care about fiction, read it, like to talk about it, wish it well.

I not only liked both these novels when I first read them and continue to like them on rereading; I think they are minor masterpieces, in the range with such esteemed works as Fitzgerald's *The Great Gatsby*, Gide's *Strait Is the Gate*, Mann's *Felix Krull*, or Greene's *The Labyrinthine Ways*. Whereupon out comes the jeer-gun: "Okay, wise guy, so you're right and everybody else is wrong. How come?"

I have a theory. In these books, Sender and Giono did not do homage to the great god Zeitgeist. Not only did they neglect honoring him; they did not even set out to flout him—flouting, after all, is an admission of importance. They simply behaved as though he were of no great consequence, no more than he had been before Hegel puffed him up. (Similarly, in more recent times, after Wilhelm Reich did his puff job on the orgasm, literary adepts of the new cult of Sex ignore any novelist who continues to treat orgasm as no more than he used to be, a bush god, the jolliest satyr of the bush.)

Before the Enlightenment and all that, Zeitgeist used to be known as the age ("not of an age, but for all time"), and the age was the liveliest, trickiest manifestation of the great god History. The historical religions, Judaism and Christianity, studied History in order to discover the will of God; historical philosophies sought in History the absolutes of man's nature. Then mighty Zeitgeist sprang forth shouting *God is dead, Everything is relative, I am where the action is*, and the nations bowed before him. His cult is known as social science (in the new pantheon, Science is so much the biggest god that his name is appropriated to all sorts of odd endeavors, Christian Science, for example), and the main occupation of social scientists is keeping tabs on Zeitgeist, for he is a god of many guises, many avatars. Uncle Tom, now a contemptuous term for a conservative American black, was a century ago a sympathetic Negro victim in a novel so radical that Z let it be thought that *Uncle Tom's Cabin* was a cause of our Civil War. His votaries have little regard for customs: at schools, our children are now taught current events or civics with the same seriousness with which formerly they were taught manners at home. What is more shameful for a true modern than falling behind, not keeping up, being out of date, out of fashion?

To artists in general Zeitgeist says, not *Make it beautiful*, but *Make it new* (think of fashionable Shakespeare productions, and Jan Kott's *Shakespeare Our Contemporary*). The large statue of an Etruscan warrior that used to be displayed in the Metropolitan Museum was generally agreed to be handsome; but then they discovered that, instead of the Etruscan spirit's having seized some anonymous sculptor to express itself through, this statue had been faked in the twentieth century for money by a jerk who was not even a proper Artist. (During the Enlightenment, divine Art acquired a new, magnifying attribute, *aesthetics;* currently, though not as powerful as Science, Art is worshiped with more fervor.) Now, they won't let us look at that statue any more (to Zeitgeist, whether a work of art gives pleasure and is beautiful is secondary to whether it reveals him). Instead, they display big plastic hamburgers and unadorned gray boxes for us to look at, and when the City of New York a few years ago paid a sculptor to have a hole dug in Central Park, put in it a nonstatue of another of the transformed deities Nothing, and then have the dirt put back in the hole, *The Times* found this amusing. Myself, I miss that warrior.

To novelists in particular, Zeitgeist says *Reveal Thou Me*, and of course they do. In fact, they were doing it before he told them to. They can't help doing it, at least a little. A *novel* brings *news* of the subtlest ways people are connected, and not even sociology and psychology between them can beat fiction at that game. If a novelist is to do much, he must know custom more intimately than scholarship and invention between them can achieve, and because he must draw upon his own social experience, local in time and place, he more than any other kind of artist is limited by his age: it is inconceivable that a novel could be faked that was both as good as that Etruscan warrior and as remote from the artist's own culture. So, one of the best ways to find out what Zeitgeist is like in any given locale is to read good novels; but that does not mean that novelists necessarily adore him, write in order to reveal him or even to understand him. Maybe a novelist is telling a story of his growing up, and uses the age, as he uses his language, not just because he has to but also because he likes to—certainly not because he thinks it his holy duty to.

Z's literary avatar is "modernism" and to literary critics he says,

If it's good it's modernist. (By "it" is meant a work of literature written in the past century and a half or two, and "modernist" is the negative of "traditional," its counter, its anti.) Many do not heed Zeitgeist, but in New York it is hard not to. For American intellectuals, New York is the holy city of the cult, to which all go at least once to make a salaam or two and where many stay. Irving Howe, a New Yorker by birth, is one of the best critics in the country, but also a true believer—not quite a zealot and certainly not a fanatic: a true, but intelligent and, therefore, saddened believer. Recently in *Literary Modernism* he gathered essays by various critics and wrote for the collection an introduction which amounts to a brief memorial to the movement now in its decline. When he and the others are speaking of such counter or anti writers as Baudelaire, Kafka, and Joyce, they are illuminating, for there is no conflict of interests. But Z is an imperialistic god, inspiring missionary fervor in his followers. Modernist critics herd such doubtful writers as Rilke, Yeats, and Faulkner into their fold—even Frost, though he not only scanned, rhymed, and never innovated, but liked to write about goofy country folk who hardly knew what century they were in. But it's a strain to get them in, as you can see by the effort it cost Robert Brustein to incorporate Chekhov as a true member of his *Theater of Revolt;* it feels pretty clear from reading the book that Brustein's main reason for including Chekhov was plain love. When the conflict of interests becomes acute, what do modernist critics do? Mostly they say as little as possible. For example, in another recent essay Howe displays great admiration for Hardy, for whose modernism he makes no claim. What do modernists do about *War and Peace?* It is, beyond serious dispute, one of the wonders of the ages, and it was published just a century ago when modernism was in the prime of youth; but Tolstoy is downright embarrassing when he blathers about History. They just don't mention it any more than they have to, preferring to talk about *The Death of Ivan Ilych*, in which Tolstoy had the minimum decency to blast the bourgeoisie. The result of such emphasis is that good modernist critics seem to obey the god's monopolistic injunction. However, if you think about it, you realize they know that the great tradition has remained alive and moderately well (though not in New York) throughout the duration of the movement. "Modernism will not come to an end," as Howe put it. "What awaits it is publicity and sensation, the kind of savage parody which may indeed be the only fate worse than death." I would join him in his mourning for the passing of literary modernism—it produced some marvels, no arguing that—except that I see publicity itself as Zeitgeist in his purest, most cannibalistic avatar.

I suspect, though I am not quite sure of this, that a novel written in obedience to Zeitgeist's command to reveal him, make it new, be modernist, revolt, will not amount to much; the best form for that enterprise, it seems to me, is journalism (think of Orwell's fiction and then of his superb journalistic essays). Norman Podhoretz is a prime devotee of Zeitgeistismus, and he has written that, though he finds fiction valuable enough, he much prefers the magazine article. Dos Passos's *USA* has faded badly, and the author long ago accepted the journalistic role his devotion to Z meant him to play all along. Currently much the strongest American writer of the cult, as you can verify from the estimates of such Zeitgeisters as Kazin and Podhoretz, is Norman Mailer. Novel after novel he immolated on that altar, and book after book the god lavished with overpraise. But in *The Armies of the Night* (occasioned by a civilian protest march against army headquarters), Mailer applied his fictional skills to experience and opinions of his own, with a result which is not only pleasing in the nostrils of the god but is a damned good book as well. As autobiography it is pretty fair; as reportage it is sloppy (so Dwight Macdonald, who is scrupulous and who was there, informs us); as fiction it is nowhere: it is Z journalism pure and strong. You don't have to think very highly of the god to admire this shrine Mailer has constructed in his honor.

Sender's *A Man's Place* is set in a rural province in Spain; the narrative time is the mid-twenties and the story reaches back through more than sixteen years into the first decade of this century; the action turns on a miscarriage of justice, and both oppressors and oppressed are vividly characterized; the narrator is a liberal. (Sender himself fought on the loyalist side during the Spanish Civil War; Malraux had already showed in *Man's Hope* how to sacrifice that experience to the greater glory of Z.) Now Zeitgeist sternly adjures his votaries west of the iron curtain, and maybe east of it, too, but I know little about that: Government is bad; the State is the enemy of the individual; all inequality is unjust; the rulers and institutions of our society must be changed; dissent, reform, rebel. (Marx, that Hegelian, seems to have in Mao his extremest descendant: Mao, I conjecture, is so zealous for Zeitgeist, believes so fanatically in the spiritually enrichening benefits of rebellion, that in the mid-60s he stimulated the young of China to rebel against his own regime. Surely this is a new thing under the sun?) Sender's story obviously contains ingredients useful for fulfilling Z's solemn adjurations. The second of the book's three sections centers on the trial, breaking, and long imprisonment of two innocent people; this is clearly one of the set occasions for high Zeitgeistery, as Koestler demonstrated in *Darkness at Noon* for the 30s, Orwell in *1984* for the 40s, and Malamud in *The Fixer* for the 60s. Sender turned down every such opportunity, doing something quite other instead. But though (perhaps because?) he did what he did very well, this novel of his has been punished by obscurity.

To begin with, the story does not force or encourage or even permit you to identify with the victims (for some reason Z seems to be keen that readers should "identify with" characters and especially with victims). Sender is impartial: he keeps you at the same distance, emotionally and morally, from both rulers and ruled. He shows both—with sympathy, true, but also with a nearly comic detachment—as part of the same social system, yet without insisting that you see The System, The Establishment, The State, as the supervillain of which even the victimizers are victims. The crimes in the novel are all impure, even the cruel ones committed by agents of the State, and so are all the characters, even the most unfortunate and victimized. So too are the reader's emotions impure; my own got so complex that I threw up my hands, not knowing whose side to take. I took everybody's side. And this is the sin against the Holy Spirit-of-the-Age for which there is no forgiveness. What the god likes is good guys against bad buys, or, at the very least, us against them.

Giono's *The Horseman on the Roof* is set in Provence in 1838 during a cholera epidemic. (Camus had already demonstrated in *The Plague* how to sacrifice such material on Z's altar.) The protagonist, Angelo, is a brave, hot-hearted, extravagant young Italian nobleman, straight out of Stendhal, with a lot of romantic-revolutionary sentiments rattling around in his head. It is a story of wandering, and in the course of it Giono invents plenty of adventures to show us how people of every stripe behave; moreover, Angelo is a great theorizer, and Giono lets us eavesdrop on his thoughts as well as on the occasional speculative discussions he becomes involved in with people he meets. We have every opportunity to find in the pattern of these adventures the book's message, for we are guided not only by Angelo's theories but also by comments which Giono makes in his own person. (An instance of his old-fashioned, tale-telling, pre-Jamesian, authorial ease with the reader: "For a heart like his, smitten with liberty, these inhuman solitudes had a certain charm." But for a novelist to manifest himself instead of Z is a mortal sin against the Art of Modern Fiction, one of Z's lesser avatars.) What we find by delving into this novel is that there isn't any message, at least not of a variety favored by holy Z. Giono instructs us on the spirit of neither that age nor ours. The plague does not symbolize anything; it is neither a punishment from God nor a product of social injustice nor a disaster in whose glare the wickedness of society may be exposed; it is just there in the world, a given, like hot weather. Again, as with *A Man's Place*, the reader is on everybody's side, even on the side of the despicable characters. Worse, he is with Angelo less because Angelo has right opinions than because he is charming and full of vitality. The novel provides victims aplenty; in fact, all the characters are victims either of the plague or of fear of it. But our delight in the fortitude with which Angelo and a few others face the horror commingles with our contempt for the abject baseness with which most face it, to impurify our victim-pitying till it does not lead to indignation or other easy sentiments but to contemplation and thence to a kind of acceptance. Giono puts these words in the mouth of Angelo's dearest friend, a conspiratorial revolutionary in exile: "Republicans have an unfortunate love for princes. Don't think they kill them for any better reason. They need them and they look for them everywhere. If they find one who's of their own skin, they're happy at last to die for him." Imagine: a republican revolutionary openly and uncensoriously acknowledging that snobbery and envy cohabit with exalted ideals in his friends' hearts! Nor is the passage untypical of this novel. For the offenses of permitting shameless thoughts like these to enter his liberals' heads and of telling a victim-story that deplores not at all and delights a great deal, that is not Relevant to any of the Problems of Our Age, Giono will not be lightly forgiven. He is even so impudent as to treat irreverently one of our solemner pieties, psychosomaticism; he has a doctor say to Angelo, "Cholera is not a disease, *it's a burst of pride*." Only the intervention of a god mightier than Z, Art perhaps, is likely to rescue this splendid *Horseman on the Roof* from the boneyard of History.

A writer of good fiction is interested in people, the world. His moral, religious, or political opinions fade when he is actually imagining the people of his story: before he likes or dislikes them, and long before he judges their opinions, he is interested in them. It is this detached, meticulous interest that both Sender and Giono display.

But these two novels subvert Zeitgeistness even more radically than I have yet suggested. For like all novels they can be quarried, whatever the intention of their makers, for a Message for Our Time. The message that I derive from them is this: *is* before *ought*. And Zeitgeist is a duty deity if ever there was one: you ought to disapprove, ought to keep up to date, ought to change the world. Oh sure, says the novelist, but let's have a look at it first. *What is there?*

Artists in general, novelists among them, tend to be viewed with suspicion by the rulers of the world, and with good reason. But revolutionaries, I think, should be wary of artists too: most revolutionaries, after all, are would-be rulers who aren't in power yet; the rest are nihilists hating order, and art is a kind of order. Rulers dread chaos and nihilists love it: novelists, an ambiguous breed, have use for it, as the stuff for the patterns they enjoy making. Nihilists rage: *Life has no meaning*. Maybe so, says the novelist, but telling stories means a lot to me. Rulers pronounce:

Our laws give meaning. Oh sure, says the novelist, so do my stories. *Deplore!* Zeitgeist commands, and the novelist says, Fine, good idea, I've been needing some blue to set against those crimsons in the upper righthand corner. The better he is, the nearer a novelist approaches the great high goods of all poetry, celebration and lament, neither of which can accommodate much deploring. *View with alarm!* I do, says the novelist, Oh I do; but then he gets so caught up in the viewing he neglects the alarm. Two characters are set on a collision course. *How dreadful!* cries Zeitgeist, efficient and dutiful and interfering the whole way, seeing in tragedy not the nobility so much as the deplorable waste. *Help them!* What do you think I've been doing? says the novelist and redoubles his efforts to help them collide handsomely. However sorry he is that things are arranged so badly, he is even more interested in how they are arranged, for without those arrangements he wouldn't have anything to make stories with. A novelist is radically conservative as well as conservatively radical, and that's not just a play with words.

Out comes the jeer-gun again: "Whose side are *you* on?" Nobody's. My own. Everybody's, when I can manage it.

4

Science and the Profession of Literature

1.

I have wondered for some time why English is supplying more than its share of intellectual wild men and rebels these days.

Partly, of course, English professors are subject to the discontent and uneasiness pandemic in American intellectual life and higher education. People who teach forestry or home economics are seldom drawn into the mainstream of thought by their disciplines, but teachers of reading and writing are likely to be affected by the currents of speculation whether they want to be or not. Moreover, undergraduates, many of whom are passionately concerned about the vast insolubles of life, keep pushing their English teachers to talk about big things. Other humane disciplines like to present intellectual subjects as problems; they aspire to train students to ask answerable questions. But how can you solve *Moby Dick?* Do you want an answer to "Who is Sylvia, what is she?" Evil, love, God, truth, justice, reality, human nature—it is hard to keep them all out of an English class all the time. And the students are, willy-nilly, going to bring them in in their contemporary dress: Vietnam, sexual freedom, who are *you* to tell *me?*, black power, the foundations of value, *why not?* It is true that there are plenty of English teachers puny of imagination, whom neither the texts nor the students can goad into thinking: the walls of pedantry are high, thick walls. But there are a lot who cannot resist or do not want to resist; they not only think, they feel about what they think.

But this general reason for ferment in English applies to several other disciplines to a greater or lesser extent: the physicists made the bomb and sociologists study current social trends; yet neither are as noisy as English teachers. But the other mainstream disciplines, especially the natural and social sciences, don't find it so easy to confuse *mea culpa* with *tua culpa:* it's easy to feel unbribable when no one has tried to bribe you. When you get $500 a day (plus expenses, first class) to advise an electronics firm on setting up a system to produce for the Defense Department a mechanism that will help kill people, you know damned well you are in it over your eyebrows; you're one of the gang. When a university press offers you $50 (without return postage, even fourth class) to give your opinion on a four-hundred-page typescript of a study of Trollope, you can quite easily feel professionally pure. If those who have great power do not seek your counsel, you are not obliged really to think about power, force, corruption, the details of political struggle and decision: you do not have really to imagine what it means to govern.

But a too-easy indignation over the wickedness of rulers, of those who support them, and of those who fail to oppose them vigorously is not reserved for English teachers. Neither is another malady, intellectually widespread these days, which English teachers are more susceptible to than they should be. This is idolatry of the Zeitgeist—substituting Current Events for History in high school curricula, tossing out Chekhov because he isn't "relevant," that sort of thing.

Literarily, the lowest version of this idolatry is keeping up with fashion. In New York, the center of literary fashion, I have met people of some power and judgment who behave as though books and writers existed to provide them with cocktail party gossip; in provincial colleges, I have frequently been asked what *they* (or I as *their* presumed spokesman) are saying about so-and-so these days in New York. A more serious version of the idolatry is using relevance as an essential touchstone for judging a work of literature. But there is no need, at this late date, to inveigh against the use of *relevance* to lobotomize us, to make the past inaccessible to us.

However, not all these reasons combined account for the incidence of wild men in college English. There is some cause in the profession itself, and I think this cause to be the increasingly unstable emulsification of science in literature. Even when the faith in science was at its strongest, the mixture was uncertain; it is amusing to learn that Balzac, Flaubert, and Zola, those preachers, conceived of themselves in their realistic fictions as taking a scientific, not moral, view of the world. But now that the apocalyptic successes of science have so drastically weakened trust in it as a human good, that mixture has become volatile indeed. By science here I do not mean scientists as characters in novels à la Huxley or Snow, or the technological consequences of science as an element of the actual world mirrored in fiction, or scientific theories as subject matter for essays or for science fiction, or even psychology (except, perhaps for psychoanalysis). I mean the scientific attitude toward the world, an attitude that both narrowed literary scholarship (which used to embrace criticism, interpretation, exegesis far more readily than it does now) and that also, through the movement called modernism, entered into the making of literature itself. Scientific scholarship and literary modernism are both in a state of vigorous decadence: either by itself is capable of disturbing a serious student; combined, they can unhinge him.

But before dealing with the two main subjects, I must first take up two lesser ones: "English" as an academic subject, and the extent to which science serves as the model for learning in American universities.

2.

What all do English teachers teach? As a subject, "English" is as ill defined as it is popular. What chiefly draws students and what originally drew professors is plain love of literature, and the core of English should be, as it generally is in undergraduate courses at least, literary appreciation and understanding. In English, the justification of scholarship, the good of criticism, the joy of exegesis, and the highest goal of teaching is to bring a student and a text together so that he may love it for itself and for what it may figure forth about reality. But English incorporates a number of other activities some of which are only accidentally related to the core activity: freshman English tries to make up for one of the things the schools did not do well, teach the young to write decent prose; "creative writing" is a craft course in revising, combined with analytic criticism; Anglo-Saxon, which is about as useful to the study of postmedieval English literature as Ojibwa would be to the study of American literature, owes its presence in English departments to the accidents of history and geography, 1066 and all that; American, like any other national literature written by English speakers, is in the English department because of the language (it is not yet clear where the literature written in English by Africans, Indians, and other colonials will wind up); linguistics, to the relief of most English teachers, is now in process of establishing itself as an academic discipline of its own, along with other "behavioral" would-be sciences. But many of an English department's ancillary activities are attached more naturally to the core: because the body of literature in English is large and rich, literary history serves an obvious function; because it is intimately tied to other literatures, English courses frequently incorporate texts translated from other languages, become in fact comparative literature (indeed, more than one new university now has a Department of Literature rather than English, French, and so on); because literature is inextricably connected with society and ideas and philosophy and religion and everything else covered by the word "humanistic," English courses often range widely.

Why not? The main thing—what happens when a student and a poem are brought together—you can't talk about directly but only by indirection. You have to talk about something in the classroom. During the long decades of bondage to scientific (or, as it was stigmatized, "Germanic") scholarship, you were supposed to teach scholarship itself in the advanced courses, though many teachers fudged and taught poetry instead or also; now, except in the most professional graduate courses, an English teacher is quite free to range. The system, even in the most permissive college, may not let you be Socrates, but neither, in any halfway decent college, will it break you down, though it will surely weigh on your spirit.

The profession of English has its ills, and they have engendered a discontent that has contributed to the rebellious zeal of many English teachers. The key professional issue is certification. On what grounds will a department certify a student as competent to go forth and profess English?

The narrow form of the question has been for decades: What do you have to do to get a Ph.D.? This of course is a question that has vexed all the humanities for a long time. William James in 1903, in an essay entitled "The Ph.D. Octopus," in a relaxed, severe, wise way, defined the harm that the Ph.D. system of certifying teachers of the humanities was doing and the greater harm it would continue to do if it was not checked (it was not), and he proposed some sensible remedies. I modify his ideas: in English, the essence of the trouble is both too many examinations and also the astonishing notion that there is a connection between the ability to write a pseudoscientific scholarly dissertation and the ability to teach literature.

The primary good of literary scholarship of the narrow kind is to establish the best version of a valuable literary text and to provide it with the necessary commentary—about political or cultural history, the author's life, literary tradition, the audience's expectations, whatever—to assist a "common reader" to enjoy it. In this endeavor, the scientific methods of scrupulous accuracy are appropriate, and all who enjoy good literature owe scholarship a debt of gratitude. But this is a modest accomplishment, as every honest scholar knows, and in English most of the job by now has been done: scholarship has established and annotated nearly all the worthwhile texts (and too many of the dubious ones as well). Emotionless, finicky, objective exactitude is fine when you are editing *Paradise Lost*, but deadly when you are teaching it to undergraduates—great when you are collecting the materials for a biography (as Richard Ellmann was scrupulous in researching for his life of Joyce), but tedious when you are writing a biography for the world at large (as Ellmann was not tedious in writing *James Joyce*)—indispensable when you are studying many great writers (Chaucer), but grotesque for a writer who isn't worth reading for any but documentary purposes. When a professor is coming up for promotion, he is asked, "What have you published?" Suppose he were asked instead, "Why did you write this in the first place—for any reason other than to get a raise?" Dozens of university presses would go out of business, there would be room on library shelves again, whole forests would remain standing that now are pulped. . . . Just how far the faith in scientific scholarship has eroded may be indicated in a small episode. Thirty years ago here at Syracuse where I teach, a course in bibliography was required of every graduate student in English; now, the course is not even offered, to the legitimate distress of the few students who really are scholarly.

Still, despite the discontents and changes—the increased hiring of poets as teachers, for example, or the introduction of a new degree which certifies that a given department thinks the person holding the degree knows enough and talks well enough to teach English although he is not a publishing scholar, poet, or critic—despite these, I doubt that any great shift in prestige will take place in English departments for a long time, for science remains the model for learning in universities and shows few signs of losing its power. The faith in science is waning as its power increases; science is the established religion and universities are its churches.

The key word is "research." Research is proper to scientists and scientific scholars, but it has little or nothing to do with what critics and poets do or with introducing literature to common readers. In any substantial university, a faculty scientist's status is more likely to be determined by the research he does than by his teaching; indeed, though he may not teach in the classroom at all, he must do research in the laboratory. The presumption is that a man who has "made a contribution to knowledge" will be more likely to have something valuable to say to novices in science than will a man who has made no original contribution. The same holds for scholars and their novices, and who could quarrel with this system? But most college students are no more future literary scholars than they are future physicists—or future critics or future poets, for that matter. Most students in English courses are best thought of as future citizens who enjoy reading. The professor can introduce them to a text, and he can help them learn how to talk about literature; these seem to me jobs well worth doing; but there is nothing whatever scientific about them. Mastery of the techniques of research is not connected with the ability to teach anything except the techniques of research. Yet it is published evidence of this mastery upon which an English professor's prestige—salary, rank—depend more than upon any other one consideration. Currently, Yale and Berkeley are the top English departments, because of the prestige of their scholars. Any ambitious English department will promote a young man who publishes "sound" scholarly articles but teaches badly, and will lay off a young man who teaches well but does not "produce." Everyone knows this system of ranking professor-teachers on the basis of their scholarship is wrong, but professional prestige requires it. The Modern Language Association is often blamed for this state of affairs, and of course the MLA helps perpetuate it; but in fact the Ph.D. octopus long antedates and reaches far beyond any professional association. American universities conceive research as being as important a part of their function as teaching: science is the model for us all.

Moreover, it is easier to assess scholarly ability than teaching ability. Love of literature, capacity to recognize and value and perhaps even to write decent English, strength of character enough to stay alive to students and poetry for thirty years, intellectual curiosity—these qualities and others like them are what the teaching profession requires and what those members of the department possess who do most of its real work. But by comparison with these, the qualities which define the prestige hierarchy are easy to judge, to weigh.

The university as Laputa.

In 1959, Louis Simpson, a good poet, got his Ph.D. at Columbia. His dissertation was on James Hogg, the Ettrick shepherd, a forgotten Romantic poet and novelist. As an honest scholar on the dissertation committee remarked, there is something odd about the system that certifies a poet as competent to teach literature by getting him to write a critical-scholarly essay on an obscure writer inferior to himself.

A poet-professor acquaintance tells of a mathematician in-law of his who did his dissertation on academic advancement. He discovered that, for a college teacher willing to move, there was a very high correlation between academic advancement and quantity—irrespective of quality—of publication. Believing his thesis, he published what he could, fast, in journals no matter how obscure, and what he could not publish in them—his thesis, every term paper he could make presentable enough—he printed as monographs issued by a publishing house of his own invention; then he mailed offprints by the hundreds all over the country. He was nineteen when he wrote his dissertation; at twenty-five he was a full professor. Another poet-professor (failed poet, assistant professor), hearing this story, had first a volume of his verse, then his dissertation, then a second volume of verse printed similarly, and within five years was chairman of the department. These events took place at two important universities with no special reputation for corruption.

As I write this, I am about to have a year off at half pay; when I requested the leave, I made it clear that I would devote my free time to writing stories and poems. But the official letter informs me that I have been granted a "research leave of absence." Decorum has been preserved.

Oh well, universities are important patrons of writers these days, and artists, hard to institutionalize, are used to being thought not very respectable; indeed, in my opinion, creative artists of all kinds should not be institutionalized too much, for the good both of themselves and of the institutions. Still, it would be fun, just once, to watch the face of a biology professor, about to launch on a big research project dissecting newts, as he read the letter informing him that he had been granted a year's "holiday to create works of art."

3.

The more intelligent a literary scholar is the more severely he is likely to suffer from being cramped into the confines of scientific scholarship. Professionally, he denies himself the humane expansiveness and refreshment of conversation about his experience of live literature; too often, even the experience itself fades from his life. Something, if he retains much vitality as a man, must take its place, and the nearest thing at hand professionally is science itself. In this section, I look at a literary scholar who made a stir in the 1960s by diverting his energies from works of literature to the works of science and technology.

Marshall McLuhan was *the* intellectual wild man of the past decade. Paul Goodman, Herbert Marcuse, or Norman O. Brown, though not so spectacular, may prove to be more influential in the long run; he ranged more widely than any of them, but how deeply he reached is not yet clear. For a while, it looked as though his star had faded as fast as it had flared, but maybe not. What his stock is on Madison Avenue these days, I cannot guess, but in the academy he is being translated into An Authority, just as in science fiction he has become A Major Influence. His books are cited in bibliographies (alongside Goodman's, Marcuse's, and Brown's). A generation or two ago, you would expect "as Kittredge said" to appear solemnly in a term paper in an English course; now, in much the same way, you come across "as McLuhan said"; I read a dissertation recently that was a McLuhanite interpretation of *Ulysses*. I believe that a considerable part of the success of his theories, of their continuing importance, and even —though this is more conjectural—of their addlement is due to his having been a sound scholar.

He began in the 1930s as a literary scholar and English professor. His articles were to be found in good journals. He was asked to select and edit Tennyson's poems for a textbook, and did a sound job of it (Rinehart Editions, 1954). He was also—like many scholars—very intelligent; he had a speculative, free-roving cast to his mind; that is, he was also something of an intellectual. Just as a modern scholar is supposed to be scientifically rational about poetry, so an intellectual is supposed to be scientifically skeptical about all human affairs, especially social ones; together they comprise a strange academic establishment, a conformity of rational skepticism, half-authoritarian and half-subversive of authority. McLuhan's erudition and the excitement of his ideas were well above average, but he was also moral, and that was a problem.

He reports (in an interview in *McLuhan: Hot and Cool*, edited by G. E. Stearn, 1967) that when he began teaching at Wisconsin in 1936, being then twenty-five,

> I confronted classes of freshmen and I suddenly realized that I was incapable of understanding them. I felt an urgent need to study their popular culture: advertising, games, movies. It was pedagogy, part of my teaching program. To meet them on their grounds was my strategy in pedagogy: the world of pop culture. Advertising was a very convenient form of approach.

The first book he published, *The Mechanical Bride: Folklore of Industrial Man* (1951), consists of fifty glosses on texts taken from the mass media, nearly all advertisements from magazines. The glosses are charged with moral outrage.

> That man counts himself happy today whose school training wins him the privilege of getting at once into the technological meat grinder. That is what he went to school for. And what if he does have the consistency of hamburger after a few years? Isn't everybody else in the same shape? Hamburger is also more manageable than beef cuts.

Nothing objective, detached, cool about that prose. The ideas are worth thinking, but the moralizing tone was mighty unfashionable, all the more so since the subject is one of science's offspring. The book sank out of sight with hardly a ripple.

In 1962 he published his second, and best, book, *The Gutenberg Galaxy*. In it he contemplates such literary texts as *Don Quixote*, and the notions these texts stimulate in him are a good deal more interesting than the notions provoked by, say, the table of contents of *The Reader's Digest* for August 1947 (one of the texts glossed in *The Mechanical Bride*). It employs his scholarship coherently; at least a fourth of it consists of quotations from other speculative scholarly intellectuals of the first order, so that you have the reassuring feeling that McLuhan is adding to a substantial body of intelligent opinion, "making a contribution to knowledge," rather than exploding on his own. In it, he also cleared his prose of that earlier tone of too-easy moral outrage: he no longer indulged himself in vatic sarcasms. In his own words: "Value judgments have long been allowed to create a moral fog around technological change such as renders understanding impossible." His moral intentions remain unmistakable, but their expression is more restrained—and therefore, of course, more effective. "Is it not possible to emancipate ourselves from the subliminal operation of our own technologies? Is not the essence of education civil defense against media fall-out?" Obversely, in *The Gutenberg Galaxy* he restrained the messianic fervor which he later famously gave way to. It is true that his tone is often prophetically arrogant and absolutist: "Cultures can rise far above civilization artistically but without the phonetic alphabet they remain tribal, as do the Chinese and Japanese." (In the context of his book, that sentence is less arrogant than it is in the context of this essay, but not much less, and makes more sense, but not much more.) But what he intends to accomplish in this book is still, for him at any rate, modest. "A few decades hence it will be easy to describe the revolution in human perception and motivation that resulted from beholding the mosaic mesh of the TV image. Today it is futile to discuss it at all." (Two years, not two decades, later, in his next and most famous book, he discusses precisely this subject at great length.) One result of the relatively calm qualities of *The Gutenberg Galaxy* is that, when he drops one of his idea-bombs, it has a more or less rational context to qualify it, to give it meaning, and it does not lose its distinctiveness by being only one of dozens of blockbusters scattered about promiscuously. "The unconscious is a direct creation of print technology, the ever-mounting slag-heap of rejected awareness." An idea like that needs room to blow up in, lots of pages on both sides to cushion its effect in the reader's mind. This idea is not given nearly enough room in *The Galaxy*, but some. Anyway, the book is not booby-trapped with so many loaded notions as to prevent you from getting through in one piece, if you're lucky.

Then in 1964 came *Understanding Media: The Extensions of Man*. Scholarship dwindled, logic and moralizing were disavowed, messianism magnified, and the book sold hot and fast. Marshall McLuhan became a power in the land. But in addition to his being the biggest celebrity among the wildmen thinkers, his ideas, as I said before, seem to me the most important intrinsically. Norman O. Brown, for example, projects a nostalgia for Innocence (polymorphous perverse sexuality for everybody) free from incursions of the devil (inhibition, repression, control) which is hardly worth discussing except as a symptom, one more instance of Rousseauistic Utopianism; its chief value, so far as I can make out, is to provide material for satire. McLuhan's teaching, however, is radical, animated by real intelligence, and capable of moving people to social action. If he is wrong, it matters.

It is not possible to give a rational summary of McLuhan's ideas, for two reasons: the attitude and tone of his writing, in *Understanding Media* especially, is at least as important as the ideas themselves, and to systematize these ideas, even in outline, would be to falsify their nature and impact. His writing is deliberately antilogical: circular, repetitive, unqualified, gnomic, outrageous. "It was thanks to the print that Dickens became a comic writer." Absurd! Still, maybe there's something to it? It's worth a thought at least.

Though his ideas do not compose a system, they are a recognizable complex. They are about the ways in which the media—a term he stretches until it includes language and technology—extend and alter our means of perception and communication, and thereby affect our nature. In his earlier writings, he, the good English professor, was appalled by what he observed in the mass media. But gradually he came to believe that the vulgarity, immorality, triviality, and imbecility which characterize so very much of what the media communicate to the masses are really of secondary importance. "The medium is the message." That is to say, what is communicated has much less effect on us than the means by which it is communicated. For example, he attributes to the introduction of movable type a "galaxy" of changes in Western man's consciousness, making it possible for us to "act without reacting" (I *think* this means something) and thereby engendering extreme specialization of social function and a sort of cultural schizophrenia; his argument in support of this thesis is formidable, illuminating, albeit extreme, and his own. He attributes equally extensive changes to the electronic media, especially TV; in gauging the effect of TV on our nature, he says the fact that TV images are made "mosaically" (I *think* this does not mean anything) and simplify their subjects to cartoons is incomparably more important than whether the program content is intelligent or stupid, in good taste or bad, honest or meretricious. His TV argument, though wobbly, is as original as his movable-type argument, and it stirs one to thought about a subject which needs to be thought about. For this, as for many isolated insights, one is grateful to him. But one is not so grateful to him for the argument as a whole, for though it pretends to be a forecast based on solid fact, it is mostly a wishful prophecy deriving from apocalyptic vision.

Things are changing so fast, he says, that we must control the media right now, not a moment to lose, if they are not to destroy us:

> The mark of our time is its revulsion against imposed patterns. We are suddenly eager to have things and people declare their beings totally. There is a deep faith to be found in this new attitude—a faith that concerns the ultimate harmony of all being. Such is the faith in which this book has been written. It explores the contours of our own extended beings in our technologies, seeking the principle of intelligibility in each of them. In the full confidence that it is possible to win an understanding of these forms that will bring them into orderly service, I have looked at them anew, accepting very little of the conventional wisdom concerning them.

Exactly how these forms are to be brought into "orderly service" is never made clear. The omission of this *how* becomes enormously important: we are being altered by TV and the other electronic media; all we have to do is to control them (but *how?*) in order to achieve the wholeness we have long lacked.

It is easy to see why McLuhan is listened to so eagerly: with high scholarly credentials, he sounds like a Future salesman assuring us that there are great days ahead and that what seems to be so terrible now arises only from our resistance to change. What if admen do use TV as a way to spread lies and distortions and idiocy? It doesn't matter much anyway since the medium is the message; and a medium is neither moral nor immoral. All in our culture are being changed by TV, those who don't watch it as well as the addicts, so why not watch? Don't resist, don't be obsolete before your time, move with the age. In plain words, Progress with Utopia in view. An electronic chiliasm. The millennium now.

In itself, McLuhan's vision need not disturb one much. It is not hard, really, to say to apocalyptoid mantics, "I'm for civilization, growing up, cities, marriage, and language," then shove them into their earthly paradises and lock the gates on them. But McLuhan is carefully listened to by admen (who never expected it would be an English professor that would justify them!), and he has many influential followers in education, active innovators, progressivistic experimenters. We shall be hearing a lot more from and about them. They accept, or agree with, McLuhan's view: "We are entering the new age of education that is programmed for discovery rather than instruction. . . . We would be foolish not to ease our transition from the fragmented visual world of the existing educational establishment by every possible means." This idea sounds fine, and it would be fine except for two considerations: one is that it encourages the impatient devastators who assert that all forms of traditional teaching have failed so that only radically experimental ones have a chance to do the job right, *let's turn everything upside down now;* and the other is the complex of ideas of which this notion is a part and the narcosis which those ideas would induce. I turn now to that complex and that narcosis.

McLuhan has become a sort of double agent. He originally went out among tribalizing media as a spy from civilization. (Spy is mine, but the tribal-civilization metaphor is his, and useful.) But he stayed there too long: in Blake's words, which McLuhan quotes tirelessly: "We become what we behold." In *Understanding Media* and in his lesser writings and speeches since then, he continues to be an agent reporting back to civilized (literate, literary) people what the tribes are up to: but he also functions among us as an agent of the media, proclaiming the destruction come and to come. To support this charge that he is a double agent, let me cite two statements he made before a meeting at the P.E.N. international conference in New York in June 1966. Challenged by the critic John Simon with having deserted literature for advertising and TV, he said that, on the contrary, he saw it as his mission to save literature from the media. He also said he did not believe a lot of the ideas he threw off; he was using them to "probe the environment." However, six months before, in the Grand Ballroom of the Waldorf, he addressed (for a star fee, I am told by a man who sells advertising and who was there) an assemblage of business and advertising executives. He did not tell them he was probing the environment or saving literature from the media. He told them pretty much what he had already said in his book. A sincere double agent: both sides are right. He often argues, quite plausibly, that "point of view" is a result of print and that he is being true to the electronic age because, abandoning point of view, he writes mosaically. But, if there is no fixed point of view, why shouldn't one be working for both sides at once? The only reason I can think of is neither typographical nor electronic but moral, and though McLuhan refuses to fog himself up with moral criteria when out to understand the media, he can't stop me from applying them when I am out to understand him. I am civilized, and maybe I'm foggy, but I don't want either myself or my world to be retribalized. Tribalization may be inevitable, as McLuhan says, though I doubt it (I'm not even sure what "global village" means). But whether it is inevitable or not, and whether he is sincere or not, I do not like defectors. He is not an open enemy. He is not even an ally who sneakily opens the gates of the city to the enemy. He is a seeming ally who sets about to persuade *me* to open the gates, using the arguments that our common enemy is stronger than we and bound to win, that we have terrible faults which succumbing to our enemy may cure if we handle him right (but *how?*), and besides the enemy can't help being barbarous, it's the environment he lives in, he's bringing his environment with him, it's irresistible and will get us, no matter what.

I wish I could confound him with erudition. But that would require an extensive knowledge of history (both political and cultural), economics, sociology, philosophy, literature, psychology, and anthropology, to say nothing of a really exhaustive knowledge of the history and practice of technology, and I have nowhere near the scholarship for the task. For example, take his notion about the "mosaic" quality of TV projection: the electronic particle which makes the images on the screen by zipping back and forth across it and also out through it can and will imprint us—our nerves?—through our skins and so change our souls; a notion that wild needs more support, if it is to convince me, than a literary scholar's repeated assertions; meanwhile, I do not know how to go about refuting it; it just sits there in my mind undigested and indigestible. I am perforce content to cite one instance of an error in a subject I know, the one standing for the many. McLuhan writes:

> In Shakespeare's *Troilus and Cressida,* which is almost completely devoted to both a psychic and social study of communication, Shakespeare states his awareness that true social and political navigation depend upon anticipating the consequences of innovation.

The statement in the which-clause and the one in the main clause are both untrue as they stand, and by the time they have been modified into truth they will be unrecognizable. (It is obvious that I think that, in the medium of language at any rate, the message too is part of the message.) Not only is his interpretation of *Troilus and Cressida* invalid, but the five lines he quotes in support of his interpretation do not in fact support it.

> The providence that's in a watchful state
> Knows almost every grain of Plutus' gold,
> Finds bottom in the uncomprehensive deeps,
> Keeps place with thought, and almost like the gods
> Does thoughts unveil in their dumb cradle.

Like other thinkers, McLuhan could have quarried Shakespeare for ideas and expressions of attitudes to offer in evidence for his own thesis. Instead, he inserts his own idea into the play, attributes the idea to Shakespeare, and claims that the whole play is about that idea. In this he is like a psychoanalytical nut who sees *Hamlet* as a study of the Oedipus complex or a linguistic nut who can't see the poetry for the morphemes. A few such extravagances in a book don't matter much, but *Understanding Media* offers an accumulation of errors—distortions, contradictions, projections, simplifications, limit smashings—so considerable that finally one says, "No, I don't trust ideas which have so infirm a foundation." McLuhan-civilized used to offer evidence which supported his insights; but McLuhan-barbarian does not deign to answer critics who point out the errors which riddle his prophecies. The arrogance is the message.

I also wish I could confound him rationally, by refuting his complex of ideas. But the complex is repetitive, "mosaic," hortatory, apocalyptic, as impervious to the discriminations of logic and common sense as to the corrections of scholarship. Worst of all, it is self-justifying. If you apply logic to it, he disposes of you by saying that you have a print-formed mind made obsolete by Hume and electricity. If you say man is being changed all right but not so drastically as he maintains, he counters by telling you to wake up, you are still in the nightmare of print-induced unconsciousness, "consciousness will come as a relief," and he quotes *Finnegans Wake* at you (*he* understands its true meaning of course, *you* don't), saying that he takes his prophecies from the "radar feedback" of great art since great art constitutes a sort of "early warning system" for society. If you judge his ideas morally, he says he is not prescribing but describing. This last statement may have some purely intellectual validity, but it certainly is not emotionally true of his practice in *Understanding Media*. There, the tone is not fairly neutral, as befits description, but high pressure, feverish, as befits admonition, and what he admonishes us to do manages to be at once vague, capitulatory, and appalling.

The last sentence of the book is a valuable opinion. "Panic about automation as a threat of uniformity on a world scale is the projection into the future of mechanical standardization and specialism, which are now past." Pared down, that makes sense. But the sentence before it betrays a *Reader's Digest*-y sentiment: *really* we are all creative and mass leisure will release our creativity. "The social and educational patterns latent in automation are those of self-employment and artistic autonomy." Pardner, when you say that, laugh. He seems to substitute, and his rhetoric urges us to substitute, electricity for divine grace: ". . . since with electricity we extend our central nervous systems globally, instantly interrelating every human experience, we can now, by computer, deal with complex social needs with the same architectural certainty that we previously attempted in private housing." Finally, having put overwhelming trust in consciousness, he makes it clear, at the end of the chapter on "The Spoken Word," what the new, electronically expanded consciousness is good for.

> Electric technology does not need words any more than the digital computer needs numbers. Electricity points the way to an extension of the process of consciousness itself, on a world scale, and without any verbalization whatever. . . . Today computers hold out the promise of a means of instant translation of any code or language into any other code or language. The computer, in short, promises by technology a Pentecostal condition of universal understanding and unity. The next logical step would seem to be, not to translate, but to by-pass languages in favor of a general cosmic consciousness which might be very like the collective unconscious dreamt of by Bergson. The condition of "weightlessness," that biologists say promises a physical immortality, may be paralleled by the condition of speechlessness that could confer a perpetuity of collective harmony and peace.

Maybe this is one of those idea-clusters he doesn't really mean; maybe he is just probing the environment with it. Well, as a part of the environment, let me respond: I don't like the idea (I don't like being probed with it either). The electronic heaven-on-earth of his vision is a world village of mutes wan with inaccessible rage, a parody of harmony and peace because the possibilities of disharmony and conflict have been lobotomized. He wants, and wants us to want, to turn most of the work of our minds over to the computers. In the name of defending literature, he would get rid of language. I know—even with my foggy, unexpanded consciousness I know—that there are disadvantages to being human. But at least it is interesting, it is various, I am for going on with it.

Hyperrational scientific thought, narrow, indifferent to our welfare, whimsical, has proved to be a great danger to mankind; no other way we have found to warp reality has released such energy; it is hastening toward us a secularized Armageddon it has already emptied of meaning. All the same, we need not therefore turn against reason even in its modest occasions. Science is not all of reason, though its devotees act as though it were. Reason—the establishing of firm, humane premises and the scrupulous, sequential linking of causes and effects—pairs off with imagination very happily, and with moral philosophy as well. Indeed, without a limited and limiting admixture of reason, imagination disintegrates into fancy or nightmare or turbulent sensation, and moral philosophy too easily simplifies into "might makes right," "I want," me.

The language of humane reason can blend with poetry, as the *Divine Comedy* demonstrates impregnably, whereas the language of pure science constantly pushes toward mathematics, toward single meaning. The strain to single-mean is what makes legal prose hard for a layman to comprehend; science's success at single meaning is not the least of what makes it emulsify so uncertainly with literature. I believe that it is natural for the mind to do with language as poetry does—to double-mean, hint, second-guess, fool around, sidestep, pry. The supersubtle paranoiac speaks, and thinks you speak, only in code; for him, language never means only what it seems to say; indeed, it seldom, to his way of thinking, means what it says at all. But not even this extreme doubleness is as hard for a poet to grasp as a statement—about something humanly important—that means all it says and nothing more. In this respect all men are poets when they are children, when they sleep, when they are emotionally engaged with others: most of their lives.

By mid-century, even we laymen could know, if we wished, that something odd had happened in physics, the uttermost science, and therefore to what it was saying and to its language. What with the indeterminacy principle and the substitution of probability for law and antiworlds and reverse time, it was apparent that even the most exact language of all was not sure what it was talking about. Science was no longer rationally deterministic, and after August 1945 only a fundamentalist true-believer could hold onto his faith in science as the savior of mankind. The scientific world-view had become scrambled, and the consequences of that scramble were manifestly affecting us, not in all respects for the better. There are various popular evasions these days—for example, drugs, astrology and witchcraft, sanitary sex. Perhaps the most common is employed by those who only seem to confront the issues; let's blame America (communism, capitalism, whitey, the Jews, *them*) for everything wrong. To his credit, McLuhan did not evade but dared face the thing itself, knowing what it was.

He said he wanted to rescue poetry from the scramble of technological change by understanding the nature of that change and the effect of the scramble on us. Just as science and engineering, as such, are outside any moral order and just as the scholarly approach to literature also claimed and strove to be outside any such order, so he would strategically divest himself of his moral scheme—he is an active Catholic—when he studied the media. This strategy was manifestly an error, for the moment they enter our lives the works of science and technology become subject to ethical considerations. He says that moral concern interferes with understanding media and what they may be doing to us; true; just so, it is handier to dissect a corpse than a living person ("we murder to dissect," said Wordsworth). "Television is bad," "advertising is bad"—he is right, it is mere impotent incantation to keep on mumbling such runes. But the alternative is not to cut the rudder, to assume that the media are beyond good and evil. That way, you lose track of where you are and where you have been, you forget which side you are on, you begin to act as though there were no choices about where we are going. In 1967 McLuhan published a little book with a title which is such a bad pun,

The Medium Is the Massage, as to suggest a real loss of bearing on his part—a chuckle, yes, but not a title.

In pure science, anything goes that can go. But if there is one thing we should have learned by now about the human condition, including the metastasis of science into our ways of willing and even of feeling, it is surely this: when anything goes, nothing goes well.

4.

A teacher is likely to be affected more than aesthetically by what he teaches, and I believe that the academic near-orthodoxy of rebelliousness—disaffection at least, nihilism at most—derives in part from the study of modernist literature. In this section, I look with attention at modernist literature and at its effects on some who profess it, especially Louis Kampf in whom its influence seems highly visible.

Literary Modernism, edited by Irving Howe, includes the best essays on the subject I have read. Lionel Trilling's "On the Modern Element in Modern Literature" is excellent in itself; it helps one understand something of what is meant by the term. Howe's introduction, "The Idea of the Modern," helps even more. All the same, I can draw only the most uncertain line between modernist and traditionalist literature on the basis of these essays. Some modernist writers, such as Pound, go in for sensational formal innovation and experiments, but others, such as Baudelaire, are as decorous formally as any traditionalist. The modernists do not have a monopoly on criticizing that whole bourgeois, respectable, secular, urban, industrial civilization of which Nietzsche is the savagest, maddest scourger; no writer worth talking about, that I can think of, speaks well of it as it is and has long been, if he speaks of it at all. Yet, despite the severe criticism of society made by modernist writers, few of them have been attracted into left-wing or socialist politics: egalitarianism has little charm for artists of any kind.

Just as the best way to define that uncertain but useful category "metaphysical poetry" is to list the seventeenth-century British poets who wrote it and to name some of the main metaphysical poems they wrote, so the best way to define literary modernism is to make two lists, one of modernist texts and avatars, the other of traditionalist texts and authors. (Literary traditionalism, not being a movement, doesn't go in for heroes and saints and leaders so much as for men who, without setting up shop as gods, write books.) This is not the occasion for full-scale taxonomy, even if I had the scholarship for the job. But maybe listing a few of the names will help sketch out a definition. The names in the modernist column have been gleaned from such sources as Howe's anthology; those in the traditionalist column occur in F. R. Leavis's *The Great Tradition* (such as *Middlemarch*), are loudly omitted from discussion by critics of modernism (*War and Peace*), or are included on my own judgment (Frost). Some big names are omitted as being too arguable: Rilke and Mann, for example.

MODERNISTS	TRADITIONALISTS
Diderot: *Rameau's Nephew*	Fielding
Baudelaire	Keats
Büchner	Jane Austen
Dostoevsky: "Notes from Underground"	Dostoevsky: *Brothers Karamazov, Crime and Punishment*
Tolstoy: "Death of Ivan Ilich"	Tolstoy: *War and Peace, Anna Karenina*
Nietzsche	Balzac
Flaubert	Dickens
Ibsen	Chekhov: stories
Rimbaud	Hugo
Joyce: above all	Eça de Queiroz
Pound	George Eliot: *Middlemarch*
Gide: especially *The Journals*	Hardy
T. S. Eliot: early	T. S. Eliot: late
Kafka	Frost
Brecht	Lawrence: stories
Genet	Auden
Beckett	Tanizaki

The main generalization I would draw from these lists has to do with attitude and emphasis. A modernist text dwells on the disorder and alienation of "modern" experience, whereas a traditional text, emphasizing the humanity of the character and author both, seeks order and values fellow feeling. Modernism is obsessed with disconnection and diseased self-absorption ("Notes from Underground"); traditionalism connects us with the man who is diseased (*Crime and Punishment*). Flaubert's cold detestation of the world of *Madame Bovary*, of nearly all the personages in it, and of Emma's mass-produced dreams, profoundly affects our relation to that world and those people; we are fascinated and estranged at once, fascinated by the artistry of the book but estranged from the life it deals with. Balzac so much enjoys detesting his mediocrities and monomaniacs and so enjoys loving his good characters that our undivisive response to his fiction is vital pleasure. "The Wasteland" is a vision of disorder and is itself disordered. Some of Yeats's lyrics, especially "The Second Coming," present a vision of disorder but are themselves masterpieces of order; moreover, Yeats also gave us a magnificent vision of imagined order in the total body of his poetry; I would list him on the traditionalist side, though the modernists claim him too. No matter. Formally, modernist literature has considerable trouble in unambiguously satisfying the emotional expectations it has aroused. Kafka famously left his two chief novels uncompleted. Flaubert in "A Simple Heart" permits us to connect with Félicité so warmly that when she comes to die we want to grieve as we would in life, and the one scene in the story which Flaubert "builds" is the death scene. But then, in the very last words, he chokes off our tears with unkind irony: the vision of glory in her mind as she dies is of a stuffed parrot. *Aestheticus interruptus*, like that other kind, leaves the reader sad and soiled. Let one of the last images of conjugation in *Ulysses* stand for modernism's impure gratifications: an (inadequate) husband kissing his (adulterous) wife (on the behind) as they lie in bed side by side (but also head to foot).

What seems to me evident is that traditional, humanist literature did not yield place to, and is now surviving, the antitraditional, modernist movement. Howe's essay is in fact a valedictory to modernism, and concludes with these moving sentences:

> How enviable death must be to those who no longer have reason to live yet are unable to make themselves die! Modernism will not come to an end; its war chants will be repeated through the decades. For what seems to await it is a more painful and certainly less dignified conclusion than that of previous cultural movements: what awaits it is publicity and sensation, the kind of savage parody which may indeed be the only fate worse than death.

Amen. To be perpetuated by the Terry Southerns of the mind, that is the living end.

Modernist literature is very strong stuff, and teaching it, especially if one doesn't balance it with a fit regard for the equally strong and far less alienating but not so imposing traditionalist literature, can be unbalancing (an example is the journal *Paunch* edited by Professor Arthur Efron). Such imbalance leads as usual to mistaking the part for the whole, mistaking a poem's version of a part of reality for reality itself. According to a modernist zealot, Flaubert's version of nineteenth-century French provincial life is not an accurate partial portrait but *the* truth. (What the zealot does about Renoir's lovely and affectionate paintings of that same world, I do not know.) And here is a sentence from Louis Kampf, an English professor whose book is *On Modernism:* "And so we continue with our experiments, with this bullying quest for order which, oddly enough, expresses itself as destructive chaos." Order expressing itself as chaos: it sounds like a parody of modernism.

The point about the political danger latent in modernism has been eloquently made by Robert Brustein. (Now Dean of the Yale Drama School, he was formerly a professor of English at Columbia, where modernist literature is more orthodox than traditional literature.) As critic (*The Theatre of Revolt*) and drama reviewer (for *The New Republic*), Brustein for some years encouraged, or at least sanctioned, extreme theatrical experimentation and rebelliousness of the Living Theater variety. In the fall of 1968 he invited the Living Theater to perform at Yale, and he was appalled by what he saw. They had been in self-proclaimed "exile" in Europe for four years (for modernists, nothing is more chic than alienation) and they had turned into theatrical guerrillas. Joyce recommended silence, exile, cunning; well, the exile of these devotees was phony and they had no silence, but they did display a certain cunning. The following is from Brustein's article in *The New York Review of Books* for February 13, 1969:

> What was finally most disturbing about the Living Theater was the content of the ideology it was marketing under the name of anarchism. . . . Love and brotherhood were continually on the lips of the actors, but no actors in my experience have bristled with so much aggression or more successfully galvanized the aggression of the spectator. . . . It was, finally, not a vision of human freedom that one took away from *Paradise Now* but vague, disturbing memories of the youth rallies in Hitler's Nuremberg. The return of the Living Theater described a full circle insofar as the company had now taken on the very authoritarian qualities it had once denounced.

From modernism to anarchism is too easy a step to take. From anarchism to nihilism is not much further; little more is needed for it than despair of the democratic, parliamentary process, and for that despair little more is needed than direct involvement in some of the gigantisms of our gigantistic society. From nihilism to totalitarianism, for those who want to take it, balked utopists, the brutal, the very impatient, is hardly a step at all.

Meantime, rebellion is *in.*

When the designers of rebellious fashions put up Che Guevara as a model for the American young, he caught on instantly. Having overthrown one wicked oppressor, he had been thrillingly thwarted from victory over another oppressor almost as bad by agents of the most devious oppressor in the world, us: martyred hero with fatigues and beard. But, I suspect, no less important to his apotheosis to *the* fad rebel was the unmentioned quality of his failures. First he, an Argentinian, failed to exercise the authority he had seized in Cuba, and then he failed in his attempt to impose a revolution on Bolivians who had not asked for one and who perhaps, if they ever got around to wanting one at all, would prefer to make it themselves. Our age has provided us with more martyrs than we can use; Che is low on my list of those to revere. I think ill of a man who refuses to fulfill the heavy responsibilities imposed on him by the success of his revolution but who substitutes imperialism for legitimate authority—an imperialism of revolution, to be sure, but no less offensive for being socialist and secular rather than capitalist and Christian. As for Che's cultists, they are less lunatic and less unsavory than the cultists of martyred John Birch but rather more ludicrous, and in the long run about equally dangerous—not very.

I heard of an undergraduate in an Ivy League shop who asked to see what they had in the way of Che Guevara outfits, preferably in olive drab. When he found just what he wanted, he asked the clerk, "But don't you have it in wash-and-wear?"

I also heard of a state university political science department that offers a major with emphasis on revolutionary movements, including a three-credit course in guerrilla warfare, two hours a week in the classroom and four hours a week "in the field."

"Join the Dodge rebellion"—a mass-media advertising slogan.

At the MLA convention in New York during the last week of December 1968, there occurred a seizure of power complete with police oppression (though, unluckily for the insurrectionists, with no brutality), guerrilla theater (with the consent of both the Americana Hotel and the MLA), and rhetoric (much of it fresh from the gutter but some of it, not so fresh, snatched and patched from the likes of Patrick Henry). It is neat to my purpose that the leader of this uprising against the main organization of literary scholars was a devout literary modernist, Louis Kampf (who claims Alexander Herzen as one of his two intellectual mentors, the other being Matthew Arnold!).

An MLA convention is dismal, first of all just because it is a convention. To be in a hotel with from six to ten thousand fellow conventioneers is enough to make a man want to run to the woods and never come out. Why this American custom of holding huge conventions? I went to an AFL convention once; the tone of it was similar to that of an MLA convention except for the parties, which inclined more toward liquor-and-whores than liquor-and-talk; worse, the professors pretend that the purpose of their convention is to exchange ideas and listen to learned papers, whereas the union men know that they are there to make deals and set policy; but the same heavy, galvanized conviviality infects them both. I have never heard anyone say he was going to an annual MLA meeting for purely intellectual reasons, that is, to exchange ideas. People go to look for a job or to hire, to glimpse celebrities, or just to see old friends. If the conventions aspired to do no more than to perform these trade functions adequately, they would, I suppose, continue to have a reason to exist, though they would be just as dispiriting as they are now. A serious exchange of ideas should—*can*—occur only in small gatherings, say in regional meetings of the MLA or in special groups such as the English Institute.

All dreary and familiar—and hardly one of the institutional evils demanding instant remedy, even unto revolution, for the good of society.

In August 1968, Louis Kampf joined the MLA. In the December 19 issue of *The New York Review of Books,* there appeared a letter announcing an open meeting of dissidents to be held at Columbia on the evening before the convention really got under way; the announcement was signed by six professors, including Kampf and his linguistic colleague at M.I.T., Noam Chomsky, the most prestigious intellectual counseling rebellion in the last half of the sixties. The meeting was well attended.

Friday morning in the Americana, where the English half of the MLA was meeting (the foreign languages half met in a hotel nearby), Kampf and some others passed out leaflets in the hotel corridors and lobby, harangued conventioneers, and tried to attach political protest signs to the walls. They had not asked for permission to demonstrate politically; their language was sometimes revolutionary in vocabulary. The hotel security staff told them to stop; when they continued, the hotel people, instead of waiting till the MLA officials had mediated, or had at least tried to mediate a more acceptable form for these activities, called the police, who arrived by carloads ready for riot. Kampf and two others were arrested; a few hours later they were released and, largely as a result of the good offices of the men in charge of the MLA, the hotel promised not to press charges and to permit limited demonstrations the next day. Friday evening the dissidents caucused again, in large numbers.

Saturday morning I happened to come upon a few score professors milling about a group of sanctioned protesters seated on the lobby floor protesting. Presumably the scraggly ones were students and teachers of high literature, but the runes of their discourtesy took the form of that impoverished dirty-talk that is now as expectable from a middle-class young white malcontent as sandals. I could not decide which repelled me more, the pinch-nosed professors, a witch-burner gleam in their eyes, hissing "How disgusting!" or the self-declassed provocateurs, assassination in *their* eyes, spitting bad names at them. I was sure of at least one thing, that I was sorry to be a member of the profession. It was as though those fundamentalist rebels, having studied up on the classical modernist revolutions, had learned (they could have found it in Ferrero's *The Two French Revolutions*) that coprolalia accompanies such disorders but, as so often, had got things turned around: they were behaving as though "motherfucker cocksucker shiteater cunt" might by some nervous magic *cause* insurrection. Both historically and psychologically, they were reverting to an early, no longer appropriate mode of behavior. The whole sibilant episode dissipated after a while without further disturbance.

Late Saturday evening, the Sunday *Times* appeared. It reported that the reformers were "laying plans for disobeying convention rules during a controversial vote" and quoted a student as saying, "If we're lucky, the police will have to be called in."

On Sunday morning, the business meeting of the MLA took place. Commonly, as with most big organizations, very few members attend this meeting: who wants to be a rubber stamp for the executive committee? It is the MLA custom each year to elect as second vice-president a distinguished professor whom the nominating committee has selected; the following year he moves up to first vice-president, and the third year he serves as president. This is merely a custom, and of course there is nothing of which Enlightened anarchists are more contemptuous than custom, especially a *middle-class* custom. A group of rebels and sympathizers attended the December 20 meeting; not even the publicity about their threatening actions and intentions had shaken regular members out of their torpor; the rebels did not have to disobey any rules at the meeting, because they found themselves in a majority (299 to 243, out of more than 11,000 members registered as being in attendance); democracy is what the Enlightened say they revolt *for*, and here it was already working for them. Once they got power, it turned out they were not Mallorys of revolution after all, ready to demolish an institution because it was *there; there* was the vast MLA, its sort of democratic arms open; they neither voted it out of existence nor did anything else very astounding to it. For second vice-president, they elected Kampf instead of the professor who had been proposed by the nominating committee, and they passed four political resolutions, three more or less appropriate to the MLA, though provocatively worded, but one, urging the United States to withdraw from Vietnam, irrelevant to the purpose of the association, one more petititon for Washington's vertical file. Kampf's statement includes this declaration of intention:

> The reformers have no desire to create a counter-organization to the MLA. They would like, instead, to create the kind of atmosphere and the necessary structures which will allow people to come to the Annual Meeting to participate in substantive activities, rather than to do business or to mingle with the great.

Apparently he is sincere in wanting the MLA convention to further intellectual discourse—the function that it has demonstrated itself incapable of performing, out of sheer gigantism—and to cease the humbler trade function it has proved halfway competent at. He would utopize it out of existence.

Or is he cunningly disingenuous? He refers contemptuously to the "secretariat" of the MLA; "secretariat" is appropriate to the top bureaucracy of a great or international power, to overthrow which would be a substantial accomplishment. He says the MLA officers panicked because of the demonstration and blames them for stirring the Americana management to call the police.

> This panic is best illustrated by the fact that a random statement by a random graduate student, flippantly reported in *The New York Times*, was taken seriously. There was no threat of violence at the Meeting—ever!

What the quoted student meant, obviously, was that he hoped they would provoke The Establishment (The Americana's, the MLA's, *some* Establishment) into causing the police to use violence. A responsible official wouldn't have to be hysterical with panic to take that hope seriously; four months earlier at the Democratic convention in Chicago, New Left young had infamously provoked and police had infamously rioted. (Indeed, a couple of years later at a national convention in Los Angeles, New Lefters tried to radicalize the most unlikely group of all, deans of women!) It is hard to believe that Kampf, an associate professor of literature at an institution as intellectually superior as M.I.T., full of ideas, widely read, one who in his writing acknowledges his intellectual debts as a scholar should, could be naïve enough to mean those words straight and to misunderstand that student's plain intention.

Still, that is not much harder to believe than something I witnessed: a young woman, a graduate student or instructor, seated on the floor of a respectable hotel, cross-legged, her skirt not pulled down between her bare legs, shouting up at the stone face of a gray-worsted lady-professor, "Motherfucker!" There are all sorts of ways to trigger a revolution, I suppose, but yelling naughty words at Mommy is not one of them.

How we could use a Henry Fielding to do up this burlesque of a seizure of power in the mock-epic style it deserves. Otherwise, in the heated obscurities of factionalism, people may lose sight of the simple fact that almost none of the ills of the profession were caused by the MLA and almost none would be cured by its abolition or reform. It did not create and does not in itself perpetuate the prestige of scientific scholarship; the main harm it does is to promote melancholy in those who attend its conventions. A shit-eating attentat against that dropsical giant? Herzen must be squirming in his grave.

But such "guerrilla theater" antics, whether politically serious like the Alice-in-Wonderland trial of the eight Chicago "conspirators" or symbolically troubling like the Living Theater's *Paradise Now* or just plain buffoonish like the Kampf seizure of the MLA, are a far cry from the aims and methods of science. Quite as obviously, modernist writing is no determinant of behavior; two Joyce scholars I know are, as citizens, on the conservative side of liberalism. If my argument is to have any validity, I must do some connecting.

My thesis is this. Qualities which are true goods in the realm of science, impersonal objectivity above all, are in most respects inappropriate to the moral, social, and aesthetic realms. Yet the manifest successes of science, especially in dislodging religion, and its intellectual prestige are so overwhelming that those qualities—methods, concepts, attitudes—have been translated wholesale into these realms of our affective lives, with frequently inhuman results. The most extensive way by which this translation has been effected in recent times is "behavioral science," especially psychology and sociology, but modernist literature has made the strongest imaginative impact. I, of course, do not view this figurative translation as what modernist writers set out to accomplish, nor do I mean a judgment on them either literary or moral for having done it; that they did it is what matters.

Let me make my point by citing the example of the highest, *Ulysses.* Fairly ordinary people going about their very ordinary lives (nothing is more democratically egalitarian than science's view of its subjects, its data); seen by a detached, remote, utterly controlling mind (without a personal God, even novelists sometimes aspire to be impersonal like scientists); in prose and narrative styles borrowing from and parodying traditional styles (leave no authority or custom unchallenged and even untainted); overwrought with arbitrary, sometimes nonsensical intellectual games (like some of those geometries mathematicians enjoy playing with); concerned, beneath all the antics, to picture the truth about those unfulfilled dwellers in that unsplendid city (not just the author's moral vision of them but the truth)—whatever else this novel does and whatever else you may think of it, if it does not leave you to some extent confused, then you have not really read it. Now Joyce was not particularly interested in science and socialism, and he was certainly not interested in converting you to scientism (or to anything else except devoting your life to studying his books). Yet *Ulysses* powerfully communicates modernist attitudes, not least because the book's god, the author, perversely leaves it unresolved and leaves you imperfectly gratified—whereas *Anna Karenina*, that elegantly shaped story of rich, beautiful, noble, passionate lovers and decent citizens, powerfully communicates a very different set of attitudes, troubling you to the classical pity and terror and then purging you of those troubles.

5.

Like literature, science is only an aspect of reality; the error of scientism is to mistake it for the whole. In this concluding section, I explore some of the consequences of this error as it ramifies in our aesthetic, moral, affective lives.

Science and technology really do progress. Only fools speak of progress in the arts. But, despite all the evidence against, true believers in scientism maintain that important social progress is possible and will improve our nature. In my view, this belief, shared by capitalism and socialism, is not only untrue but, being very influential, has contributed, not least by experimenting with human beings, to the dreadful state the world is in now. The discouragement is that progressives, in their bigotry, see as the only remedy to our dilemma more progress.

To pure science, no fact or thing has more intrinsic value than any other fact or thing. Transported into the social world, this provides support for the glorious ideal of equality before the law—and can also be used as illegitimate, surreptitious sanction for that envious leveling which is the special hazard of democracy.

Science, taking nothing on faith, accepts only those ideas which can be proved rationally, tested by experiment, and built into a construct of logical thought. But, since our motivation is mostly irrational, those who put their trust only in the rational easily lose control of their irrational forces—indeed, as in totalitarian regimes, the irrational makes a bondservant of reason and apes logic, with monstrous results. Reason's highest *moral* job is to govern our impulses well; to accomplish this, it must not only know but respect and delight in their fearful, holy strength, including the might of aggressiveness. (Where better to learn this awe than in great literature?)

Science admits no limits but the possible. Translated, this becomes contempt for every authority that is not wise, good, and true, and denial of all taboos. But very few authorities, being people, are wise, good, and true all or even much of the time; and if, as I believe, we are taboo-makers by nature, then surely the consequences of smashing recognized taboos (currently the sexual ones) must be that we will make unrecognized ones in their stead: noisily to emancipate sex may be surreptitiously to immure love. Such an intellectual as Norman Mailer has speculated on violating even the taboo against murder, and some of the young nihilistic terrorists are trying it out. Weakening the murder taboo might lend strength to the cheerless new prohibition against having children. Of course something must be done about overpopulation. . . . Then what?

Science, to stay vigorous, must constantly press on (like a military avant-garde) into unknown territory. In art and society, the avant-garde has degenerated into guerrilla bands, crazy for novelty, scornful of the past, and demanding relevance to present concerns: ME NOW.

Over and above these transmutations and others like them, there is the straightforward impingement, not only ecological but also spiritual, of technology on our inner lives, through the media and the arts. In this respect, literature, being less accessible to technological intrusion, is luckier than painting, sculpture, and music, to say nothing of the technological arts of photography and cinema; language just about *has* to make sense to keep going, and making sense is a kind of order, a purely human order at that; to use words powerfully, you have to think, because words fight back in a way that electronic sounds, poured concrete, paint, and light on film do not. John Cage, that destroyer of music, simply could not have made it in poetry.

When Beckett abandoned language, he tried such dodges as having sighs set to music; but even sighs, howls, moans, shrieks mean something human, and an opera even of sighs is a structure that does whatever it is art does. Let the tombstone of modernism be Beckett's Nobel Prize, and its epitaph be his statement that he will never write again, never create anything new again. (And let us also give thanks that he has disdained his celebrity and refused to degenerate into the mod and the pop.)

The career of I. A. Richards should be exemplary for the profession of English. In the 1920s he published books which formulated scientific principles for analyzing language and poetry, that is, for taking them apart; in the 1950s he began to publish verses and plays, putting language and poetry back together. In his entry in *Who's Who in America*, he no longer lists the scholarly, would-be scientific books that made him famous.

Science adjures: "If a problem is stated correctly, it can be solved. Observe. Experiment." And everything science deals with is turned into a problem. But this does not so much translate as transmute when it is imported into the moral world. It becomes something like the following: There being so much obviously wrong with mankind, there must be endless behavioral problems to solve. (I heard a physicist, subsequently renowned for his speculations on antimatter, assert that within twenty years we would have the body-mind problem solved. That was fifteen years ago.) If physiology, electricity, and chemistry don't solve a human problem, then the problem must be psychological or social or, more accurately, a combination of both. (Or maybe it was just an evidence of *mental illness*, that convenient cesspool into which to dump and half-forget all sorts of behavioral problems that won't go away, won't get themselves solved by some other means.) We must constantly press for new social arrangements (even though the harder we press the more *insane* we call society, since all too often *insane* is applied to those who resist our version of the way things are). Never rest content, never accept what is, never submit to the given. If a social arrangement isn't downright wrong, at least it can be improved (unless it is too *sick*, in which case better get rid of it, of the whole *sick* society, and start all over). The correct way to think of any injustice is as a problem, first to be correctly formulated and then solved; if you cannot formulate it successfully into a problem solvable by social action, then it must be evidence of mental illness, a new sort of problem for which there is a simple pseudosolution—forced, indefinite sequestration in mental hospitals. (In fact, things get dreadfully muddled in the category *mental illness:* most of the inmates of these jails masquerading as hospitals are poor and weak, more likely the victims than the perpetrators of injustices. Whichever, the problem is put away. See Thomas Szasz's *The Manufacture of Madness.*) Hierarchy is to be abolished, as is ceremony. Aggression is a tough problem because it seems to be a built-in feature of the beast; best eliminate it by genetic change. Worst of all is religion, that tool of the ruling class, for it counsels resignation to this unjust world (though not to all the injustices in it) and acceptance of the authority of God and so of authority itself, and it says that the paradise of justice and love and freedom is attainable only in heaven. How unscientific! What lies!—So far as I can tell, one of our privileged young, molded by behavioral science to see his world and himself as thronging with problems he should try to solve, is more likely to be malcontent, disaffected, solipsistic, spiritually wretched than is a slave in a society which held slavery to be in the nature of things (so long as it also had halfway humane laws to protect him from too brutal a master and to give him, if he were exceptional and lucky, a chance to rise, a legal escape): the slave's enemy is external, and there is a great deal to be said for having your enemies *out there*, as pseudoproblems are not. Slavery at best was a deplorable institution, and to revert to it now would be depraved; but it never was misconceived as subject to rational solution; it was a vice to be combated with passion and force. Imagine being a young person trying to solve your sexual problem. I remember seeing the phrase somewhere recently, "death as an emotional problem." If "Who am I?" is a problem, no wonder drugs are so popular.

I have a sociologist friend who assumes that applying the methods of science to social problems will be good for us. He wants us to be happy, and, a good liberal, he also believes in democracy and egalitarianism. But his own research, a study of the attitudes of college students, has told him that students are happiest in an institution with an authoritarian, undemocratic governance, not with a more or less participatory, republican one, much less a permissive one. He has looked for the mistake he must surely have made somewhere, but he cannot find it. Science tells him he must publish his findings; liberalism tells him not to, for publication might harm the cause. He had never supposed it possible that for him to tell a scientific truth might be bad, that to do good he might have to suppress or distort a truth. If he were a man of spleen, in this dilemma, he would take vengeance on the world by publishing: our unhappiness would make him feel better. If he were self-sacrificing, he would withhold his knowledge, buying our happiness with his guilt. He does not strike me as being either splenetic or self-sacrificing; I don't know which he will do, or for what ultimate reason.

I am in a dilemma myself about which choice I want him to make. Since I do not believe in the liberal cause as extensively as he does and since I doubt that publishing his findings would cause much to happen one way or the other, I am chiefly interested in the results the decision might have on him. By publishing, he would publicly undermine his trust in egalitarianism. Good. By withholding, he would betray his duty to (behavioral) science and so undermine that faith instead. Not quite so good, for science, on its marvelous, remote, stark island, is worth a man's faith. Either way, I hope he begins asking some first questions: "Is what I am doing really scientific? Even if it is, should I be doing it?"

Of course he might wind up deciding he had misspent most of his life. . . .

One who imposes the values of science upon the moral and social life is likely, if he is of an emotional nature and has much spleen, to be in a state of chronic restlessness. The usual form this takes is rebelliousness and hostility toward those who are not with him. Rapid and extreme social change becomes for him a necessity, without regard to the anxiety which such change generates in ordinary people and to their reactive cruelty because of that anxiety. When rebelliousness is elevated to orthodoxy, then courtesy, respect for authority, and obedience are likely to become despicable; but to put on discourtesy, contempt for authority, and disobedience, as is so fashionable these days among with-it blacks and privileged young whites, is by no means the same as to be genuinely revolutionary. Indeed, often it looks like desexed masochism: to take a noble course, as Martin Luther King did, which entails attack on you by your enemies is one thing; to employ noble-sounding words in order to provoke attack on yourself by both enemies and friends is quite another. To discriminate between these two modes of action is not always possible and seldom easy; "Notes from Underground" is the best guide to this scientific-rebellious masochism I know of.

What reason says about a true revolution is: for it to succeed, a sizable portion of the people must want it and an even larger portion must acquiesce to it, and the state must be weak, that is, the rulers must not be able to give clear and consistent orders and/or the soldiers and police must be disaffected enough to be ready to refuse to obey orders or even to mutiny. What reason says about the situation in the United States now is this: a large portion of the people want not to have a revolution but are willing to accept reforms, and the state is strong. It also says that large numbers of blacks and of the young are disaffected with our social values and are tempted by amorphous violence. What threatens us is disintegration, not revolution.

The antireformist rebel who is willing to seize power and exercise authority, like Lenin, can hold together, for he bows to reason: if his revolution is unlikely to succeed, he sits tight and studies hard. But when reason itself has been unhorsed, the rebel disintegrates: like the Black Panthers he may go through the conventional motions of revolution, to win chiefly a delusional martyrdom (anyone who has read the papers knows *cops kill cop-killers*); like a fascist he may parody revolution and impose a travesty of authority and order, brute, pseudolegitimate force; at the extreme he may degenerate into a real *Sadiste*, like Bernadine Dohrn, leader of the Weatherman faction of the SDS, who said of the Manson murderers: "Dig it, first they killed the pigs, then they ate dinner in the same room with them, then they even shoved a fork into a victim's stomach! Wild!"

The archetypal modernist antihero is Dostoevsky's Underground Man (1864):

> I am a sick man. I am a spiteful man. I am an unattractive man. I believe my liver is diseased. However, I know nothing at all about my disease, and do not know for certain what ails me. I don't consult a doctor for it, and never have, though I have a respect for medicine and doctors. Besides, I am extremely superstitious, sufficiently so to respect medicine, anyway (I am well-educated enough not to be superstitious, but I am superstitious). No, I refuse to consult a doctor from spite.

Now that modernism is in its decadence as a movement, the symptom has become part of the orthodoxy. At the outset of *On Modernism*, Kampf says of himself:

> Being modern, and naturally diseased, I cannot leave well enough alone; being an intellectual with some pride, I assume you will be only too happy to take the plunge with me.

That this "diseased" literary anarchist, who wrote "if an intellectual is to carry out his task of criticism properly, he must necessarily be a revolutionary socialist," should have bothered to "seize" the second vice-presidency of an association of scholars for whom he had expressed his contempt in this stale hyperbole, "an army of vermin," and that he should be a professor at a respectable university that pays good middle-class salaries out of funds derived mostly from the government . . . See what dealing with modernism did to that sentence? There is just no satisfying way to conclude it.

The first, and a very instructive, portrayal of what modernism can do to a man was drawn by Diderot, that exemplary philosophe, in *Rameau's Nephew*. With the dark side of his splendid mind, Diderot (who is the reasonable, balanced *I* of the dialogue) guessed one kind of character his Enlightenment was going to produce. The *he* of the dialogue, Rameau, is a compendium of Enlightened (rationalistic, anti-religious, "scientific") attitudes and of spite. "*He:* The spleen that's corroding my dear uncle's innards seems to fatten his dear nephew." It is a toss-up whether he feels more spite against power or against goodness, but there is no question what makes him feel worst of all: to be confronted with excellence in any form. "I've never yet heard a genius or great man praised without feeling secretly furious. I'm envious. When I hear some little degrading thing about their private lives, I always listen with pleasure. It brings them down to my level." He can't keep from loving good music; so his nastiness for musicians knows no bounds, and he is careful to pollute or abort his own performance of music. Not that his vices are new in the history of things; and though he expresses a good many Enlightened notions, he obviously could not have been reared on them. "My sole merit is that I have done systematically, out of clearsightedness and a reasonable and just view of things, what most other people do gropingly, by instinct." What Diderot was doing was speculating on what might happen in a fellow with unpleasant impulses—Diderot was not as gullible as Rousseau about the nobility of man's nature—should those impulses be freed from the old restraints by a rationalistic subversion of morality and custom. "Since I can manage to find happiness through vices that are natural to me, acquired without labor and retained without effort—vices condoned by custom and congenial to my protectors—vices that are closer to their own little private needs than any virtues would be, because virtues, like so many reproaches, would make them uncomfortable the livelong day—it would be strange if I tormented myself like a soul in hell just to turn myself inside out and be something that I am not. . . . Virtue inspires respect, and respect is uncomfortable. Virtue commands admiration, and having to admire someone is no fun. I have to deal with people who are bored, and I have to make them laugh. Well, nonsense and madcap pranks are what provoke laughter; so I have to be nonsensical and madcap. And even if Nature hadn't made me that way, the best I could do in that case would be to act as if I were." (Had Diderot not been a decent and almost conventional man himself, he might have gone whole hog and invented *Sadisme*, thereby saving the Marquis the trouble of writing all those vile novels.) Diderot did not dare publish *Rameau's Nephew* in the 1760s when he wrote it—bad for the Enlightenment. (It was first published in 1805, in a German translation made by Goethe.) Now, every English major should be required to study it, for monitory as much as for literary reasons: *See what can happen to you if you don't take care.* For *he* is not just our contemporary; he has become our colleague too; the scholarly establishment has, confounding everything, opened its doors to him and he is of it, he presides.

Will it do him in—or will he destroy it first? Myself, I am rooting for both sides: I hope they both win. Soon.

Perhaps what I am doing is reawakening a dream I first had years ago when I began to teach and have had off and on over the years since; a beautiful dream; I'll never let it go to sleep again: that literature belongs to the common reader, and also to the teacher who, scholar or not (probably not), loves it and wants to help young people who love it quarry it for ideas about reality and, sometimes, for instruction on how to live, on their duty toward their fellowmen, on love's maze, on what to do about guilt, on forgiveness, on the contract each person makes with himself. The teacher does this in the civilizing faith that to know story and drama and poetry can help us toward the core good of mind, self-knowledge, that without some of which all other knowledge, especially impersonal knowledge, is dangerous, can become a source of great evil.

5

Teaching Writing

I

Nowadays there is much discussion of a civil war that is said to be raging in American education. On one side are the powerful: the public school system, including nearly all administrators and teachers and reaching out through boards of education into the governing institutions of our society. On the other side are the weak: the children, a few teachers, possibly a very few administrators, and some champions such as Edgar Z. Friedenberg. The system (Bad) cripples the children (Good) to fit the requirements of this society (Bad) instead of setting them free to be creative (Good). Even according to this manichean Good/Bad scheme, things are a lot more complicated in college than they are in school. College students are not children any longer, though it is an American custom (Bad) to treat them as children. A lot of college teachers and even a few administrators are intellectuals (Good), so that in any halfway decent college the students, at least in the social sciences and humanities, are led to question (Very Good) the values by which America lives. Nevertheless, basically the same war is raging in the colleges as in the schools, because in both the ultimate power, money, is controlled by governing boards chosen from The Establishment, i.e., people important in business, church, and state.

In more activist moods, I pretty much accept this scheme. But now, wielding a pen—a tempering, cooling instrument of thought—I am made uneasy by it. Good/Bad makes me skittery. Children don't seem to me all that weak; they generate strong emotions both in themselves and in adults, and that is a considerable power. Their chief weakness, obviously, is ignorance; in addition to not knowing how the world is put together, they don't know how best to use their power—for which good reason the job of education is to give them some truths and no lies about how the world works and some training and advice about how to direct their powers to fruitful ends as well as to restrain them from sterile ones. I believe, like a proper liberal, that children are naturally creative and full of love and that everything possible should be done to let them grow up that way; but I also believe, after Augustine and Freud, that every child is a compendium of vices which must be controlled if he is to grow up to be a tolerable member of society. How to accomplish both these ends at once, I have no notion; I think they are ideals to be striven for, like justice and freedom, in the knowledge that they can never be attained and that to attain either would be to destroy the other. I believe that society, politics, the law, is a necessary evil ("Democracy," Churchill is supposed to have said, "is the worst form of government ever invented except for all those others"). That is, I do not see the loose federation of small true primitive communities dreamed of by idealistic anarchists as being a real option available to us; I see as far more probable the mere anarchy of nihilism, which I dread, or the totalitarian State of nihilism, which I dread quite as much. Finally, in this whole matter of school against child, society against the individual, I am suspicious of the metaphor of war. War, including civil war, seems to imply victory or at least a possible cessation of conflict, and it certainly implies an unhappy state of affairs disruptive of that most desirable condition, peace. But I conceive struggle as being in the nature of human life, itself a source of vitality, never-ending; I do not see the combatants Law and Impulse as being in themselves just good or just bad, nor do I see the struggle between them (in any form, including School versus Child) as being just good or just bad. But I do see the alternatives to this struggle as being just bad. Such struggle could be eliminated on the one hand only by our annihilation, which is an unreality suddenly made actual in 1945, or on the other hand by our attaining utopia, which is equally unreal though genetics seems to be bringing it within the realm of possibility. In my view, utopia was a pleasant dream so long as it was clearly unobtainable because of our nature; but genetics may very well be giving us the power to change our nature, and that appalls me as much as does the power to exterminate ourselves which physics gave us. For even if we should endeavor to perfect ourselves by breeding out our destructive passions—and I see little reason to suppose that that would happen since we as we are now are the ones who must do the breeding—even so, I am against that endeavor, on the grounds that we are perfectible only in certain ways, not in all, and that to make ourselves lopsidedly better is a form of denaturing, dehumanizing ourselves. I hope people don't decide to attenuate into Houyhnhnms, just as I hope they don't allow themselves to congeal into Yahoos: I hope they decide to remain human. And I don't take "human" as synonymous with "good": Stalin was human, Martin Luther King was human, and so are you.

No one in his right mind supposes perfection is attainable in teaching college English, especially teaching writing. But it can be done better than it is commonly done now, and I have some ideas, derived largely from experience, about how to do it better. They won't effect an immediate and radical reformation of American institutions, for even figuring out how to start such a reformation is a full-time job and I'd rather teach and write; but they do involve subverting those institutions enough to get your work done, to teach better than you're supposed to.

My first teaching job was in a ratty private high school in Berkeley, and towards the end of my year there I learned two things that have since influenced me a good deal. One was that it was the student's IQ more than his grades which decided our principal on whether to recommend him for college; indeed, she often changed grades, up or down, without consulting the teachers. Ever since discovering that, I have viewed grades, credits, admissions standards, degrees, nearly all that goes on in registrar's offices as mostly irrelevant number-jumble of the sort with which our lives generally are cluttered. The only trouble with this contempt of mine is that it was so easily come by and is shared so wearily by so many of my colleagues: the corrosions of cynicism. The other thing I learned happened in the midst of a class discussion of Blake's "Garden of Love." A diligent, worried-looking, phlegmatic C-student in whom I had thus far detected no spark of soul suddenly said, "I get it! Poetry's double-talk!" Light, and on a couple of other faces reflected light. I have no idea whether he has continued to read poetry or just how much I had to do with that moment but I know that such illuminations are among the high goods of teaching. I also know that the main contribution an educational system can make to such experiences is to get students, teacher, and books into a room together—not so much, though you can't do without it. Once you are in the room with some students, what practical measures can you take to produce such moments? I have never found out. Like instants of grace, they come according to a mysterious scheme over which we have only a negative control: we can keep them from happening by the relentless pedantry of legalism and factology, by denying imagination, by disciplined dullness.

The next year I got the deadliest teaching job I've ever had, teaching bonehead English at the University of California to freshmen who failed, as most did, an entrance exam in reading and writing. Syllabus, grammar, spelling drills, red ink, the works: it was a higher rigid system intending to remedy the deficiencies of a lower rigid system. It worked impeccably in suppressing imagination in all the Americans in my three sections, but I was lucky enough to have also a Mexican Indian who had begun to learn Spanish at the age of twelve and was only now, new to the States, beginning to learn English. He was as handsome a man as I have ever known, with the most intense gaze, and he turned in the livest writing I saw from a student for years, until I began to have near-professional writers in advanced writing courses. He wrote a prose rhapsody entitled "When Socialism Come to Mexico," which I marked meticulously and graded 10 (10 was to F as F was to A). In conference I talked to him about idioms, conjunctions, dangling participles, the run-on sentence. He turned in another paper, snatches of which I still remember, on the execution of Emperor Mamilliano and G'ral Miramon. System to the teeth, I red-marked it as before. I don't remember what else he wrote that term; nothing much. I didn't feel particularly bad about this at the time: I was busy with my own affairs; I had the merest glimmer of what teaching could be. System makes many things easy, including hardness of heart, and it safeguards the perplexed, the slothful, from many dangers. It is here to stay.

After the war, I got a regular teaching job at St. Mary's College near Berkeley. At the first faculty meeting of the year, the president told us to "keep a united front against the students." The charitable interpreted this, "don't knock your colleagues in front of students." This seemed to me mere decency, and still seems so; it is not hard to discourage students' impertinent probes; by your recommendations, you let them learn as much as good manners permit them to know of your private opinions of other teachers. Maybe this is what the president meant at that meeting, but it is not what he said. I think he meant what he said literally, as too many others rigid with system so mean it. However, I think no better of those who in effect adopt the other extreme as a sort of motto for action, secretly keeping a united front with the students against the faculty. Teachers and students should no more be like lovers, in my view, than like guards and prisoners. They should be like parents and children: authority *with* love.

Fortunately the president did nothing to unite us against the students beyond telling us to, which united some of us, all right, against him; in the classrooms we were free to use our authority as we saw fit. (An indolent despotism leaves you far freer than a diligent democracy: committees. At St. Mary's in those days, we had no committees; next door in democratized Berkeley, the chancellor appointed a committee to select the committee on committees.) Though I used that huge word "love" to suggest something of the relation of teacher and students, I cannot claim to have individually loved many of mine very much over the years, roughly as many as I have hated. All the same, I began to notice, at St. Mary's where I learned most of what I know about teaching, that an odd thing kept happening in my classes—not in all of them, just in those I felt to have been reasonably successful. At the beginning of the semester, I would enter the classroom cold, stiff, full of system; I was ready to be disgusted by the ignorant indifference of the students, their stupidity, their poor language. But sometimes, late in the semester, I would look forward to going into the same classroom with pleasure, charged up by the students' energy, their improvement, their sprouts of imagination. I did not talk much about this experience to other teachers, not wanting to seem boastful, fearing it might be illusory or a symptom of some sentimentality in myself. A Chaucer man helped me define it—the Chaucer men I have known have tended to be wiser than most. You can tell a good class, he said, by the way it pulls together late in the term into a kind of community. He did not know how it came about or what he contributed to bring it about; he did not think such a class learned more in the testable way than another; but he felt, as I did and do, that only such a class can be called successful. This is an occasional community; a year later you can't remember most of the students' names; there is no possible way of quantifying the experience, regulating it, reducing it to system. You do not feel separated from the students by your authority in such a class but united to them; you certainly do not personally love them all and may even dislike some of them; yet not only is the experience of such a fragile community a good in itself but also, as I believe, it heightens the experience of literature, which is among other things a form of communion. I have no practical measures to recommend for achieving this happy condition. The ones I employ myself vary from class to class, and none are foolproof. Recently I had two freshman honors classes discussing the same texts, which I had chosen because I was interested in those books at that time; ideal conditions, apparently; yet one class was a success and the other a total failure (to complicate matters, the successful class contained the least cooperative student and the disastrous class the student who wrote the best paper). But it is not just that I have no measures to prescribe; I would not prescribe them even if I thought I had some. For it is of the essence of community that its members make it themselves, learn their own ways to make it. With each new class you must strive for it all over again. Rather, since it is like love, is a kind of love, it does not come by being striven for directly (the people I have known who talked about "working hard at our marriage" wound up divorced); the hard work goes into removing and preventing obstructions, that it may come if it will and stay awhile.

The most effective obstruction within a teacher's personal control is knowing too well ahead of time what he is going to say. The first lecture class of my career was surely the worst, not because my opinions were disreputable or my knowledge inadequate but because I was so scared that I carefully outlined my lectures in advance; at the time I was speaking to the students, I was not thinking, much less feeling, what I was saying; I was repeating what I had thought days or weeks before. You may be repeating the best ideas of the best scholars and critics; you may be repeating opinions you yourself generated spontaneously a year or two before; you may be repeating lecture notes you jotted down thirty years ago. It matters, of course, how good the opinion is; but to utter opinions, even the best ones going, without meaning them at the time you are speaking is the surest mode of pedagogical contraception I know of. System at its worst can do no more.

One day a few years ago a dear friend came to town, and we stayed up till four in the morning talking and drinking. The next day at ten past one in the afternoon, I walked into a classroom with seventy or so students in it and began to talk about the Book of Job. I knew it well, though I had not reread it for a long time and had not taught it before. I had spent ten minutes looking blankly at the text before class. I had only the foggiest notion about what I was going to say, and seventy-five minutes to fill. What in fact I did was to ask a central question to which I did not have an answer in mind, explore all the answers I could think up and dismiss them one after another, and then with a minute to go come up with a good one. The stillness in the room that last minute and the opening of my voice as I said what came into my head constitute the finest classroom experience I have ever had. I discovered afterward that the answer I came up with was ancient and respectable, the sort of chestnut you'd expect to yawn over in a college-outline series; in fact, for all I know I had come across it long before and forgotten it. No matter: at the moment of talking I was discovering something worth discovering, and I was doing this because of the people I was talking to, for them and for myself at once. The closest thing to it in my experience is writing a story, as I have done a few times, the whole thrust of which is toward a final revelation which I know only when I get there. In Karl Shapiro's figure: "I paint myself into a corner and escape on pulleys of the unknown." That class of Job remains for me the model. Since then, I have constantly aspired to open the classroom door each time with my mind full of the text for the day, whether it is *Lear* or a student's first draft of a story, but empty of ideas about it, and then dive in. This method doesn't always work, of course, but when it does, there's nothing better. I would rather fail at trying to teach this way than to have spent a lifetime successfully not-failing.

Spontaneity is all very well, you may object, for professors who only have to teach two or three courses a semester, courses pretty much of their own choosing, and who have sabbaticals to refresh themselves in. What about freshman English teachers? How spontaneous can they be at ten, eleven, and two o'clock every Monday, Wednesday, and Friday for five, seventeen, thirty-odd years? Maybe there are a few workhorse saints of freshman English, but what about ordinary folk?

If I am not to be convicted of elitism and dreaminess, I must respond to this legitimate objection. The rest of this essay is that response.

II

To begin with, I accept it as a given that most teachers are ordinary folk—always have been, always will be. But I believe that ordinary folk, respectable, a bit timid, decent enough, though they are likely to assume those pedagogic postures which have forever been legitimate butts of satire, do not have to assume them. An alternative to squatting sequestered in the fastness of pedantry is to strive in the classroom to let come into being a fragile community. It is in our nature to make such communities, though of course we can be prevented from doing so both by our own negative wills and by too constricting a system (which it is also in our nature to make). The extraordinary ingredient in making communities is not possessing the power to make them but exercising that power, wanting them enough to risk failure. Our life is so far from nature now, so abstract, and system so obstructs us that many no longer know they have the power of communion, of making even fragile communities, and many have too little hope of exercising that power successfully even to try, even to want to try. The faith must be restored. What can we who are believers but not great prophets do to restore this faith except exercise that power as best we can? "We must love one another, or die," Auden wrote many years ago. Later he changed it to "and die." He was right both ways, but the first time much more profoundly.

I also accept it as a given that mass literacy is here to stay for a while as an American ideal. I don't think much of it as an ideal; so far as I can see, a lot of people seem to have no use, much less desire, for any more literacy than it takes to drive a car or to shop for soap in supermarkets, and I think ladling literacy out to them as we now do is not only wrong in itself, like a dole instead of jobs, but generates in them troubles which do not need to be. However, the ideal of mass literacy flourishes, and so long as it continues to be implemented in the schools, freshman English will continue to be with us in college in one of its many forms, few very good, many very bad. In my experience, the worst as well as the most obvious of its forms is bonehead English—system pure, every response rehearsed. The best is one in which the students' main homework consists of writing essays to be revised according to the teacher's corrections and the classroom time is spent in literary appreciation or in discussing ideas derived from good texts or in going over a student paper. Students at every level, from grammar school to graduate creative writing courses, learn how to write adequately by writing and rewriting rather than by studying rhetoric as a conscious discipline. Indeed, the prose which linguists write in their essays makes me doubt whether the power to join words well is in any way connected to the knowledge it takes, say, to distinguish between an ablative absolute and a schwa. A class in which ideas are discussed and papers are written from those discussions may fail, but it is not doomed to the certain death of bonehead English; it has a chance, at least, of coming to life.

Moreover, I believe it is true that teaching freshman English well is important for the good of our society, which, as everybody recognizes, is in a perilous condition. In my hierarchy of values, our gravest dangers are less those peculiar to us than those we share with the other great rationalized nations, and very few social ills are greater threats to us now than the degradation of our language. In the article on the fused participle in *Modern English Usage*, the brothers Fowler, those glorious pedants, wrote this: "It is perhaps beyond hope for a generation that regards *upon you giving* as normal English to recover its hold upon the truth that grammar matters. Yet every just man who will abstain from the fused participle . . . retards the progress of corruption." Let me spell out how seriously I view the corruption of language. If the general support were to be withdrawn simultaneously from medicine till it reverted to leeches, from marriage till it became a euphemism for shacking up, and from money till a cup of coffee cost three million dollars, our society would not suffer more than it will suffer if the mass media are permitted to triumph utterly. McLuhan prophesies, and many agree, that the media must triumph; if I believed that, I would not want to live, I would go get a job in advertising where the pay at least is better than it is in academia, I would certainly not be writing this essay. Before electronics, illiteracy safeguarded the language of large populations from the incursions of the media, and they used their own words, sometimes well; in this age of electronics and mass semiliteracy only a certain sophistication in language among large numbers of citizens can safeguard it. The language of ecstasy is used to sell perfumed toilet paper, words of passion to name automobiles, the tongue of trust and family intimacy to persuade the oppressed that they want this rich man instead of that to govern them, the vocabulary of all elevation has been repeated into triviality, shoots of spontaneous slang are repeated into self-conscious sterility before they can replenish the body of language with vigorous grafts, the terms of aesthetic judgment have been repeated into a blur, praise is a noisy blur, contumely is a noisy blur, blur reigns. I have heard, though I do not know, that, much as the media have done to degrade language in our nation, they have done worse hurt in Russia; there, such opposition as they are pestered by comes mostly from poets, those very unacknowledged legislators. One of the reasons some vigor of language is still with and of us in the United States is freshman English, which has been at war against clichés, distortion by innuendo, great vacuous assertions, quicksand logic, against agitprop and adspeak, as long as I can remember; and if we do not succumb finally to some computer-made Esperanto of efficiency, one of the reasons will be freshman English. An early act of a stupid totalitarian regime in this country would be to abolish freshman English; an intelligent regime would sanction and accelerate the conversion of it into bureaucratized business English and call it "communication skills."

Perhaps I exaggerate. The homogenization of language is my worst fear next to Nothingness and my worst nightmare. Nightmare is provided with images not by Nothingness but by the approaches to it, and of these the unsouling of language is the one that hits me hardest. But whether I exaggerate the threats to which our language is subjected and underestimate its power to resist them, surely I do not exaggerate the pedagogic importance of making an English class into a little community. In any kind of class, the experience of community is important of itself; but insofar as the purpose of a class is to impart information and skills on the order of geology or auto repairing, community is obviously not essential as it is in football or chorus. In this respect, language is ambiguous: nowhere can an individual retreat more intimately than into that supreme social creation, and The Word simultaneously joins you to others and brings others into yourself. Learning language by rote from books is to the intercourse of living speech as masturbation is to marriage; and ambiguous marriage itself is an intercourse first of words and then of bodies. Your job as English teacher is to get the students to use language your way in large part as a result of wanting to, not having to, be together with you. The teacher from whom a student learns English best is the one to whom he is most connected, and though personal connection may be the finest, the connection of classroom community is as much as an ordinary English teacher need aspire to; it is enough; it can do the job.

The teacher who stays alive is the one who is always learning something new, about his subject, about students, about teaching itself.

When studying a text in class, let the students know your likes and dislikes, your ignorances, your shortcomings.

Don't make them do their reading by forcing them to take factual tests on the assignments. In fact, don't *make* them do anything; let the system do that; that is what it is needed for.

Commend every spark of imagination they show on paper and in class. The better the student, the more scrupulously you must point out his weaknesses—he won't trust unadulterated praise, for he believes he is flawless no more than you do. Overcorrect only those whom you want to keep from writing, for overcorrection is a form of punishing discouragement and only that.

In formulating topics for themes, exert all the imagination you have; seek counsel from books and colleagues; ask your students to help you.

Curtail the talkative, but not by sarcasm; entice, do not harass, the shy out into the open.

When you have been wrong, admit it. When you have hurt a student's feelings, apologize to him. Tell the class ahead of time what constitutes a transgression and how you intend to punish it. When they or you feel like straying from the subject, stray a while. When you feel like smiling, smile. Use your eyebrows, your lips, your hands.

When a session is a bust, dismiss class early, or, if you'll get in trouble for doing that, let the rest of the period be a reading time —if you have any talent for it, read aloud to them. And tell them why you are doing what you are doing: one way to teach students how to communicate is to communicate with them.

Tell them early what you think of having to give grades.

Always hold in mind: much that is old to you is new to them. Speak to their freshness, that your weariness at making a point for the seven hundredth time may not show. This, like a good deal else that goes on in a classroom, is a matter of courtesy.

Know the text at hand far better than what you are going to say about it, even when you are going to repeat what you have said before.

Think of yourself as an actor or rhapsode who must say the same thing over and over, yet each time afresh. You must have a primary faith in the opinions you are uttering, wanting the students to share those opinions or at any rate to consider them seriously, above all to look at the text from which the opinions derive. How to make your utterances sound fresh? Partly by mere technique, but more by not thinking about them between times, by a forced forgetting. Yet, sooner or later, you are likely to hear yourself saying something important not because, not even as though, you mean it at that moment but just because you have said it before: time to change texts.

Words are motions of the air between mouth and ear. Writing makes silent signs for living sounds. It can take on a fine life of its own, but that life is of necessity parasitic on speech. Poetry is a form not of writing but of saying, and the analytic way of teaching it which is dominant in our colleges now is by no means superior to teaching students to read it aloud. To teach English is to present models of ways of talking.

Dickens, that handful of dust, speaks to me; whereas a tepid sack of guts who avidly corrects my spelling errors, ignores my unassigned gropings for words by which to understand the strangenesses I see in the world, and chides my wit for its clumsiness and my lovely phrases for their softness, neither speaks to me nor makes me want to speak. He is not teaching, he is antiteaching.

Socrates and Jesus, those teachers, seldom said what they meant. Socrates was a great ironist; Jesus used paradox and dazzling nonsense ("the meek shall inherit the earth"); both told good parables, stories which are not exhausted by the morals attached to them. More often than not, if you can say what you mean, you don't mean much.

Don't cheapen irony by using it as a mask for timidity.

To teach writing at every level does not mean to prescribe

rules, assign topics, or recommend forms. To teach writing is to help to rewrite. The only point at which I, either as teacher or as writer-friend, can legitimately enter into the work of another, however humble it may be, however exalted, is to suggest ways by which or at least areas in which he might improve it.

The metaphor of writing as organic, a natural, spontaneous expression of the writer himself, has proved to be immensely valuable in criticism; but it does at least as much harm as good for the teaching of writing, for it leaves nothing for the student, much less the teacher, to do once the soil is prepared and the seed planted (and exactly what do those metaphors mean?). It is better to compare a sentence, a paragraph, a whole essay, even a story or poem, to a mechanism with replaceable and movable parts; for in this way revision is thought of less as a tampering with something uniquely the writer's own than as a sort of puzzle which can be assembled in more than one way, but in one way best. Yet the mechanism must seem a living artifice, like one of Yeats's Byzantine hammered gold birds set upon a golden bough.

System.

To teach English well is to conspire within and to some extent against the system that employs you, however good it is. (If it is bad enough, you can hardly work in it at all, even conspiratorially.) For it is in the nature of system to begin to ossify as soon as it takes shape, and as an educational system ossifies, it more and more tells you ahead of time what to say. The only kind of class I know of that approaches bonehead English in dullness is a graduate seminar in which trainee professors are working diligently to learn what to say ahead of time in the classes they will soon teach: they think their jobs depend on it. Such a class would not be dull if only they would concern themselves that seriously with the kind of speech their lives depend on. In fact, not even their jobs depend on dullness as much as they think: the conspiracy is an open one.

I hope that Friedenberg and Co. do not get stuck in the habit of demolition and I especially hope they never get it into their heads that system can be replaced by some nonsystem, by love. I hope they create and disseminate a strong conception of a good educational system and of how to get there from here. But the moment their system succeeds I shall begin to subvert it. In the classroom at least. Though not wholeheartedly. For as a matter of fact, you can have too little of system, procedure, the law.

One of the reasons I like teaching in the Syracuse English department is that I am not obliged to do any committee work. Being unforced, I have served on several committees willingly, including one to find a new chairman—distillate of system! Moreover, I have helped to institute a new committee (after all, "committee" means "a bringing together") that we needed because of the creative writing program of which I am a part. In this program, we give an M.A. to a student who fulfills the course requirements demanded for a regular scholarly M.A. and who also submits, instead of two expanded and polished seminar papers, a thesis consisting of a novel or a small book of poems or short stories. (A system is not yet ossified which can stretch "thesis" to include, say, a novel on the love and drug lives of far-out college students.) But suppose a candidate's writing is, in our judgment, not of acceptable quality. Who is to tell him so, and when? Nobody wants to, for we may all like him and think him intelligent, just not gifted. If all of us professors in the program were of stern moral fiber, there would be no problem. But we are not. We need a procedure and a committee. We "creative" teachers, egged on in part by shaggy, subversive, antisystem students in whom our lack of procedure was generating unnecessary anxiety, have made a system for ourselves and like it.

A very long time ago in Europe when a thesis was still a thesis, a candidate for a high degree had to stand in a public hall before learned examiners whose peer he hoped to become and defend his thesis against their probing, attaining his degree only if he succeeded orally in protecting that thesis well. The defense of thesis became an established part of the educational system in the West, and we at Syracuse have required it of, say, a girl who has written a batch of poems about how she was bugged by her parents and who is she anyhow.

One such defense I sat on (examining professors no longer attack a thesis, they sit on it) was for a young man who had written a novel which we who made up his committee thought well of. By the time this last formality was due, we had already passed him and he knew it. As we examiners ritualistically had him wait outside the door while we conferred, we agreed that we would keep him only half the legal hour. But in fact we stayed the whole time, because we got involved with him in a conversation we were enjoying too much to break up. One of the professors, a critic, was annoyed by a shifty statement in the candidate's required summary of thesis and by his stubborn refusal to modify it. He had written that his purpose in writing his novel had been to tell a good story, and when asked why he had done this, that, or the other thing in the book, he would reply with steadfast shiftiness that he had done it because he thought it would make the story better. He already had a teaching job lined up for the fall. "Well," said the professor in exasperation, "if you were teaching this novel in an English class, what would you say about it?" "Oh, I'd go on about themes and point of view and symbols and that. But they aren't why the guy wrote the story or why I chose it to teach, and I'd let the students know that. Still, you got to keep talking."

My little story is not yet over. In the letter of recommendation I had written for him that spring to send around with job applications, I had mentioned that he, an Alabamian who had served his tour of duty in the Air Force, had been recently active in peace and civil rights demonstrations. One afternoon a month before the defense of thesis, I had received a telephone call from the chairman of the English department of a new Virginia college. This stranger, who identified himself as a retired Air Force officer, said they were considering our candidate and wanted to know more about the political activities I had mentioned in the letter. System had not obliged me to mention his politics; but he and I and the world at large agreed that such activities were an important part of a man, of a teacher, even though not connected with his literary studies or capacities. I told that officer on the other end of the wire the truth of what I knew and my true opinion on it. And I felt somewhat like a betrayer because this student had become something of a friend by now. The next day he dropped by to tell me that the previous evening that same chairman had phoned him, in part because of what I had said about our candidate's politics, to offer him a job, which, partly because they wanted him politics and all, he had accepted.

I guess I'm not absolutely convinced that what we most need is a total revolution of the educational system right this minute. For though at its worst it can outright forbid, and though even at its best it somewhat hinders, the community of classroom, yet our system never commands us to make such a community. Freedom to make or not make a community of a class as you choose is essential if you are to make it at all. Yet much freedom means much responsibility. It is up to each of us to lay himself on the line in every class.

6

The Novelist as Meddler

1.

The word "novel" has been used to describe almost every sort of long fiction. The *Odyssey*, an epic poem, is sometimes called the first novel. *Tristram Shandy*, a satiric autobiography with no plot whatever, is called a novel, and so is *Alice in Wonderland*. But "novel" has also been used more strictly a good deal of the time, to describe the sort of long prose fiction which has been dominant in Western literature for over two centuries. In this essay, "novel" means this one species and not the larger genus.

Not many novels are formally pure in this restricted use of the term "novel." None of the three books listed above is properly a novel, though *Tristram Shandy* is partly one; neither are *Don Quixote*, *The Castle*, and *Moby Dick*. T. S. Eliot and André Gide have said that as pure, as "novelistic" a novelist as ever wrote is Georges Simenon. Perhaps they are right; if so, the lack of strength in his pure novels only suggests the necessity to adulterate fiction, as gold or silver must be adulterated, with some baser alloys, to make them strong. Flaubert and James are commonly referred to as formal masters of the novel; an inspection of *Ma-*

dame Bovary and *Portrait of a Lady* would disclose the extent to which these books are strengthened with alloys of romance and satire. *War and Peace, Bleak House, The Red and the Black, Huckleberry Finn, The Brothers Karamazov, Remembrance of Things Past, Tom Jones:* all these celebrated books are commonly called novels, and all are by any formal criterion manifestly imperfect. In other words, the novel is odd in this: great representatives of the form are impure and imperfect.

The novel, the realistic species of long prose fiction, is differentiated from realistic drama by far more than the form in which it is printed. James's advice to the novelist to disappear into his material, which he must *render, present, dramatize,* pushes the novel toward drama and away from essay; yet a true novel is not just a realistic play with stage directions spelled out and speakers described rather more fully than is conventional with printed plays. A novel presents the characters' hidden life with an extensiveness, intimacy, and analytic subtlety which drama forbids, and it is a story controlled by a narrative voice.

Here is a formal definition of the (realistic) novel.

In the novel, (1) objects, behavior, and social customs resemble those existing in some actual society at some actual time, and motivation is probable, which is to say that the characters are mostly in the middle range of experience without being altogether consistent and if their behavior is extremely irrational it is presented in the light of convention as criminal or mad; (2) the principle for selecting and arranging the parts derives primarily from concern to reveal and to explore the pattern of relations, both hidden and open, of characters with one another, with social institutions, with ideas, with the natural world, or each with himself and his own beliefs; and (3) the reader's relation to the imagined characters is appreciably modified by the attitude of the narrator (who may or may not also be the author) toward the reader, toward the moral and social values of the world he is describing, and toward the characters as imagined persons, including the narrator's earlier self if that self is one of the characters.

The content of the novel, as here defined, is intercourse among a few credible characters and between them and the reader, who knows them by their public actions, their intimate words, and their unrecognized impulses. But this is also the area of moral concern. Both in fiction and in life, an attitude toward the behavior and motive of individuals related in and to a natural and social world almost necessarily becomes moral as it becomes engaged. The scientific attitude toward behavior and motive is that of detached observation; Balzac, Flaubert, and Zola all announced their intention of assuming this disengaged stance, but in fact neither they nor any other novelist worth reading ever did so consistently. The aesthetic attitude of pure interest is much more congenial to a writer than the scientific one, the novel being, after all, a form of art. "Let us become epicures of experience, valuing it according to its refinement and intensity." Gide is the practicing apologist of this attitude. It is possible to read his *Strait Is the Gate* and *Lafcadio's Adventures* in such a way as to value Alissa's spiritual agony above Lafcadio's zeal for gratuitous malice only because imagining her agony is a more refined and intense pleasure than imagining his malice. Pleasure of this kind is of course a part of the enjoyment afforded by even as nonaesthetic, propagandistic a novel as *Uncle Tom's Cabin.* But Gide's theoretical amorality is in fact extremely rare in fiction; it is also possible to read his finest novel, *Strait Is the Gate,* as a work of moral commitment. The very process of writing a novel and imagining characters engages the spirit, and this engagement almost necessarily assumes a moral quality. Even Gide the aesthete trembles on the verge of *ought;* his position can be imagined as this: "To purify experience to its finest and then to explore it, either actually or imaginatively, is my (the?) highest good." In sum, it is possible for a novelist to take the position of purely aesthetic engagement with matters that are the heart of moral concern, but it is rare for him to do so and the results at best are lacking in strength.

Meanwhile, perfect or imperfect, great or small, whatever the moral stance, novels and part-novels all face certain problems in common. Formally, the most important of these is point of view. The ideal held up by James the theorist and by his critical descendants is of an invisible, inaudible author; preferably there should be no narrator; if he is there he must meddle with the characters and their world only ironically, that is, in such a way as to reveal his own character; to author and reader, a narrator should be only another personage in the story. But since almost all substantial novelists do in fact meddle (including James the novelist) and since such meddling is apt to be not just formal but also moral in nature, this essay will concern itself both with ways in which author-meddling does not damage a novel but instead leaves it pretty much unscathed and also with ways by which such meddling can be turned to a novel's advantage, and then at the end with the one sort of meddling for which there is no forgiveness.

2.

A harmless sort of intrusion is for the author to turn from the story to expound his theories on some subject or other directly to the reader. His justification for doing this is that you should understand the true nature of old maids, the gods, social upheaval, storytelling, whatever, in order to appreciate the significance of his characters' acts and thoughts. But what ordinarily happens is that you listen for a while to what the author as a private person has to say, and then you go back into the world of the novel with your own opinions on the subject intact and with your connection with the characters untouched; for as a man of opinions a novelist is no better than his neighbor.

> In devotion woman is sublimely superior to man. It is the only superiority she cares to have acknowledged, the only quality which she pardons man for letting her excel him in.

I doubt it; but this disagreement does not interfere with my understanding of Eugénie Grandet, of whom it is said, or with my affection for Balzac, who said it. Tolstoy's long quarrel with the French historians, in *War and Peace*, and his elaborate theory of history have so little to do with what is valuable in the novel that a disagreeing reader takes to skipping those sections. The most to be learned from those chapters is the hardly surprising knowledge that a novelist, who is primarily concerned with individuals, finds the way of a historian, who is primarily concerned with social movements, exasperating and uncongenial. Meanwhile, however, the long asides do not damage the novel proper, because they are presented openly and separately and because an understanding of the characters' behavior does not depend upon them. One can find Tolstoy's notions about how to write a history of the Napoleonic invasion of Russia silly and yet find, while reading the novel proper, that every action and thought of every important character during his account of that invasion rings absolutely true. For the worth of the novel, the truth of this ring is what matters.

So long as an author is saying *This is what I think,* all goes well enough; when he begins to say *This is what you ought to think,* the reader is likely to resist. Even so, if this preaching is open and is separable from the novel proper, it will do no essential harm.

> That is the whole history of the search for happiness, whether it be your own or somebody else's that you want to win. It ends, and it always ends, in the ghastly sense of the bottomless nothingness into which you will inevitably fall if you strain any further.

I feel Lawrence pushing me with his rhetoric to accept this as true not only for the character who is dimly supposed to be thinking it, but for the world at large. I not only doubt the truth of this opinion, I also balk at being pushed. Even so, my pleasure in *The Fox* remains unimpaired, and my regard for Lawrence continues only slightly impaired.

When a novelist's comments on experiences strike you as true and good, your pleasure is increased.

> There are in the music of the violin—if one does not see the instrument itself, and so cannot relate what one hears to its form, which modifies the fullness of the sound—accents which are so closely akin to those of certain contralto voices, that one has the illusion that a singer has taken her place amid the orchestra. One raises one's eyes; one sees only the wooden case, magical as a Chinese box; but, at moments, one is still tricked by the deceiving appeal of the Siren; at times, too, one believes that one is listening to a captive spirit, struggling in the darkness of its masterful box, a box quivering with enchantment, like a devil immersed in a stoup of holy water;

> sometimes, again, it is in the air, at large, like a pure and supernatural creature that reveals to the ear, as it passes, its invisible message.

This passage has little or nothing to do with any of the characters in Proust's novel, except as it is one of the opinions of Marcel the narrator, who in such respects is Proust himself. But it and a thousand others of its kind constitute much of the excellence of the book. It has a legitimate if slight tonal function in the section in which it occurs, *Swann in Love;* but its main virtue is to give elegant expression to something true, something with which one cannot disagree and for which one could not possibly have found better words.

To a novelist with the urge to tell the reader what something of the world is like, the best, hopeless advice is: Be subtle, be wise.

3.

A description of surroundings is likely to be closer to the heart of a novel than is a general comment on life, because the circumstances in which a character acts modify what he does and our understanding of him. The operative principle here is plain enough: the amount and intensity of the description of anything should be proportionate to the importance of that thing in revealing character but should not be determined by the author's personal interest in the thing described.

Descriptions of nature are notoriously long winded and are commonly skipped—for example, those in the romances of Scott and Cooper. Descriptions of hunting and fishing sometimes go on longer than necessary, even the famous set pieces of Tolstoy in *War and Peace* and of Hemingway in many of his fictions. Readers who like hunting and fishing for their own sake find the passages delightful, but those who are indifferent to those sports find the descriptions excessive for presenting character—though they are not very damaging to the novel since they are abridgeable by the impatient reader. Surely the authors dwelt upon these scenes at such length mostly because they themselves loved those sports.

But here is a description of nature, from Mary Webb's *Precious Bane,* which is wholly justified.

> When I look out of my window and see the plain and the big sky with clouds standing up on the mountains, I call to mind the thick, blotting woods of Sarn, and the crying of the mere when the ice was on it, and the way the water would come into the cupboard under the stairs when it rose at the time of the snow melting. There was but little sky to see there, saving that which was reflected in the mere; but the sky that is in the mere is not the proper heavens. You see it in a glass darkly, and the long shadows of rushes go thin and sharp across the sliding stars, and even the sun and moon might be put out down there, for, times, the moon would get lost in lily leaves, and times, a heron might stand before the sun.

It is a novel of country people who see the world alive with mysterious connections, as the narrator in this description does; and none of the novel's descriptions go on too long.

Closer yet to the heart of fiction are descriptions of man-made things, for the artifacts a character has made or has chosen to exist among affect him, reveal him. Here, the usual advice is to let concrete things speak for themselves, and Flaubert is the model. Emma goes with Léon to the house of the wet nurse who is taking care of her baby.

> The ground-floor bedroom—the only bedroom in the house—had a wide uncurtained bed standing against its rear wall; the window wall (one pane was mended with a bit of wrapping paper) was taken up by the kneading-trough. In the corner behind the door was a raised slab for washing, and under it stood a row of heavy boots with shiny hobnails and a bottle of oil with a feather in its mouth. A Mathieu Laensberg almanac lay on the dusty mantelpiece among gun flints, candle ends, and bits of tinder. And as a final bit of clutter there was a figure of Fame blowing her trumpets—a picture probably cut out of a perfume advertisement and now fastened to the wall with six shoe tacks.

The author imposes on the reader no attitude toward this room and the items in it he has chosen to describe; "a final bit of clutter" does not exceed the bounds of reasonable observation. Two sentences later, Léon's attitude is given: "it seemed to him a strange sight, this elegant lady in her nankeen gown here among all this squalor." Indeed, this is about as meticulously hands-off as a novelist can be. But here is a passage from *Our Mutual Friend* which operates on another principle entirely.

> Mr. and Mrs. Veneering were bran-new people in a bran-new house in a bran-new quarter of London. Everything about the Veneerings was spick and span new. All their furniture was new, all their friends were new, all their servants were new, their plate was new, their carriage was new, their harness was new, their horses were new, their pictures were new, they themselves were new, they were as newly-married as was lawfully compatible with their having a bran-new baby, and if they had set up a great-grandfather, he would have come home in matting from the Pantechnicon, without a scratch upon him, French-polished to the crown of his head.
>
> For, in the Veneering establishment, from the hall-chairs with the new coat of arms, to the grand pianoforte with the new action, and upstairs again to the new fire-escape, all things were in a state of high varnish and polish. And what was observable in the furniture, was observable in the Veneerings—the surface smelt a little too much of the workshop and was a trifle sticky.

This description is not so concrete as Flaubert's, but surely it is fictionally valuable to learn a little about this house in such a way as to learn far more about what its owners are like; and Dickens's openly satiric view of the Veneerings is surely no less legitimate than Flaubert's professedly objective but, in the whole novel, covertly satiric view of the world of *Madame Bovary*. And here is a passage from *The Ambassadors*. Strether is visiting Miss Gostrey's place in Paris.

> Her compact and crowded little chambers, almost dusky, as they at first struck him, with accumulations, represented a supreme general adjustment to opportunities and conditions. Wherever he looked he saw an old ivory or an old brocade, and he scarce knew where to sit for fear of a misappliance. The life of the occupant struck him, of a sudden, as more charged with possession even than Chad's or than Miss Bar-

> race's; wide as his glimpse had lately become of the empire of "things," what was before him still enlarged it; the lust of the eyes and the pride of life had indeed thus their temple. It was the innermost nook of the shrine—as brown as a pirate's cave. In the brownness were glints of gold; patches of purple were in the gloom; objects, all, that caught, through the muslin, with their high rarity, the light of the low windows. Nothing was clear about them but that they were precious, and they brushed his ignorance with their contempt as a flower, in a liberty taken with him, might have been whisked under his nose.

This is literary impressionism: there is not a concrete image in the passage; yet, by suggesting the effect the room makes on Strether, James succeeds in creating in the reader's mind a sense of the room, its owner, and its viewer. And though James's own attitude toward the room is as scrupulously absent as was Flaubert's toward the wet-nurse's room, one is in no doubt of James's aesthetic love of it.

In *Laocoön,* Lessing suggests that, in a competition between a visual and a verbal representation of a thing, the visual must win. If he is right, as he probably is even for people with strong image-making faculties, the usual advice about the best way to describe things in a novel needs qualifying. It is no more valuable to let the things in the room speak for themselves as Flaubert does than it is to give the impression of a room as James does or to give both that and also the narrator's opinion of the room and its inhabitants as Dickens does. Words can carry a thing-in-itself not at all and an image of the thing vividly but imperfectly; but they can, marvelously if less vividly, carry someone's impression of it and relation to it.

4.

Because a point of view is, literally, geographically fixed, there is a kind of assumption that the metaphorical "point of view" of fiction should be fixed too. To a writer who feels bound to maintain one consistent point of view and to keep the same distance from events and people, all sorts of special benefits come from his restricting himself to one clearly defined consciousness, which ordinarily means using *I*. The most obvious benefit of *I* is the increase of credibility: "I was there, I saw it." That the body of *Wuthering Heights* is narrated by Nelly Dean, the respectable housekeeper, to Lockwood, the respectable lawyer, gives the book a credibility and solidity it could not possibly have had if told in the free manner of a Gothic horror story. Another benefit of *I* is that certain of the actual author's narrative or stylistic peculiarities can be put to use by being so disposed as to reflect upon and reveal the character of *I*. Conrad's fondness for generalizing was never put to better use than when it became part of Marlow's character as he tells *Heart of Darkness*, nor James's famous ambiguity than as it opened depths in the story within a story of *The Turn of the Screw*.

But it is only theoretically that lack of consistency in point of view matters very much. Critical prescriptions are to be reached inductively: if many good novels violate a formal prescription, then that prescription must be modified or discarded; and many do violate the one about consistent point of view. *The Possessed* is told by an *I* most of the time, but when it is inconvenient for the *I* to be present at a scene, he simply disappears from the book and the scene is told by Dostoevsky from the unspecified point of view conventional in narratives of all sorts; nor does the book suffer from it. And in *Crime and Punishment*—which is surely one of the greatest novels—Dostoevsky begins one chapter:

> It would be difficult to describe the exact reasons which gave Mrs. Marmeladov the idea of the absurd funeral meal.

For the rest of the paragraph, Dostoevsky speculates on her possible motives. But during the course of the chapter he gets more and more involved with her—presenting her, to be sure, by external description and by objective reporting of what she says—until early in the next chapter he is close enough to say:

> Mrs. Marmeladov remained standing in the same place, as though thunderstruck. She could not understand how Mr. Luzhin could have disavowed her father's hospitality, for by now she believed in it blindly.

Only a narrow theory would object to such a shift in how much the novelist should allow himself to reveal of what is going on in a character's mind. Fielding is sometimes reproved for his intrusions and shifts, even though *Tom Jones* is as much satire as realistic novel.

> [Jones] returned the fellow his empty pistol, advised him to think of honester means of relieving his distress, and gave him a couple of guineas for the immediate support of his wife and his family; adding, "he wished he had more for his sake, for the hundred pound that had been mentioned was not his own."
>
> Our readers will probably be divided in their opinions concerning this action; some may applaud it perhaps as an act of extraordinary humanity, while those of a more saturnine temper will consider it as a want of regard to that justice which every man owes his country. Partridge certainly saw it in that light; for he testified much dissatisfaction on the occasion, quoted an old proverb, and said, he should not wonder if the rogue attacked them again before they reached London.
>
> The highwayman was full of expressions of thankfulness and gratitude. He actually dropped tears, or pretended so to do.

Here Fielding moves from a rather distant reporting of action, to an author-comment which would break any illusion, back to an even cooler reporting. But the shift is open, the author's voice is clear, and the story and characters have vigor enough to survive the comments of writer and reader alike. *Here is the way to look at my characters:* this is bad only if the author's way of looking is stupid and the characters but half-alive.

The theory that the Dostoevsky-Fielding-Balzac method is so inferior to the Conrad-Joyce-Flaubert method as to render their novels inferior as works of art makes one huge assumption: that the reader of a novel should not feel himself in the hands of an artificer or storyteller and that the novelist's true art is to create an illusory actuality, appearing to have no art. But this assumption goes too far. It is the equivalent of that theatrical assumption that the audience can be looking through a fourth wall into an actual room. Just as a spectator never really forgets that he is in a theater watching actors, so the reader of a novel does not really forget he is being told a story. When the narrator is open about his role as storyteller, as most have been in every sort of fiction, the reader happily allows him all sorts of liberties of point of view: everyone recognizes the artifice and enjoys it. Only when consistency is promised must inconsistency disturb.

As for fixity of remove—the steady distance which "point of view" metaphorically promises—it is made nothing by the example of the best, Tolstoy. He moves at will from the most panoramic aloofness above a battlefield to an account of the inmost feelings of a man at the moment before his death, and he moves anywhere between when and as it pleases him; and it is hard to imagine this lordly freedom troubling a reader for any reason but a narrow literary theory or his own private and uninteresting pathology. There is a great peace in delivering oneself into the hands of a writer who *knows:* "Tell us what you know, any way you will."

5.

In fiction the point of view that matters most, and is least like the geographical one, is the author's set of values, what he considers important, especially morally; for this gets at the heart of the novel, the character's being and doing. The subject is so important, and so tricky, that I am looking at it under two aspects: first, the relation of the author's values to the reader, and then the author's relation to the characters he is creating.

Before going on, I must spell out an assumption: that everyone concerned with a novel, reader, writer, and character, has a set of attitudes, preferences, judgments, or values about human conduct, and that, whether these values are conscious or unconscious, articulated with logical coherence or only manifest in sometimes contradictory acts, they must finally be considered, if the word moral is to mean anything, moral values. This is no more than an *ad hoc* definition, much too loose to satisfy any ethical philosopher. Its justification in this essay is to insist that everyone says, or at least implies, "good" or "bad" when he looks at human conduct or when he himself acts: the hyperconscious aesthete for whom the high good is savoring refined experience; the self-indulgent reader who seems to ask no more than that a novel remove him from moral concern but who is also asking for the author and the story to assure him, at least temporarily, that self-indulgence and sloth are all right; even Faulkner's feebleminded Ike Snopes, whose great good is to love, though he knows that the world thinks he should not love, a cow. These are extreme cases. Typically, people accept the code of conduct of their society, class, religion, province, whatever, without much distinguishing between convention and morality. It is a considerable part of the novelist's art both to let the reader understand the code of the imagined world and also to define the characters as they conform to, modify, rebel against, ignore, affirm, use this code.

The novelist's understanding of the imagined society's code of manners and values is essential to the reader's understanding of the characters, but the novelist's own code need not be and seldom is identical with the imagined code. Even where there is a substantial agreement, as with Jane Austen, the excellent novelist yet has a moral vision which much of the time perceives in the characters, including the narrator if there is one, a disparity between official reason and private motive, between society's requirements and the heart's need, that delights the reader and rings true to what he knows. One may say that a novelist will be interested in manners and convention, if only because he needs them to portray his people, and that his code of moral values may greatly differ from that code of manners but cannot utterly deny it. Any sort of writer who, like a mystic, says that social mores are of no importance or who, like a nihilist, says that all actual societies deserve destruction will have little interest in writing novels. Tolstoy the radical prophet necessarily rejected the works of Tolstoy the novelist. To this extent a true novelist is conservative: he says that the society he is writing about is worth at least our attention, for within it and of it are people worth noticing, worthy of our concern. The coherence of a novel depends in part upon the coherence of its characters and of their society. No doubt the society which every novel presents could or should be improved;

meanwhile, something has been presented worthy of improvement. Nobody who can be considered an adequate reader of fiction requires that the code of conduct in the novel's world be the "right" code, if only because a part of what a novel can do is to bring news of strange parts, news of people with unfamiliar customs or with different attitudes toward familiar customs. Similarly, no reader asks that the novelist's own moral code be the "right" one; for those who think they know exactly what the right code is and how to apply it to a given occasion are happier with sermons than with a form so relative, so much a network of relationships and opinions, as the novel.

Nevertheless, since the narrator, whether the novelist himself or a character, is in fact going to have his own personal and moral opinions about the characters, his expressing them openly need not interfere with the reader but may very well please and help him. Both Dickens the novelist and David Copperfield the narrator dislike and disapprove of Uriah Heep, and any reasonable reader so fully shares this attitude that the expression of it adds to his pleasure. But in *Bleak House* Esther Summerson's view of herself is not likely to be identical with a reader's view of her; her humility is too conscious and she is too keen to report the praise of others for her to be accepted at her own evaluation, or, for that matter, at that of the other characters; and in this very disparity Dickens's own estimation of her reveals itself—to the reader's pleasure—as being not identical with any of those in the book. When the expressed view of a character is neither acceptable in itself nor dramatically acceptable as being a character's but is eccentrically the author's own, trouble may enter in but it need not be very serious. Fielding's excessive affection for and approval of Sophia in *Tom Jones* need interfere only slightly with a reader's somewhat reserved fondness for her; and Richardson's almost commercial equating of virtue and virginity in *Pamela* impairs the book but does not prevent one from seeing Pamela's holding out for marriage as a matter of some moral interest and complexity. In both these cases, the authors have created characters and situations of sufficient vitality to flourish apart from their creators' opinions of them. Bad trouble comes when the characters lack this vitality—in which case the author's opinion of them will not help or hurt much anyway. Worst of all is for the characters and actions to exist chiefly to demonstrate the author's views—whether Dostoevsky's anemic saints or Genet's evil-be-thou-my-good satanists or Katherine Mansfield's only-to-be-pitied victims. For in such cases the author's opinions come to be what matters, not the characters, and the reader has experience of polemic in the guise of fiction.

The relation of reader to writer is like that of two acquaintances talking about a mutual friend (in this case a character in a novel). The writer may express his opinions and the reader may share those opinions or allow himself to be persuaded by them; but finally the reader wants to make up his own mind on the evidence of the character's actions and thoughts. The trouble is, he can't. The analogy to the friends and their mutual acquaintance breaks down, because all the reader can know of the character is what the writer tells, shows, arranges, and comments on. The reader may think he is free to make his own connection with a character but in fact he is controlled.

Flaubert's ambition in *Madame Bovary* was to do nothing but present the evidence. However, what reader is (or should be) allowed to admire Homais? Every novelist, even if he does not overtly develop his personal and moral opinions as such, has those opinions and they will manifest themselves whether he intends them to or not. "In a corner of every notary's heart lie the moldy remains of a poet," Flaubert opines like any Balzac and then ducks back into the story out of sight. But whether it shows itself overtly, the author's moral judgment will—must—inform the very structure of action and delineation of character. That Emma Bovary should kill herself at the end of the book is right and inevitable in every way, including that of reflecting the author's moral views; but that the details of her dying are reported so extensively and with such vividness mainly reflects Flaubert's punishing cruelty, just as the hideous blind man's improbable appearance outside Emma's window at the moment of her death singing a love ditty reflects very little more than Flaubert's weakness for romantic irony.

If a novelist is wise enough, he need manifest his moral views only in the actions and contours of his characters and in little cues along the way; if he is not wise enough for that, at least he will do no harm by telling the reader his opinions openly so the reader can estimate how much the novelist's opinions are affecting the presentation of characters and his response to them.

6.

The reader prefers not to trouble himself over the writer's attitude to the character, though he will keep an eye on the narrator when the story is told in the first person. When he agrees with the writer, as he agrees with Dickens about Uriah Heep, or when the writer is so powerful and wise as to give the ultimate illusion "life is really like that," as Tolstoy often does, then the reader happily pays attention only to the characters and actions. But the novelist can never afford to neglect the reader. He must never forget that his connection with a character does not exist for its own sake only but exists partly to create the reader's connection with the character.

In this the most intimate and crucial of novelistic relationships—the writer creating character—there is, finally, the necessity on the novelist not to meddle. He may like the character as a person, and say so; he may disapprove and say so; he may develop all sorts of general theories about the type of person the character is or the social institutions he belongs to; he may be close to the character sometimes and far off at others; he may do all he can to control and direct the reader's response to the character when the character's acts or thoughts are not the instant focus of attention. But at the moment of action, of speaking, of thinking, of choice, he must not interfere; for if at that moment anything whatever gets between the character and the reader, nothing good will be created. Dickens notoriously could not let a dying child alone. Here is the death of Jo in *Bleak House*. The trouble is not with Dickens's comment at the end but with what Jo is represented as saying:

> "Jo, my poor fellow!"
>
> "I hear you, sir, in the dark, but I'm a-gropin—a-gropin—let me catch hold of your hand."
>
> "Jo, can you say what I say?"

"I'll say anything as you say, sir, for I knows it's good."
"Our Father."
" 'Our Father!'—yes, that's wery good, sir."
"Which art in Heaven."
" 'Art in Heaven'—is the light a-comin, sir?"
"It is close at hand. Hallowed be thy name!"
" 'Hallowed be—thy—' "
The light is come upon the dark benighted way. Dead!

Dead, your Majesty. Dead, my lords and gentlemen. Dead, Right Reverends and Wrong Reverends of every order. Dead, men and women, born with Heavenly compassion in your hearts. And dying thus around us every day.

Plato loved Socrates, Boswell loved Dr. Johnson, in *Heart of Darkness* Marlow had strong and complicated feelings about Kurtz; yet the deaths of those three subjects affect us far more than Jo's does because their telling is clean. Tolstoy himself sometimes falters even in his greatest fictions. At the moment of the death of Ivan Ilych, Tolstoy does not just report what was going on in the character's mind but makes his wish Ivan's.

"And the pain?" he asked himself. "What has become of it? Where are you, pain?"

He turned his attention to it.

"Yes, here it is. Well, what of it? Let the pain be."

"And death . . . where is it?"

He sought his former accustomed fear of death and did not find it. "Where is it? What death?" There was no fear because there was no death.

In place of death there was light.

"So that's what it is!" he suddenly exclaimed aloud. "What joy!"

The reader knows he is no longer seeing Ivan's experience plain and responding to that, as he feels he has been doing up to this passage of the story; he also sees this as Tolstoy's wish and must shove Tolstoy aside in order to get cleanly to Ivan.

Here, ultimately, technical advice to a novelist becomes moral advice to any man. Grant others their otherness. "Justice," says Socrates in *The Republic*, "means minding one's own business and not meddling with other men's concerns"—which concern, for a novelist, is the intercourse of reader and character. At the moment of greatest intimacy, of creation, do not judge, or you will be judged for having judged. Like a god, grant your creatures their free will. Like a father, give your children their independence. Like a friend, love them and leave them alone.

7

The Person of the Maker

If you want to produce a complicated reaction in a storyteller, try telling him his fiction strikes you as being inevitable. He will of course be grateful to learn that his stories have hit you right, but, remembering all the false starts, wrong turnings, bungled opportunities, all the revisions, he knows how far from inevitable it was that this story was told in these and only these words. I have never heard of a novelist so Platonic that for him there was for *this* novel a preordained and perfect arrangement of words which it was his art to discover. It just doesn't feel like that to a writer when he is writing. So, you sophisticate your compliment; how beautifully he has created the illusion of inevitability. This will really bug him; for, if he was doing more than just amusing the reader, if he was trying to figure forth a truth, illusion was only a means to a substantial end. Terms such as necessity, organic unity, the inevitable form for the material, can make even a novelist with Platonic views splutter: but but but. So you decide poets don't understand what they're saying any better now than they did when Socrates gave up on them.

I think we do, though, we writer-critics. There have been so many philosopher-critics and scholar-critics over the centuries, tidying up too much, getting things wrong here and there, explaining what can't be explained, that in mere defense we have said quite a lot about what we do, accumulated some wisdom on the matter, not enough to satisfy a Socratic probing, but some. Nor is there much chance that this dialogue between writer-critics and nonwriter-critics will dry up. Tolstoy said of "a true work of art, that its content in its entirety can be expressed only by itself." [1] If this is true, as I take it to be, then so long as literature is being made there will be speculation on whether *that* material would have been better served by another shape than *this* one, and writers will continue to receive generous but inadequate praise which will evoke from them extensive, tricky, often impassioned, but sometimes less inadequate explanations.

A good many years ago I read a couple of novels by Ivy Compton-Burnett and was moved to do likewise. That is, I felt like writing a story in which the plot problem is announced at the outset, developed in clearly marked stages, and resolved near the end, and in which all the characters are connected with the same family and speak concisely and hyperconsciously. I had no story or characters in mind, just the desire to play with this form. I was not concerned that my story might sound like a pastiche of Compton-Burnett. The world I lived in and knew well was the San Francisco Bay area in the mid-twentieth century. This raw material would oblige various modifications on the Compton-Burnett style if my story was to be at all credible—no large family mansions with servants; blurred, uncertain formalities within the family; different idiom and speech rhythms. For me to imitate her very closely would be to violate my experience. Besides, direct imitation would not have been as much fun as playing my game by some of her rules. The impulse to play by other people's rules obviously has a great deal to do with the game of parody, whether the parody is smooth, like Beerbohm's "The

[1] *Talks with Tolstoy* (1922), ed. A. B. Goldenveizer, trans. S. S. Koteliansky and Virginia Woolf (1923). As cited in Miriam Allott, *Novelists on the Novel* (New York, 1959), p. 235.

Mote in the Middle Distance," or rough, like Fielding's "Shamela." But it would not be surprising to learn that Dostoevsky got a similar impulse when he went to Dickens or Raymond Chandler when he went to Dashiell Hammett, and it would be even less surprising to learn that when Faulkner read Molly Bloom's soliloquy he thought "I want to do it too" and invented Benjy.

However the storyteller comes to make his initial formal choices, once they are made they will powerfully affect the material of the story. I based one of the characters in "A Family Matter" on myself; but what I chose to select and rearrange from my own personality conformed less to my knowledge of myself than to the requirements of that comic artifice, and the character is but a cousin to another one I based largely on myself in a novel, cousins twice removed. A far more substantial example of a consequence of formal choice is to be found in *Huckleberry Finn.*

Before he came to write that tale, Mark Twain had already invented the character of Huck, and I think it likely that, if he had chosen to tell this new tale in the third person, in the voice of adult indulgence that he used in *Tom Sawyer*, then *Huckleberry Finn* would have been little more than its predecessor. To be at his best, Mark Twain had to get away from the respectable world into which he had married, in the guise of Samuel Clemens, and which he pleased for a living, which he dared displease only in private. To get away from respectability without displeasing it, this he could manage only at the double distance of speaking an idiom not his own and in a boy's voice. The choice to do this was, literarily, the most important Mark Twain ever made. Perhaps it was also the most fearful; at least, so one can speculate from the facts that he underestimated the book—he thought *The Personal Recollections of Joan of Arc* far better—and that the parts of *Huckleberry Finn* he liked to read aloud were the tamest, those which were most like *Tom Sawyer,* involving naughty-respectable Tom himself. Of course, writing in Huck's voice did not ensure excellence: *Tom Sawyer Abroad*, narrated by Huck, is poor stuff. All the same, it is displeasing to think of the Grangerford episode narrated in *Tom Sawyer* manner, and it is really painful to imagine Huck's temptation to betray Jim told that way.

As it could have been: Mark Twain's decision to speak in Huck's voice looks a good deal more inevitable to us, I dare say, that it looked to him before he made it. In fact, he may not have decided at all; maybe he just fell into it.

I interrupted "A Family Matter" to write another story, "Children of Ruth," which originated not in a desire for formal play but in experience. I knew two upright, intelligent, strong, liberal women in Berkeley, both of whom had had serious difficulties with their children. Since I liked and admired them both, I was troubled to understand what had gone wrong, and since my intellect jumbles when my emotions are strongly engaged, I would be able to understand these two women only if I wrote a story about a third woman somewhat like them, with children of my fostering. As for form, I took the one nearest to hand. That is to say, the story is formally conventional, traditional: here's a situation; first this happens, then that happens and means so and so, then something else meaning such and such; here's the outcome. I had only two special formal concerns, neither of them very important. The first was to make everything quite clear, so that I might understand the better and also because I was tired of hearing my friends complain that my fiction perplexed them; the second was to relieve the heavy, slow movement of the story by introducing midway a contrasting new element startlingly. But most of my attention went to working out what that woman and her children should do and say, not for the fun of it but for the understanding of it. The result is a longish story of considerably more force than comeliness, a kind of synoptic novel—a dwarf of a novel, head's all right but not enough body.

A good deal of fiction derives from the writer's impulse to understand or cause the reader to understand the true nature of part of the world. Whether he does it for himself primarily or for the readers he wants to affect does not matter as much as that he is pressed by the need to understand the world, to order experience. Often he is too pressed. Frank Norris, Theodore Dreiser, James Farrell, they did not play enough, and neither, like most autobiographical first novels, did *Stephen Hero*. If Harriet Beecher Stowe had slogged away naturalistically at her heavy job instead of playing in the manner of Scott and Dickens, *Uncle Tom's Cabin* would never have occasioned the comment, "So this is the little lady who made the big war." If Boswell had allowed himself to play with his material even more than he did, not only would Dr. Johnson be the greatest character in English literature but *The Life of Samuel Johnson* would be the greatest novel.[2]

Not long after writing these two stories I found myself arguing with a theologian who maintained that Aristotle was right, some people are natural slaves. Imagine: slavery not unjust? Since I can't think abstractly about anything as highly charged as this was for me at that time, I had to write a story. Of course I had heard the idea before, but it had had about as much meaning for me as phlogiston or Menippean satire, other people's vapors. However, shortly before arguing with my theological friend, I had met in Berkeley an American woman (black) who had been kept in slavery for twenty or more years by another American woman (white). At the time I knew her, the former slave was working, for wages, as a domestic servant for a gentle, civilized, liberal archaeology professor and his psychoanalyst wife. The children of the slave's former mistress, now grown, had recently freed the slave by bringing suit against their mother and having her put in prison. By what underground route the former slave found herself working as a domestic for my friends, I forget. But it was clear to everyone that she was far happier than my friends about this legal, just relationship: they were barely able to behave like employers, but she went on just like a slave out of Aristotle. "I shall serve you," she declared, and they said, "Please." Of course, I could have written a story based on that experience, a fantastic-seeming but actual story; and there were armed, well-trained, ready battalions of liberal emotions mutely demanding to be commanded forth by this real-life story. However, at the time, I had had a free and equal wife for several years, and a child with a will of her own. Aristotle's notion, illiberal and color free, stayed in the forefront of my mind. In the apologue—or maybe it's a Menippean satire?—I wrote out of all this, "Sandra," I cut most of

[2] I owe this notion to Cecil Y. Lang.

the ties to my own experience: the slave in the story is white, parents are off in the wings, slavery is imagined to be a twentieth-century American custom and the narrator is a conventional young executive. The story is a playful meditation on authority and obedience.

Clearly a good many storytellers are failed philosophers whose intellectual ladders are not long and strong enough to get them out of the foul rag-and-bone shop of the heart. They may tell a parable as I did, or sprinkle their novels with essays as George Eliot did, or intellectify their characters like Mann in *The Magic Mountain.* They may attach the story to the idea with paste, like C. S. Lewis in *Perelandra,* or weld story and idea as Dickens did in *Bleak House,* vitalizing symbol, symbolizing life. No matter how, it is clear that the root and central stem of a lot of fiction is moral thought.

Idea, play, experience, these are important sources of fiction, though not the only ones. "Among the Dangs" was given me in a dream. I have produced a headless monster or two for money. Dickens was sometimes moved to effect social reform. Tolstoy in *Resurrection,* Richard Wright in *Native Son,* D. H. Lawrence sometimes, the Marquis de Sade always, they are out to convert their readers, and if William Burroughs is not intent on disordering his reader's mind, I can't guess what he is up to. No doubt there are more sources yet—lust for fame, revenge, plain competitiveness. My point is that for a writer no story is inevitable but that to a reader an excellent story will feel inevitable. I think one must locate the source of this feeling of necessary order, not in any of the things I have mentioned thus far, but in that which finally unites them when they are united.

I take my texts from Tolstoy. "The most important thing in a work of art is that it should have a kind of focus, that is, there should be some place where all the rays meet or from which they issue. And this focus must not be able to be completely explained in words." [3] What makes a story more than a story? ". . . not the unity of persons and places, but that of the author's independ-

---

[3] Allott, *Novelists on the Novel,* p 235.

ent moral relation to the subject."[4] By putting these two passages together, one from Goldenveizer's *Talks with Tolstoy*, the other from Tolstoy's preface to a Russian translation of Maupassant, I mean to suggest a reciprocal relation between fictional materials, ideas, forms, on the one hand, and the person of the maker, on the other: they reach out toward and converge upon him; he reaches out toward and unites them with his moral vision. I have already been playing with some of the convergings; let me deal more seriously with moral vision, the ultimately important matter in making as well as in judging a novel, that which the maker, while he is writing, can do little or nothing about since it is the essence of his person.

Fortunately, there exists a kind of paradigm upon which I can elaborate my argument. First there are Robbe-Grillet's novels and films, and his theoretical essays collected under the title *For a New Novel;* then there is a critical study of Robbe-Grillet by an American, Ben Stoltzfus, and now Stoltzfus's own "new novel" based on Robbe-Grillet's fictional methods. I argue from no special knowledge of either of these writers. I must confess that I have read only two of Robbe-Grillet's novels, *The Voyeur* and *Jealousy*, and have seen only one of his movies, *Last Year in Marienbad*. I shall speak primarily about *The Voyeur*.

The obvious question posed by this novel is: Did Mathias, the central character, rape and murder the girl (perhaps two girls?) or did he only fantasy the crime? Similar questions of fact are posed by *Jealousy* and *Marienbad*, as well, I understand, as by all Robbe-Grillet's other works. Some commentators treat the novels as puzzles and look for solutions. I throw in with those who think that it is part of the author's plan to raise such questions and leave them unanswerable. My primary reason for thinking he plans this is that the fiction is so very well put together. Here is a writer who knows what he is doing and does it expertly; if he leaves you asking what happened and who did it, surely he meant you to ask these questions, meant you to be unable to answer them. I find it an amusement—a tiny amusement, to be sure—to watch the puz-

---

[4] *Ibid.*, p. 131.

zle solvers take sides: Yes, Mathias killed her; No, he only fantasied it. For by the odd terms of this fiction, the ordinary question *Did he or didn't he?* changes character. Doubt about the facts of the story does not indicate an imperfection of plot but becomes, like the meticulous, objective description of the visual appearances of things, an essential part of the novel's strategy against the reader.

Moreover, we have the author's word in his essays. Of similar questions addressed to *Last Year in Marienbad*, he says in the essay "Time and Description": "Matters must be put clearly: such questions have no meaning. The universe in which the entire film occurs is, characteristically, that of a perpetual present which makes all recourse to memory impossible. This is a world without a past, a world which is self-sufficient at every moment and which obliterates itself as it proceeds. . . . There can be no reality outside the images we see, the words we hear." [5] Hume would have enjoyed this film, composed on his principles of cognition. Robbe-Grillet goes further: "Similarly, it was absurd to suppose that in the novel *Jealousy*, published two years earlier, there existed a clear and unambiguous order of events, one which was not that of the sentences of the book, as if I had diverted myself by mixing up a preestablished calendar the way one shuffles a deck of cards. The narrative was on the contrary made in such a way that any attempt to reconstruct an external chronology would lead, sooner or later, to a series of contradictions, hence to an impasse." [6] Now

---

[5] Alain Robbe-Grillet, *For a New Novel: Essays on Fiction*, trans. Richard Howard (New York, 1965), p. 152. Acknowledgment is made to Grove Press for permission to quote from this work.

[6] *Ibid.*, p. 164. As Jessie L. Hornsby suggests (in "Le 'Nouveau Roman' de Proust" in *L'Esprit Créateur* for Summer 1967), a "new novelist" is like a pygmy Proust. Imagine knowing of Albertine and Marcel only what the love-affair portion of *The Captive* tells. Our understanding of the relationship between the characters is inextricably involved with a reasonable understanding of Albertine's sexual actions and impulses. But on the basis of that "new novel" portion of *The Captive*, she would be unknowable, and the relationship between the lovers and their own personalities would remain for us flabbily, emptily ambiguous. In the whole of *Remembrance of Things Past*, however, Albertine's character and her relationship to Marcel become established for us about as they might be in actual life. What is a limited strategy in Proust becomes a new novel's reason for being. And Proust himself (in *The Past Recaptured*) disposed of Robbe-Grillet's

it is possible to assume, as Robert Martin Adams does,[7] that Robbe-Grillet's theoretical criticism is a lot of trickery, a big put-on: he contradicts himself, he applauds exegetes who contradict him, some of what he says is phenomenological nonsense. True. But I think that at least in "Time and Description" he is not kidding or horsing around. That is, what he says there about his fictional intentions is the best explanation I have seen; it jibes with what I think he is up to; even if he meant to be pulling the reader's leg there, too, I will take this essay straight, for it states accurately what I take the intention of his work to be; his admirers warn us that he is shifty, but to be absolutely untrustworthy is to be in a sense trustworthy, and no one claims that for him. One does not need to trust the person of an essay-maker much to trust the essay's words: they are only conscious. Here is the last half of the paragraph I was just quoting on *Jealousy*. ". . . there existed for me no possible order outside that of the book. The latter was not a narrative mingled with a simple anecdote external to itself, but again the very unfolding of a story which had no other reality than that of the narrative, an occurrence which functioned nowhere else except in the mind of the invisible narrator, in other words of the writer, and of the reader."[8] Adams was right: Robbe-Grillet is a put-on artist. In the most literal sense, far more intimately than by flaying you and wearing your skin, he puts you on.

Ben Stoltzfus in his study *Alain Robbe-Grillet and the New French Novel* contradicts his master and asserts that Mathias in fact, not in fantasy, raped and killed one girl. "The plot, which revolves around the murder of the thirteen-year-old girl, Jacqueline, is not a tale told by an idiot, but visualized by a 'sex maniac.' The novel is full of 'violence sans objet' since the murderer, Ma-

---

would-be scientific descriptive method: "One may list in an interminable description the objects that figured in the place described, but truth will begin only when the writer takes two different objects, establishes their relationship . . . and encloses them in the necessary rings of a beautiful style."

[7] Robert Martin Adams, "Down Among the Phenomena," *Hudson Review*, Summer, 1967.

[8] *For a New Novel*, p. 164.

thias, has no 'reasonable' motive for his crime."[9] How can Stoltzfus be so sure? By importing the psychoanalytic technique of interpreting and applying it to selected cues (somewhat as Ernest Jones did to *Hamlet*). "We can say that Robbe-Grillet is initiating a new naturalism based on Freudian determinism."[10] So sure of this is Stoltzfus that in his own novel, *The Eye of the Needle*, published in 1967, he not only adapts Robbe-Grillet's fictional devices, which are admirable for suggesting a severely deranged consciousness; he also puts into practice the psychologizing he attributes to him. Here is a naked instance of literary influence: Stoltzfus read Robbe-Grillet, was moved by him, misunderstood him, then went and did somewhat likewise. At the outset of the novel, Stoltzfus's main character is unequivocally established as being insane; the story provides sufficient evidence for us to understand how the character was driven mad; all blurs, doubts, evasions, shifts, jumps in the story are attributable to his troubled mind and help us sympathize with him. In my view, Stoltzfus is wrong about Robbe-Grillet, but correct about how to write good fiction: though there is a certain awkwardness in *The Eye of the Needle* which is not to be found in *The Voyeur* or *Jealousy*, it is a better novel than they, because of the author's moral vision.

I take psychoanalysis to be a variant of the Jewish-Christian ethical system. The arrogant dogmatism of the religious moralists is founded on their conviction that they have the revealed word of God to build on; the arrogant dogmatism of psychoanalytic moralists is founded on their conviction that they are not speculating on the contingent but building on scientific discoveries. But beneath their arrogancies, both are fundamentally concerned with the same nexus of motive, guilt, authority, love, responsibility. What are the rules of behavior, and how should they be modified? How keep from transgressing? How cure the ills of having transgressed? What are we like and how should we live? Because Stoltzfus is concerned with such matters, he distinguishes among his own person as maker, the person of his character, and you the

---

[9] Ben Stoltzfus, *Alain Robbe-Grillet and the New French Novel* (Carbondale, Ill., 1964), p. 59.
[10] *Ibid.*, p. 64.

reader, and this discrimination is not just literary in quality but also moral.

Robbe-Grillet, however, could not care less about such niceties of discrimination. He does not permit you to love, hate, or remain indifferent to Mathias, as you love, hate, or are indifferent to a person who is an other. You are to identify with Mathias, become him. Since Mathias is cut off from others, as disconnected as a man can be short of solipsism, catatonia, the padded cell, you are not permitted to connect with any of the other characters—not characters, named vacancies—in *The Voyeur.* Moreover, Robbe-Grillet is not an other for you to be connected with either. That novel imprisons you in a fearful, mad self. If, that is, you play its game. If you don't play its game but insist on otherness, on connections, if you straight-arm the author, you find yourself indifferent to all the named vacancies, including Mathias, but connected to Robbe-Grillet—by intense resentment at what he has tried to perpetrate on you. The one benefit I gained from reading *The Voyeur* was some notion of what a phenomenologist sees when he looks at the world. Case history. A document. Not a work of art.

I believe that there is no greater literary transgression than for the writer to put the reader on, that this is the ultimate possible fictional violation, and that Robbe-Grillet does it as well as it has been done. Stoltzfus, however, psychoanalytically moral through and through, says Robbe-Grillet puts the reader in the position of analyst. "His attack on psychological analysis in reality masks an intense fascination with the working of the mind, insomuch as his novels are the re-creation of a subjective world. It is the reader who, through the effect of his participation, is the analyst, and, by virtue of his insight into the projected images of things, sees and understands the mechanism of the protagonist's mind." [11] But that is not what Robbe-Grillet himself says. "Far from neglecting him, the author today proclaims his absolute need of the reader's cooperation, an active, conscious, *creative* assistance. What he asks of him is no longer to receive ready-made a world completed, full, closed upon itself, but on the contrary to participate in a

---

[11] *Ibid.*, p. 65.

creation, to invent in his turn the work—and the world—and thus to learn to invent his own life." [12] That is to say, he intends his fiction to supply you with materials, and a few guidelines, which you are to employ in making your own creations—of a novel (your *Jealousy*, not the *Jealousy*), of the world, of your self.

Not even Joyce was that immodest. All he wanted was for you to spend *your* life reading *his* books. Robbe-Grillet wants you to become him. As writer and novel-maker, he becomes Mathias; as reader and novel-maker, you must become Mathias; both you and he become that same person, unholy three in one. According to the New Novelists, it is old fashioned to reimagine a novel which the author imagined in the first place; since the New Novel exists only as it is becoming without having a defined form to become, since it is created each time the first time, the reader creates the novel just as the author did; the author's contribution, presumably, is to give the reader the materials and a few rules for making his own novel—a do-it-yourself kit. But you are not to create just the novel: you are also to create the world and your own self, since the world and the self also have to be created each moment afresh. The best term I can find for this attitude is a pretty, if flimsy, oxymoron, creative nihilism.

Robbe-Grillet is a sort of anti-guru, an Ignatius of nothingness. According to his instructions, to read one of his novels is to go into spiritual training for perpetual creating. Well, speaking for myself, thanks anyway but no, I'm too slothful to play the strenuous game of creative nihilism, and if I did feel like playing it I know better rules than Robbe-Grillet's to play it by. Or maybe he is out to get me to make up my own rules? Thanks again, but the answer is still no. I can't get it out of my head that the world was already here, equipped with rules of its own, when I was born into it, and as for that sad little sack of self I was born with, I guess maybe I've had a hand in shaping it up, but so did lots of other people and institutions and forces, many of which I don't so much as know to thank.

I have a friend, a subtle, honest, quick woman, herself a novelist, who is much drawn to the New Novel. Each of us, she says,

---

[12] *For a New Novel*, p. 156.

goes about in the world unable to know the most important part of it, his own head, the space behind the eyes and between the ears where his self, the *I*, is located. The New Novel brings things to focus exactly on that space, saying in effect, "You can't know who you are; here is somebody to be." My friend was thinking primarily of *Jealousy* and of Nathalie Sarraute's *The Golden Fruits*, not of Robbe-Grillet's theoretical essays, which she had not read.

As I see it, this opinion renders meaninglessly arbitrary the fundamental human assertion "I am"—the "I am" in which is implied "you are" and after which comes "I am myself; you are yourself." I don't know how to go any further in than those assertions go. There are in fact people who cannot say "I am," and there are those who say "I am not anybody." Surely it is well to help them get back to the beginning "I am," and to aim them at "I am myself." Surely it is ill to do as Robbe-Grillet does, to get them to say "I am nobody" and then aim them at "I am somebody else." The religious teachers tell us that in order to become yourself you must lose yourself. But there are ways and ways of losing yourself. To do it by becoming simultaneously a rapist-murderer (or fantasist of rape-murder) and a put-on artist, surely there is a better way to lose yourself than that.

Let me quote Tolstoy again on the unifying principle in fiction: "the author's independent moral relation to the subject." And, I would add, his independent moral relation to the reader. One hardly goes to fiction for moral instruction in such matters as the evils of raping and murdering little girls. Fiction is an inextricably moral art not because of prepackaged admonitions and exempla but because of the complex, intimate relationship of author to subject matter and of author to reader. Tolstoy said: "Whatever the artist depicts, whether it be saints or robbers, kings or lackeys, we seek and see only the soul of the artist himself." [13] Myself, I much like one of the ways Chekhov took. In "Ward Six" he in his own person invites me in my own person to go with him into the small wing of a dreadful provincial hospital. "If you are not afraid of being stung by the nettles, come with me along the

---

[13] Allott, *Novelists on the Novel*, p. 131.

narrow path leading to the annex, and let us see what is going on inside." [14] He introduces the keeper and the five madmen, and tells me what he thinks of them—of one especially. "I like his broad pale face with its high cheekbones, an unhappy face in which a soul tormented by perpetual struggle and fear is reflected as in a mirror. . . . I like the man himself." [15] Chekhov then retires and lets me get to know the doctor well, allows me—makes it possible for me—to follow the doctor's terrible descent into confusion and unredemptive loss of self and life. Because I do not confuse myself with the doctor, my pity for him does not mask pity for myself. Because I do not confuse myself with Chekhov, my enormous gratitude to him contains no self-congratulation. I did not create that story, he did. He made it and invited me in.

I am well aware of the objection to these views of mine: out of date, relativistic world, twentieth century, era of individualism is over, humanism, we have changed all that, spirit of the age. Robbe-Grillet is a bit conventional—even respectable perhaps?—in bothering in his essays to belabor the stupidity of applying archaic, quaint, nineteenth-century moral standards to contemporary life and literature. For example, he permits himself the banality of observing that in the Balzacian novel "time played a role, and the chief one: it completed man, it was the agent and measurement of his fate." [16] But after this stumble he catches his balance and does what is only de rigueur for an up-to-date French intellectual in his position these days, he disposes of practically everything else. "In the modern narrative, time seems to be cut off from its temporality. It no longer passes. It no longer completes anything. . . . Here space destroys time, and time sabotages space. . . . Moment denies continuity." [17] I do not know what he means by all this, but I think he means it. It is a coherent extension into blatant inscrutability of his other less extreme opinions and practices.

Perhaps what drove him so far was emulation of the other arts.

---

[14] Anton Chekhov, *Ward Six and Other Stories*, trans. Ann Dunnigan (New York, 1965), p. 7.

[15] *Ibid.*, p. 9.

[16] *For a New Novel*, p. 154.

[17] *Ibid.*, p. 155.

They have pretty well got humanness out of them—architecture and music without much trouble; sculpture, painting, and dance with rather more effort but considerable success; even drama, with Artaud's assistance, by cutting out intelligible language. (Cinema is still all cluttered up with people, but it is trying.) But what is a writer to do, especially a writer of fiction? Without language and people, no fiction. "The novel is dead." That generations-old slogan, never true, might be translated: "The novel is an offense against modern aesthetics." Currently, William Gass in his role as aesthetic theorist of fiction keeps asserting that fiction isn't about people, *really*. Fortunately his own stories belie his theory. The odd thing is that he, best of several, should feel compelled to make the assertion. It is as though novelists with radical aesthetic views were trying to keep *those others* from realizing just how disgracefully conservative storytelling is.

I take all this as being interesting chiefly as a symptom of the greatest modern intellectual idolatry, adoration of the Zeitgeist—not the *Geist* of our particular *Zeit*, but Zeitgeist as a god—not a good god but a powerful one, necessary to obey, to keep up with, not to fall behind, never never to deny or challenge. But this is not the occasion for taking on Hegel, and besides I lack the intellectual artillery to do the job right. So far as I can see, the Hegelian Zeitgeist operates as a sort of cosmic CIA with all halfway-conscious people in its pay whether they are knowingly spooks or not.[18] Well, Robbe-Grillet is a spook all right, but I don't think Chekhov was and I hope I am not. I don't see why you have to write evil stories just because the age is evil. There are other powers to be secret agents of.

I could—one could—find out a good deal about M. Alain Robbe-Grillet, the man in history, even meet him and talk with him; but when I read *The Voyeur* I have only a blurred, hollow sense of the person who made it. I know little of Lady Murasaki and nothing of the nameless Icelander who wrote *Njal's Saga;* but when I read either of them, I have a strong, clear sense, which I cannot define in words, of the person of the unknown maker.

---

[18] I owe this simile to R. V. Cassill.

8

"Not Me, My Stories"

His narrative style is intended to keep you at a certain aesthetic distance whether the story is ironic or straight, realistic or fantastic, short or novel length, in verse or in prose. Partly this is to make sure that, if you read the story at all, you must have done some of the work yourself: he freely employs such methods as juxtaposition and reasonable-seeming, mad logic, and he omits a good deal, especially of emotional rhetoric in passages of intensity for the characters. If you do not imagine the story, you will probably quit reading it.

More, he seldom wants you to "lose yourself" in one of his stories, and never for long at a time, because he intends you to think about it, too. The sort of literary imagining he values most highly involves not only the senses and the emotions but also the mind. Hence his style is a bit cool, on the intellectual side, seldom sensuous, seldom gorgeous, never opaque. The sentences make narrative sense before they do their other things. Frequently, ambiguity turns a phrase, an odd possibility thickens a paragraph, a satiric patina colors a whole story, but he almost never relies on parody, literary allusion, or special knowledge on the reader's part. For he, a literary traditionalist, wants you to thinking-feel about the matter of the story but not about the author's having done so—and certainly not about how he did it, as a modernist fiction requires. He wants you to be somewhat aware of the verbal surface but even more aware of the people in the story, the pattern of their changing connections, what that pattern and those changes mean.

He aspires to be the kind of storyteller whose books are read for their own sake but whose biography only a cultist of creativity would be drawn to read because of those books. It is in part to accomplish this end that he keeps the narrative surface lucid and cool, for you will be less inclined to look at the writer if his style performs a mediating, revealing function than if it excites your imagination. He wants you to imagine the characters' world and to be more or less conscious that you are doing so, but he does not want you necessarily to be conscious of how he got you to do it. If the story is in the first person, he wants you to realize that the "I" is a character in the story and not the author of it; if it is in the third person, he intends the means he uses for controlling and directing your responses to be so unobtrusive that you are not impelled to succumb to him and his analytic comments to seem so true to the givens on which the story is based that you will not quarrel with him, will not feel him there to be quarreled with. He wants you to feel yourself in the hands of a storyteller who knows what he is doing and who exists in history, but not necessarily in the hands of *this* man who has *this* history of his own. If the story is, as it should be, ordered by the author's vision, you will learn something essential about his self but you need not be concerned with those unmysterious accidents and quirks which are most of what we know of each other in ordinary life. He knows far more about the family next door than about Lady Murasaki; but, in and of itself, the little he knows (and wants ever to know) about her through reading *The Tale of Genji* is infinitely more valuable to him than is the neighboring clutter (about which, all the same, he *could* write a story someday).

But his main rationale for the style—formal-seeming, of a certain polish, rather distancing—is moral. Ultimately though not proximately, his stories are meant to bring the reader to felt understanding; and, since intense emotion, in fiction as in life, interferes with lucid thought, he intends his characters to have feelings, sentiments, passions which may overwhelm them sometimes but the reader never. The complex relationships among storyteller, characters, and reader are, he believes, intrinsically moral; and without aesthetic distance there is not likely to be much moral clarity.

This all sounds neater than it really is, for storytelling entwines aesthetics and psychology and ethics inextricably, at least in his experience. Life offers him few higher or more enduring pleasures than making moral-psychological discriminations, especially in the narrative mode. But it does offer at least one.

Occasionally, at moments of intensity which occur only when you have got well into the story, he wants you to disregard literary techniques and philosophical distinctions and ethical judgments and suchlike for a while and just feel with a character, secure by then that the meaning of the character's behavior will be told you by your very feelings and that the intensity of these feelings will not be in the least diminished by reflection. Whether getting to the state of powerful, no longer critical, yet understanding sympathy with a fictional Other is moral or psychological or aesthetic or all three, more this than that, high in this scale but low in that, in fashion or out, he does not much care; it is the thing in the world he most likes doing.

9

Discovering the Dangs

In the good old days, when magic was a useful art and the stars sang in the heavens, it was commonly believed that the circumstances under which a child was conceived might affect his whole character and development. A reasonable theory, but genetics, being even more reasonable, has pretty well done it in. However, until there is a genetics of artistic creation—which God forbid—I for one am going right on believing that the circumstances in which a story is conceived may very well condition its whole future growth and development. In me this condition often operates on the principle of opposition. "Among the Dangs" concerns some savages who in bleak surroundings are living a life dominated by religious practices, and it was conceived in as civilized, sumptuous, and secular a place as I had ever stayed in.

In Saratoga Springs, adjoining one of the racetracks, there is a large, parklike estate called Yaddo, which, according to the will of its makers, has been used since 1925 as a retreat where writers, painters, and composers might go for a few days or a few weeks to do their work without expense and free of any external care.

Yaddo was built in the late nineteenth century by a tycoon named Spencer Trask. The opulent furnishings of the two mansions reflect the taste of his arts-loving wife, Katrina, whom he adored and who wrote. The smaller mansion contains Katrina's special bedroom, painted bone white, with a wall-to-wall faded pink rug, windows on three sides looking across expanses of lawn and flower beds into a nearby elegant little forest of assorted conifers, the whole room some forty-five feet long and twenty-seven feet wide with a fireplace, some pretty little statues of nymphs, and its own sunporch. To Yaddo I went to stay for a couple of weeks in June of 1957.

I was assigned the maid's room just off the large pink bedroom. I felt right in the maid's room, which was only about twice as big as any bedroom in any place I'd ever been able to afford to rent. Moreover, I came straight from serving a one-year sentence in a New York City apartment, writing on a card table in a tiny, jam-packed storage room the window of which had a sunless view of a brick wall ten feet away. Psychologists have discovered that people behave very oddly when deprived of their dreams even when allowed to sleep all they want. For me, New York is a huge dream-deprivation depot; there, my dreaming powers are so occupied with resisting the alarms of the city that I seldom have dreams of my own. In Yaddo suddenly to have silence, spaciousness, no interruptions of any kind all day long, a stately view, the society of pleasant companions, good food, nothing to do but write—it was too much for me. After a day of it I came down with a fever. It wasn't enough fever to worry about; it didn't come from a cold or flu; it just kept up for a couple of days—though it abated for meals—burning the poisons out of my system, as my father would have said.

I was lying in a single bed on a quite firm mattress, flat on my back without a pillow, with one sheet stretched over me for it was a warm afternoon. I had the bodily discomforts that come with a temperature, but I was really quite content for I could feel that fever doing me all sorts of good. I was half-asleep, perfectly willing to let any fever images enter my mind that wanted to. The fever made my skin so sensitive that it seemed to me the sheet was binding me tight, with only my head free. Abruptly I imagined that I was lying bound in hides, with a poisoned spear point so close to each temple I dared not move my head, and with this chant stomping in my ears: The Dangs and the Urdangs, the Dangs and the Urdangs. After I had lain there stiff for a while, terrified and enchanted, I realized that I had just conceived a story. As soon as I realized this, I knew that the climax of the story would occur as the protagonist lay in the position I had half been in, half imagined myself in, and that it would have something to do with prophesying. I also thought at first that there would be two tribes, the Dangs and some sort of ancestors of theirs, the Urdangs—like *Hamlet* and the Ur-*Hamlet*. As it turned out, the Urdangs never emerged from the hills where, for all I know, they're still dwelling in caves. That night my fever broke. The next morning I began the story, and eight or nine days later it was finished, though I had to fiddle around with the ending off and on for a month or so longer.

For me to compose a longish story at the rate of a thousand words a day, particularly a story as complex as this one, is to go at two or three times my usual speed. However, I have occasionally done it, before and since then, though always *after* having thought through the details of what I was writing. What is extraordinary not only for me but for any writer is to sit down to write a sizable story the day after having got the idea for it, especially since I began with no plot in mind, no conception of any of the characters, and an utter lack of experience with any primitives whatever. Yet I wrote with excitement and less difficulty than usual: it flowed from my pen not only fast but easily.

The standard psychological explanation to apply to such an experience—an experience out of the ordinary but by no means unique—is that the story had been gestating in my unconscious mind and this accident merely started its parturition; that the writing of it was a sort of writing it down from internal dictation; that it was produced as a dream is produced, its order and components determined in the way Freud has best described. The classic instance of this process is Coleridge's composing "Kubla Khan." Coleridge wrote of his memory of writing in that opium dream: ". . . during which time he has the most vivid confidence, that he could not have composed less than from two to three hundred lines; if that indeed can be called composition in which all the images rose up before him as things, which a parallel production of the correspondent expressions, without any sensation or consciousness of effort." Then came that accursed emissary from common sense, "a person on business from Porlock," and after an hour of conversation with the person, Coleridge found to his mortification that "with the exception of some eight or ten scattered lines and images, all the rest had passed away like the images on the surface of a stream into which a stone has been cast." The creative impulse had ended with the dream; he was never able to reenter the poem again, nor to recollect the rest of the lines composed while he was asleep. All we have, all he had, left of this loveliest of fantasy poems is fifty-four lines. Coleridge's experience certainly appears to support the usual explanation of these matters: the subject of the poem is a dream; the mood of it is marvelously dreamlike; it was composed while he was dreaming; it faded from the waking author's consciousness just as a dream fades. Now there is probably enough truth in this explanation to make it dangerously easy for one to subside into it profitlessly—though I doubt that there can be any way of determining the gestation period of dreams and stories, and indeed I see no reason why some should not be delivered full-blown from their creator's head the hour they are conceived. The whole truth, I would judge from my experience, is far less comfortable, far more difficult and essentially mysterious.

To begin with, "Kubla Khan" was not a dream. According to Coleridge's own testimony, which I think it presumptuous not to take literally, "Kubla Khan" was a poem composed at the same time the author was dreaming. The dream provided images for the poem. Those images may have been no more than the manifest content of the dream, but as embodied in the words, they are of the very structure and essence of the poem. Why should a reader, while he is enjoying the poem, give a hoot about the analyzable meaning latent in Coleridge's mind behind these images? The images, the rhythms, the sound patterns of the words, these *are* the poem. It seems to me amazing that Coleridge could have composed any poem, much less so beautiful a one, which used the manifest content of a dream even as the dream was going along, amazing that his poetry-making powers worked so well so fast. But I am often amazed by what our minds can do. At the dinner table one evening I told a friend about an algebra problem which my daughter had brought home that afternoon and which I had wrestled with unsuccessfully for a couple of hours. In four or five minutes, while eating and keeping up his end of the general conversation, he solved the problem accurately. These separate actions of his mind were wholly conscious. The unconscious is yet more versatile and multifarious. I see no reason why a man of Coleridge's powers, supersaturated in poetry, should not be able simultaneously to dream and compose a poem about the dream; nor why one should not consider these actions, while intimately connected and to some degree similar, as being nevertheless radically different, quite as different as passing the salad, commenting on the weather, and solving an algebra problem.

Perhaps composing a dream and composing a poem ultimately derive from the same creative source. Freud's speculations on dream formation did not penetrate beyond those elements in the psyche which he could treat as determining and determined. The power in us to shape, what Coleridge called the *esemplastic imagination*, that power as such Freud said little about. How could he? The prime wonder of dreams is that everyone has the power to create them. Confronted with this, all the how's and why's of dream formation fade a bit. Freud, a master strategist, did not confront the mystery, and his speculations on how and why have had the limelight since the turn of the century.

Ultimately the power to make dreams and the power to make works of art may derive from the same root. But my own experience, available to me through memory, is that, wherever the ultimate power may come from, creating a story is as much unlike as it is like creating a dream.

In writing "Among the Dangs," I was faced with the literary problem of preventing a reader from worrying about the inconsistencies between the fantasy and the actual world. This is especially a problem at the points where the two conflict, as they always must. The writer must keep the reader from thinking about it. Suppose a real-seeming story opens with these words: "As

Gregor Samsa awoke one morning from uneasy dreams he found himself transformed in his bed into a gigantic insect." At no point in that story ought the writer to allow the reader to speculate on how it is possible for a man to turn into an insect. For when fantasy and reality collide, reality wins, hands down. As a writer I recognized and dealt with this problem as best I could. But the problem does not exist for a dreamer: the dreamer is his own spectator, the dream is its own reality. My work in composing "Among the Dangs" was made the easier because I was so little interested in all those aspects of the world which are recognizably arranged in a realistic story. The whole thrust of my story was to get away from the familiar world and deeper and deeper into a fantastic one. This left me quite free to use my odds and ends of knowledge about primitive customs and psychology in any way that pleased my fancy; in the story these bits and pieces are analogous to the manifest content of a dream. It also left me free to fabricate any details that suited my purpose. The idea for the vatic drug came from a recent article in *Life* magazine about trance-producing mushrooms; but the custom of disposing of corpses by floating them down the river, I just made up. The idea for making the protagonist an anthropologist came from my hearing about an anthropology professor, a dignified doctor of his science, who had entered a tribe of savages and taught them one major technical advantage (something like the wheel); his purpose was to observe the effect of this novelty upon their behavior patterns over the years; one thing they did was, in gratitude, to make him a god—Professor John Johnson, Ph.D., LL.D., God. But the equally important idea of making prophecy the chief activity of the Dangs does not correspond to the practice of any actual primitives I have ever heard of. The word Dangs does not derive from the tribe of that name in India; I first heard of the actual one seven or eight years later. It derives from Urdang, which was then no more to me than the name of an editor of an anthology in which one of my stories had appeared. In other words, what I included, omitted, distorted, or fabricated depended scarcely at all upon the actuality either of primitive customs or of my daily experience and almost entirely upon what the internal order of the story called for, as in dream-making; but unlike dream-making it depended also upon various literary considerations, which can be suggested by the question: "What will this mean to a reader?"

For example, I had no notion that the protagonist was going to be a Negro until I got well into the first paragraph. It was obviously a convenience to me for him to be dark skinned for the simple reason that, since all the primitives left in the world are in fact dark of skin, it would be a huge and distracting element if the story were to make them beige or peach colored. However, there is the difficulty that the moment an educated Negro is introduced into a contemporary American setting, The Problem rears its ugly head. The Problem may matter to a dreamer or it may not. But to a storyteller it must matter just because it matters to so many of his hoped-for readers. I had to work consciously at my craft to control the reader's response to The Problem. There is another reason for the protagonist to be a Negro. The story is partly a social satire, and satire is an undreamy quality depending for its existence on an audience of others; it was appropriate enough that a character torn between two cultures, between America and the Dangs, in but not of either of them, should be a contemporary, intellectual American Negro. Indeed, this and not the narrative convenience is the chief justification for his color.

The crux of the similarity and difference between making a dream and making a literary fantasy is to be found, I believe, in the question of revising. In a sense a dream may be said to undergo revision: when a dream or portion of a dream is repeated with variations. It is as though the unconscious dream-making mind wanted to disguise some latent content yet more effectually or else to taunt the soon-to-be conscious sleeper into an open understanding and recognition of this content. Quite apart from the aesthetic considerations involved in revising a poem, the poet may revise his fantasy with a similar intention—to disguise yet more or yet less revealingly the fantasy's hidden meaning. But the poet aims to shape a fantasy which will preserve this power and be able to exert it over many, whereas the dream's power is over no one but the dreamer and it fades with waking. Poems aspire to perfection of form and meaning; dreams aspire to keep the dreamer from waking up, by releasing some of his enlabyrinthed spirits.

To revise a poem means to intensify it, deepen the significance of what it says, prune it, mold it, improve it—none of which has anything to do with dreaming or redreaming.

What I was given as the germ of this story was an image from a dream. My fevered imagination had taken my actual physical situation and made of it an image which, even at the time, my dim consciousness knew to be fantastic; but this image, as I also knew at the time, was somehow surcharged with significance. The movement of the story is from here to there—from the recognizable order of our civilization to an imaginary world ordered barbarously. That strange world I aimed to render with the vividness of hallucination and yet also with suggestions of meaning referring not back into my own private mind but out into what a number of readers are concerned about. This fictional movement, of which I was aware and which affected the execution of the story in many ways, corresponds very closely to the movement of my imagination in writing the story—from here to there. I knew where I was: sitting with a pen in my hand, conscious and excessively rational, at a table in a room in Saratoga Springs. I knew where I was going: to a re-creation and comprehension of that image which had been the seed of the story, its mummied sperm. My whole purpose was to get from here to there—from that straight cane-bottomed chair in a maid's room in Yaddo, into a swathing of deerhide flat on my back in peril of my life among the Dangs, whoever they were. I was bent on discovering what complexities of meaning were latent in that image, discovering them, however, not just for my own benefit, as in a dream, but in such a way as to make it possible for a reader to make a similar discovery. I could discover for myself what it meant only as I revealed it to you.

My aim in this story, like Coleridge's in "Kubla Khan," like any science-fiction writer's, was to make my fantasy the reader's fantasy. Doing this is as different from dreaming as it is different from telling a dream to a friend in conversation, and as like them too. What this shaping and transferring power is I cannot really know. The hair on the back of my neck stands up when I try to imagine it.

When the fantasy image reaches out in a story to the conscious minds of others, ceasing to refer back only into its creator's unconscious mind, when it becomes public, then its nature essentially changes. In talking about it, one must use psychoanalytic insights only with tact and discretion. For a new mystery has entered—language, the language which is common to stenographers gossiping during a coffee break, and to Coleridge's sleep-created but not dream-created poem, and to an essay on logic assembled by Bertrand Russell, that conscious man.

Though the dreaming mind ordinarily uses language, it has no essential need of words: sounds are enough to make a dream with. A dream's words, when it uses words, serve their function quite as well nonsense as sense. "Zumbly doo" can serve a dream as well as "the Dangs and the Urdangs," and both can serve it as well, and in the same way, as "How are you, my dear?" or "Please come in." For a news reporter a given word is like a little boat which always carries the same cargo; the cargo is what matters. For a dream a given word many carry the usual cargo or any other cargo the dream unconscionably wants, though the dream usually disguises its special cargo as the customary thing. The word "toothless" always means about the same thing to reporters, "without teeth," and usually, for convenience, it means that to a dreamer. But it can mean all sorts of things to a dreamer; as a dream greeting, "toothless" could melt him with joy, as a curse it could scare him half to death. To the society which gave him his language, the dreamer's unconscious is wholly irresponsible in its choice, use, and fabrication of words. However, to a creative writer, to one making with words, and especially to the writer of a fantasy, all this is different. Language is given to the poet by society, by those before and about him, and it means to him what it means to them. Yet his writer's fantasy enters into those very words; it is nowhere if not in those words and in the way he arranges them. He must return the words to society from whom he got them, return them recognizable and changed at once.

The words of a reporter are as little his as "hello" and "goodbye" are yours or mine; the community, far more than the individual, is responsible for the way they are used. The words and word components of a dream come from the community, or at least from the outer world, but only the dreamer is responsible for the way they are used. The words of a creating writer are both at once. This is true even of *Finnegans Wake*. By the time Joyce came to write that huge simile to a dream, he was as solipsistic as a sane man gets—every dreamer of course is a total solipsist. Joyce altered the word-boats and changed their cargoes to suit his special purposes. Yet he did not so do it that he was his only audience. I find it possible to enjoy a few passages of the book quite as I enjoy any other poem or story, and some say they have worked hard enough to enjoy all of it. The words of *Finnegans Wake* retain most of their communal function most of the time. The words of "Kubla Khan" retain all of it. Joyce the waking solipsist used words in a more dreamlike way than did Coleridge the poet, who kept the rest of us in mind even in his sleep. Except for a couple of words which Coleridge invented but which are obviously proper names, every word in "Kubla Khan" means what it means in the dictionary, that guide to social custom. He makes the language his own by shearing it of all but its syntax, its sound, and its image-making power.

In "Among the Dangs," I aimed to use words in a sociable way, but I also aimed to make them the story's by playing a few rhetorical tricks—by juxtaposition, by ambiguity, by figure of speech. The turning point of the story occurs when the protagonist understands the words "Stone is Stone." Those words as words are about as simple as words get. "Stone" appears to mean here what it means in the dictionary. Yet in the context, that little boat "Stone is Stone" just about founders; its tiny social cargo just barely disguises its huge private cargo—not private to me but private to the story and therefore accessible to you when you read the story. This is the crucial sentence in which it occurs: "I understood Stone is Stone, and that understanding became my consciousness." Now that sentence communicates a meaning only as it is prepared for within and as the climax to the story; and even then one cannot easily say what the meaning is. Structurally, narratively, the function of the statement seems as clear as its dictionary meaning does. The tricky problem is: What real-life experience, what possible revelation can that simple tautology refer to?

This problem is made all the more acute because the situation of the narrator is so fraught with conventional symbolisms. He is in a cave, lying with his head emerging from a channel at the bottom of a large boulder, on which are two breastlike protuberances. Well, I guess: REBIRTH. "Stone is Stone" is a magic formula involved in his being reborn—that fits into this archetypal interpretation all right, though it hardly explains why it should be this formula rather than some other. Moreover (as the students in a class taught by a friend of mine pointed out), the narrator, who has been prophesying the story of Christ, has endured up to this point experiences which have a great deal in common with the essential events in Christ's story. He has appeared to them from on high; he has performed what must seem to them a miracle with fishes; he has just been prodded in the side with spears till he bled; he is lying as it were in bonds of death with spears sharp as thorns pointed at the sides of his head; he must endure this torment in order to save his people who are not his people. At this moment he identifies himself with Christ, and "Stone is Stone" is a sign of that identification—though, once again, why it should be this formula rather than some other is hardly clear. But aside from the psychoanalytic and the Christian interpretations, how can the tautology be justified in the story?

In itself, "Stone is Stone" means no more to me than it does to you. The statement refers back into the story, not back into its author. I happen to know where the formula came from. I'd come across it, in slightly different form, earlier that year in Suzuki's book on Zen Buddhism. "One of the masters remarked: 'When I began to study Zen, mountains were mountains; when I thought I understood Zen, mountains were not mountains; but when I came to full knowledge of Zen, mountains were again mountains.' " The idea charmed me. But "Among the Dangs" is not a story about Zen. That I got the notion from Suzuki's book is as little relevant to this story as the fact that I got the notion for the Dangs' custom of standing on the left leg with the right foot against the left knee from a photograph in a picture magazine in a waiting room in a dentist's office.

What the narrator says at that crucial moment can be said to have this public meaning: "I understand that this boulder over me is a big rock and is also what both geologists and Dangs think it is; this sensible fact is at once the thing and its meanings, and I accept this state of affairs; what is, is." Very well. But even in paraphrase this sounds dangerously near to Margaret Fuller's famous "I accept the universe," to which Carlyle answered for all people of good sense, "Gad, madam, you'd better!" Now, as a matter of fact, I didn't intend "Stone is Stone" to mean much in a dictionary way when I wrote it; but I did intend it to seem to mean a lot, at least it seemed to mean a lot when I was writing it. It is wise-sounding and obscure, like "I am Who am." "Stone is Stone" has the aura of portentousness without having, outside the story at least, enough content to justify the portentousness. For this revelation which the narrator experiences is not so profound as he thinks it is; it is temporary; it becomes his consciousness for a while but that's all of him it becomes. Ninety-nine percent of the purpose of those words in this story is not denotative but structural, in a way analogous to, but only analogous to, the dream use of words. They mean the little they would mean in ordinary speech, but mostly they are vehicles and instruments to accomplish a purpose peculiar to this story.

Within the story "Stone is Stone" is asked to mean: a thing is itself and is not another thing; also a thing is what science says it is and is simultaneously what religion says it is. The narrator's salvation is to reach the point of accepting this difficult meaning as true. Yet all he can salvage of this experience next day in the light of common sense, in ordinary language, is the mere tautology. This tautology lacks the power to preserve the experience, either for him or for the reader, with anything like the profundity it promises.

I do not mean that the narrator's experience was phony. Earlier, to be sure, he recited the story of Christ not because he believed it was true but because he believed it was useful. Now, in danger of his life, he has to some extent identified himself with Christ, and his experience is as genuine as it can be. At this point he does not utter Christ's message. He utters a tautology which lacks the power to hold his experience.

I, flat on my back in Yaddo, in imaginary danger of my life, uttered words even emptier than his: "The Dangs and the Ur-dangs." But I, sitting at a desk, set about finding words public enough to generate an experience analogous to mine and strong enough to hold it once it was created. Only as I wrote did I discover the nature of this experience. I had to identify myself with a character who was identifying himself with Christ before I found the meaning my experience had generated. This meaning is not Christ's message, nor is it "Stone is Stone." As nearly as I can paraphrase it, this meaning is: Without words adequate to contain it, insight may not endure but seems to be, perhaps is, illusory.

At least that's what I find the story means when I reread it, I who am by now able to reenter this story only as another reader.

10

Confessions of a Repentant Symposiast

After a symposium, the simply polite look at you sympathetically and half smile; the polite for whom even a little hypocrisy is a great strain cast their unhappy glances anywhere but at you; the polite-and-kind murmur, "Very interesting, very stimulating," or even valiantly take issue with one of your points for a minute or two. There are also the impolite.

Last year after a symposium, a young man caught me at the Party After and, writhing in an agony of embarrassment, blurted at me, "Why did you do it?" The true answer, I suppose, was vanity, but I was not about to say this to a stranger: I don't go in for cocktail confessions much. Besides, I'd guessed ahead of time that this was likely to be a bad evening—the topic, the occasion, the symposiasts, all had promised the tedious disaster we'd just been in; and knowingly to participate thus in public folly implies a vanity too depraved to dump on even a rude young man under such circumstances. Anyhow, I'd also come to this bash out of a sort of loyalty to an editor, paying off an old debt, a fact which was none of the young man's business. The decibels in the room were approaching the five-jackhammer level. "Money!" I shouted. "Money? But you can't need the money." "No, but I like it." He writhed away. My special, campy (i.e., perverted), secret satisfaction came from knowing that I'd be clearing less than fifty dollars from this turn; at least he hadn't asked *how much* money and so spoiled my antinonjoke. After the Party After, thinking about this episode, I felt like something out of Susan Sontag; and believe me, whoever you are, I don't enjoy feeling like something out of Susan Sontag.

Once, years ago, at a regional meeting of the MLA in Seattle, I was on a good symposium. Somehow, the demon in charge of keeping symposiums lousy had been negligent: things went well for us. Everybody stayed on the subject, which is nearly unheard of; but, odder yet, the subject was worth staying on. It wasn't The Future of the Novel, or The Function of Drama Today, or Form and Content in Modernist Poetry. It was defined by a critical essay, the first chapter of Sheldon Sacks's then unpublished book *Fiction and the Shape of Belief*, which both the five symposiasts and the audience of seventy had read ahead of time. The essay was intelligent, disputatious, and moral, and the subject mattered to us all. We enjoyed that fine sort of intellectual intercourse in which things worth listening to get said. But, as I mentioned, the demon had fallen down on his job, in a way and to a degree I have not detected in him before or since. Nearly always, the question to be asked about a symposium is *how bad?*

The least bad one I have been on was rigged. A dear friend and I were invited to be on a symposium with one moderator and no other symposiasts. Seeing our chance, we unscrupulously plotted between ourselves to pay no attention to the subject or to whatever the moderator might say, but to continue in public our years-long argument, most of the terms and twists of which we knew well by then. Our collusion fooled the demon all right, though the inconsecutiveness between our argument and the moderator's comments made for some mighty rough bumps. As we were leaving the Party After, our host professor, whom we had known for several years, said, "I want you to know that was the best symposium I was ever at, and I sure have seen some bad ones in my time."

Post symposiasm, omnis intellectualis tristis est.

The worst one I've ever been on—or maybe the next worst, it's hard to make these delicate discriminations—took place at St. Mary's College (California) where such things had never been known before. No two of the four of us talked on the same subject (The State of Literature in America, or some such ilk, had been announced). Alfred Kazin, the symposiarch for the occasion, droned a passage from a book he was writing. I droned a passage from a book I was not writing. Evan Connell, who had never talked in public before, talked to the five hundred before us, and has never done it again. Herb Gold, who is defter at the craft of symposiastry than anyone else I know, said nothing wittily for ten minutes. His joke that day was to begin, "There are three respects in which. First we see that." And all the earnest coed pencils flashed. But there was no Second, no Third. Pretty little foreheads puckered, pencils drooped, heads leaned and touched, they gave up. Then came Questions from the Floor, and the wrangle. The next day, a student on the committee which had perpetrated the occasion said to my best friend on the faculty, "Wasn't it awful?" "Absolutely disgraceful." "I can't understand how they could have done such a thing. . . . Let's have another."

Which poses the question I could not even conjecture an answer to for years: Why do people arrange and throng to symposiums? For a while, I thought they went to learn something. Plainly sentimental of me. Then I decided they must be going out of sheer masochism. Good enough, but hopelessly vague.

I narrowed this down to one manifestation of the common American urge to be cheated, the urge which advertising exploits in a myriad ways—50 Girls Count Them 50—and which is as good an explanation for the popularity of pornography, for the chicness of voyeurism, as I know. But this cheat-me urge, though it seems to be important all right, baffles me. I keep looking for another explanation so as not to be stuck with this utterly perverse insanity. I've come up with a pretty good one.

The lousiest symposium I ever witnessed took place at Buffalo a few years ago. David Posner was the moderator. Robert Creeley was on it. De Snodgrass was standing in for Randall Jarrell, and Robert Graves for Hugo Williams. Appropriately enough, Marshall McLuhan happened to be in town at the time, for this poets' symposium had no real content but the symposiasts themselves. Posner, who was handsome, profiled to nonexistent TV cameras. Creeley mumbled earnestly. Graves sort of picked his nose, flirted egregiously with a woman in the third row, and collected his thousand dollars. Snodgrass was a boob: he tried to say something. Under such circumstances he actually said something! Graves, no boob he, threw his left arm across Snodgrass's shoulders and with his right hand slipped a blade between his ribs. "I can't understand all these big words you're using. Why don't we get down to poetry again?" And he lapsed into Greek. In the middle of the Party After, I found myself chatting with Mrs. Leslie Fiedler, when up rushed De. "Wasn't it awful?" "Absolutely disgraceful. He ought to be shot." "I've never felt like such a fool in my life." "Oh, Mr. Snodgrass," said Mrs. Fiedler and I hurriedly introduced them, "I thought you did a fine job." "*Wha-at?* You saw what that son of a bitch did to me?" "Oh, yes, but that's nothing. There're just two reasons for a poet to get up in front of an audience, to read his poetry or to display himself, and I thought you did a fine job of displaying yourself."

Ah ha. She was right: spectacle. But I still couldn't figure what the audience was getting out of it, really. A poet on display without his poetry? I'd rather watch 50 Girls Count Them 50 any day, and so, I assumed, would anyone else in his right mind.

Then last year came that symposium after which I lied to the young man about why I'd been on it, and things fell into place. The next day I talked on the phone with the editor who had arranged the whole bash. People had been telling him what a great occasion it was; so I told him, with a sort of New-Year's-resolution fervor in my voice, that I was never going to be on another symposium in my life. (I've only contracted for one since then, only one, the *very* last one.) I assured him that all the other symposiasts, except for the symposiarch (a reviewer famous for his unkind wit), shared my view of the occasion. Then the editor said something to this effect: People come to see some writers they have read and heard about perform. It's like releasing four or five dangerous animals in a pit to see what they will do to each other. They sniff, they snarl, they scuffle, they . . . Even if they do nothing more, that is in itself interesting.

He was right.

Think of the best symposium that ever was or is likely ever to be, that Platonic all-night drinking party of which Socrates was the symposiarch, of which the subject was love. Then imagine their doing it for money in front of a thousand paying spectators avid for gore. . . .

By setting intelligent or talented people against each other under circumstances which make them appear stupid, silly, vicious, and cheap, the symposium gives a crowd the leveling pleasure of being intellectually cheated and gladiatorially satisfied at the same time. Any way you look at it, the audience gets what it came for. And the beasts? Some publicity anyhow.

II

Against Pornography

So much has changed in attitudes toward pornography, as toward sexual matters generally, since this essay first appeared in 1965 that I thought of updating it, even though my opinions on the subject have not changed in any major respect. But who knows what further shifts the seventies have in store? The only thing one can be sure of is that there will be plenty of them. Built-in obsolescence is not for cars alone. This is the original version, polished a bit and with a note appended.

Pornography is like a squalid, unnecessary little country which owes its independence to a vagary of history. But, though pornography is seldom of much importance, it may be of considerable interest, for to talk about it is unavoidably to talk about the Great Powers adjacent to it. Pornography speaks the language of Art; in recent centuries it has come within the sphere of influence of the Law; Psychology and Morals have vested interests in it. Moreover, occasionally pornography becomes genuinely important—when it is used as a seat of operations by the erotic nihilists who would like to destroy every sort of social and moral law and who devote their effective energies to subverting society as such. One who undertakes to discuss pornography finds himself, willy-nilly, falling back upon some of his ultimate positions in matters aesthetic, social, psychological, ethical. If a reader agrees with these opinions, he is likely to view them as principles; if he disagrees, prejudices. Here are some of mine.

Before plunging ahead, I had better indicate two mutually antagonistic dispositions, one liberal, the other conservative, in my opinions on pornography. On the one hand, I favor the liberal view that the less power the state and the police have over us private citizens the better, that the less the state concerns itself with the individual's thoughts, entertainments, and private sexual actions the better, and that we should do what we can to counter the drift toward totalitarianism. In other words, let us have no censorship because it strengthens the state, which is already too strong. Also let us have none because most of the things that in fact get censored are less harmful than some of the things that do not—for example, large circulation newspapers and magazines. Society is harmed far less by the free circulation of a book like *Fanny Hill* than it is by routine and accepted practices of the daily sensationalist press: let a man inherit ten million dollars, pour acid on his wife, or win a Nobel Prize, and reporter and photographer are made to intrude upon him and his family and then to exhibit to public view in as gross a manner as possible his follies, shames, or just plain private affairs. Such invasions of privacy are not only allowed, they are allowed for the purpose of letting the public enjoy these same invasions vicariously, all in the name of freedom of the press. I believe that this accepted practice has done more damage to society as a whole and to its citizens individually than massive doses of the most depraved pornography could ever do. So much for my liberal views.

On the other hand, I favor the conservative view that pornography exists among us and is a social evil, though a small one. That is, in a good society of any sort I can imagine—not some daydream utopia where man is impossibly restored to sexual innocence but a society populated with recognizable, imperfectible men—in a good society there would be active opposition to pornography, which is to say, considerable firmness in the drawing of lines beyond which actions, words, and images are regarded as indecent. Furthermore, the opinion that pornography should not be restrained I regard as being commonly a symptom of doctrinaire liberalism and occasionally an evidence of destructive nihilism.

A liberal suspicion of censorship and a conservative dislike of pornography are not very compatible. Some sort of compromise is necessary if they are to live together. Their marriage, being of the earthly sort, will never be without tensions, but maybe the quarrel between them can be patched up well enough for practical purposes.

Originally the word pornography meant a sort of low erotic art, the writing of and about whores with the intention of arousing a man's lust so that he would go to a whore. But some centuries ago, the word, like the practice itself, came to include considerably more than aesthetic pandering. It has come to overlap with obscenity, which originally meant nothing more than the filthy. Obscenity still means that primarily, but notions about what is filthy have changed. Defecating and urinating, instead of being just low and uninteresting, came to be viewed as filthy, obscene, taboo. Apparently, down in the underworld of taboo, things and functions easily become tinged with sexuality, especially functions as near the genitals as urinating and defecating. In any case, since in common practice no clear distinction is made between pornography and obscenity, I am offering, for the sake of convenience, a definition in which the single word pornography is stretched to include most of obscenity. The definition is mine, but not just mine; it also reflects the usages and attitudes of my society.

Pornography is the representation of directly or indirectly erotic acts with an intrusive vividness which offends decency without aesthetic justification.

Obviously this definition does not just describe but also judges; quite as obviously it contains terms that need pinning down—decency, for example. But pornography is not at all a matter for scientific treatment. Like various other areas of sexual behavior in which society takes an unsteady, wary interest—homosexuality, for example, fornication, or nudity—pornography is relative, an ambiguous matter of personal taste and the consensus of opinion. The grounds for this definition are psychological, aesthetic, and political.

Psychologically, pornography is not offensive because it excites sexual desire; desire as such is a fine thing, and there are happy times and places when desire should be excited and gratified freely and fully; moreover, even in inappropriate times and places there is plenty of free-floating desire abroad in the world; it doesn't take pornography to excite excesses of desire among young men and women. Nor is pornography offensive because, in its perverted and scatological versions, it excites disgust; in the proper context disgust serves the useful function of turning us from the harmful. Psychologically the trouble with pornography is that, in our culture at least, it offends the sense of separateness, of individuality, of privacy; it intrudes upon the rights of others. We have a certain sense of specialness about those voluntary bodily functions each must perform for himself—bathing, eating, defecating, urinating, copulating, performing the sexual perversions from heavy petting to necrophilia. Take eating, for example. There are few strong taboos around the act of eating; yet most people feel uneasy about being the only one at table who is, or who is not, eating, and there is an absolute difference between eating a rare steak washed down with plenty of red wine and watching a close-up movie of someone doing so. One wishes to draw back when one is actually or imaginatively too close to the mouth of a man enjoying his dinner; in exactly the same way one wishes to remove oneself from the presence of a man and woman enjoying sexual intercourse. Not to withdraw is to peep, to pervert looking so that it becomes a sexual end in itself. As for a close-up of a private act which is also revolting, a man's vomiting, say, the avoidance principle is the same as for a close-up of steak-eating, except that the additional unpleasantness makes one wish to keep an even greater distance from the subject.

Pornography also raises aesthetic questions, since it exists only in art—in painting, literature, sculpture, photography, theater—and my definition implies that it is offensive aesthetically. The central aesthetic issue is not whether certain subjects and words should be taboo, but what distance should be maintained between spectator and subject. Because of our desire to withdraw from a man performing private acts and our doubly strong desire to withdraw from a man performing acts which are not only private but also disagreeable or perverted, we wish aesthetically to remain at a certain distance from such acts when they are represented in art. Nothing whatever in human experience should, as such, be excluded from consideration in a work of art: not Judas betraying Christ nor naked starved Jews crowded by Nazi soldiers into a gas chamber nor a child locked by his parents in a dark closet for months till he goes mad nor a man paying a whore to lash him with barbed wire for his sexual relief nor even husband and wife making love. Nothing human is alien to art. The question is only, how close? But the criterion of distance is an extremely tricky one. Aesthetically, one good way to keep a spectator at a distance from the experience represented by an image is to make the image artificial, stylized, not like us. If it is sufficiently stylized, it may be vivid and detailed and still keep a proper distance from the viewer. One would normally feel uneasy at being with a lot of men, women, and children engaged in every imaginable form of pleasurable erotic activity. Yet the vivid throngs of erotic statues on certain Indian temples create in the viewer no uneasiness but are simply delightful to look at. The viewer is kept at a considerable remove by the impossible poses and expressions of the statues; he cannot identify with the persons performing the acts. For the statues do not represent lustful, passionate, guilty, self-conscious, confused people like you and me, but pure beings to whom all things are pure, paradisal folk who are expressing their joy in generation and the body by erotic acts: these are stylized artifices of blessedness. Another way of keeping the spectator at a proper distance from a private experience is to give very little of it—make the image small, sketch it in with few details. One does not want to be close to a man while he is defecating nor to have a close-up picture of him in that natural, innocent act—not at all because defecating is reprehensible, only because it is displeasing to intrude upon. One would much rather have a detailed picture of a thief stealing the last loaf of bread from a starving widow with three children than one of Albert Schweitzer at stool. However, Bruegel's painting *The Netherlandish Proverbs* represents two bare rear ends sticking out of a window, presumably of people defecating into the river below, and one quite enjoys the sight—because it is a small part of a large and pleasant picture of the world and because the two figures are tiny, sketched in, far away.

To be sure, a satiric work of art may purposely arouse disgust in its audience. Even the breast of a healthy woman is revolting when inspected too closely, as Swift knew when he had tiny Gulliver revolted by every blemish on the breast of the Brobdingnagian wet nurse suckling a baby. Our revulsion at the description of her teat sticking out a good six feet, with a nipple half the size of a man's head, is necessary to Swift's satiric purposes, and it is kept within bounds by his reminding us that if proportions had been normal—if Gulliver and she had been about the same size—both he and we would have been pleased by the sight of her breast. When the artist's purpose goes to the limit of satire and he intends, as Swift does in the fourth book of *Gulliver's Travels*, to disgust us with man as such, then he will force us right into the unpleasantly private, as Swift gets us to contemplate the Yahoos copulating promiscuously and lovelessly, besmeared with their own excrement. The aesthetic danger of such powerful evocations of disgust is that the audience may and often does turn not only against the object of the artist's hatred but also against the artist and work of art for having aroused such unpleasant emotions. Swift, just because he succeeds so powerfully, is often reviled for his misanthropy in the voyage to the Houyhnhnms; the fourth book of *Gulliver's Travels* is even called a product and proof of madness—which is convenient and safe, for of course the fantasies of a madman may be pathetic and scary but they don't apply to us; *we* are sane.

There is a special problem raised by realism, because it aims to present people as they actually are. How can a realistic artist be true to his subject if he is forbidden direct access to an area of human behavior which is of considerable importance? The aesthetic problem is for the realistic artist to represent these actions in such a way as to lead to understanding of the characters without arousing disgust against them or a prurient interest in their activities. When he can accomplish this very difficult feat, then he is justified in including in a realistic work of art representations that would otherwise be pornographic. Here are two instances of intimate erotic acts realistically represented, one of a kiss which is pornographic, the other of a copulation which is aesthetically justified and hence is not pornographic.

In the movie *Baby Doll*, made by Elia Kazan, a healthy young man and woman who desire one another embrace. By this point in the movie the spectator is convinced that their lust is powerful but banal, and a brief and somewhat distant shot of their embracing would adequately suggest to him how intensely they wanted to consummate their desire. Instead, he is subject to a prolonged series of images, especially auditory images, the effect of which is to arouse his own lust and/or disgust, to no aesthetic end. The kiss becomes so severed from characters and plot that the spectator does not care how the couple are related, but cares only that they are given over to desire, and he is encouraged by the very depersonalization of that desire to give himself over to a lust of his own. He may be excited to want some sort of sexual activity with the next available person, but, more probably, observing and sharing in that movie embrace becomes a kind of substitute sexual activity on the part of the spectator. For, just because the scene in *Baby Doll* arouses its spectator vicariously and in a theater, the chief appetite it whets is not for casual fornication but for more voyeurism—which is good at least for the movie business. Even if *Baby Doll* were a good work of art, as it surely is not, this episode in itself would remain aesthetically unjustified and therefore pornographic, and would merit censoring.

The other example of an intimately presented erotic act is from the novel *Pretty Leslie* by R. V. Cassill. The reader is given an emotionally intense account of a young man and woman copulating in an abnormal way; the man hurts the woman, and the reader understands how he does it and why she lets him do it. This would seem to be essentially pornographic, yet it is not. The art of this novel redeems its ugliness. The reader is not encouraged to use this episode as an incitement to casual fornication or voyeurism. Instead, what is aroused in him is a profound understanding of the characters themselves, of a kind he could have got in no other way. To understand what these people were like, how they were connected, and why they did what they did to each other, the reader must be close to them as they make love, and because he knows this is necessary for his understanding, he will not use either the episode or the whole novel for pornographic ends, unless he himself is already perverted. In *Baby Doll* a natural private act, by being brought close for no legitimate reason, excites an uneasy desire whose satisfaction can only be indiscriminate or perverse. In *Pretty Leslie* the account of an unnatural private act is not so close as to create disgust but is close enough to lead toward moral understanding and aesthetic satisfaction: there is no other possible way for the novelist to accomplish this legitimate end, and the emphasis he gives the episode is in proportion to its contribution to the whole novel.

The aesthetic problem has been stated succinctly by Jean Genet. As a professed immoralist and enemy of society, he has no compunction about using pornography. But as a writer, he has this to say about his art (in an interview in *Playboy* magazine for April 1964): "I now think that if my books arouse readers sexually, they're badly written, because the poetic emotion should be so strong that no reader is moved sexually. Insofar as my books are pornographic, I don't reject them. I simply say that I lacked grace."

Nothing said thus far would justify legal suppression, official censorship, for, though the effect of pornography in a work of art is aesthetically bad, it is no business of the state to suppress bad art. The effect of pornography on an individual psyche is that of an assault, ranging in severity from the equivalent of a mere pinch to that of an open cut; but in the normal course of things one can avoid such assaults without much trouble, and besides the wounds they make are seldom very severe one by one, though they may be cumulatively. To be sure, there are people who want and need pornography, just as there are those who want and need heroin, but such a secret indulgence is not in itself socially dangerous. Here again, the state has no business intruding: a man's soul is his own to pollute if he wishes, and it is not for the state to say "Be thou clean, be thou healthy, close the bathroom door behind you." It is only when pornography becomes public that, like dope, it takes on a sufficiently political cast for censorship even to be considered. It is unlike dope in that it sometimes acquires political overtones by being used ideologically, when put in the service of nihilism. But in one important respect it is like dope: it usually becomes public by being offered for sale, especially to the young.

The classic example of pornography is a filthy picture: it is ugly; it is sold and displayed surreptitiously; it allows the viewer to intrude vicariously upon the privacy of others; it shows two or more men and women posing for money in front of a camera, in attitudes which sexual desire alone would lead them to assume in private if at all. An adult looking at such a picture is roused to an excitement which may lead either to revulsion or to satisfaction, but whatever his reaction, he should be left alone to decide for himself whether he wants to repeat the experience. The state has no legitimate political concern with his private vices. But the effect on young people of such a picture, and especially of a steady diet of such pictures, is another matter. A common argument against allowing young people to have unrestricted access to pornography runs somewhat as follows:

About sex the young are curious and uncertain and have very powerful feelings. A filthy picture associates sexual acts with ugly, vicarious, and surreptitious pleasure, and helps to cut sex off from love and free joy. At the most, one experience of pornography may have a salutary effect on the curious, uncertain mind of an adolescent. To be shown what has been forbidden might provide him a considerable relief, and if he has feared that he is warped because of his fantasies, he can see how really warped are those who act on such fantasies. Moreover, by his own experience he can learn why pornography is forbidden: experience of it is at once fascinating, displeasing, and an end in itself, that is to say, perverse. However, too many experiences with pornography may encourage the young to turn their fantasies into actions ("in dreams begin responsibilities") or to substitute fantasies for actions, and so may confirm them in bad habits.

Whatever the validity of this argument, it or something like it is the rationale by which our society justifies its strong taboo against exposing children to pornography. For my own part, I would accept the argument as mostly valid. The state has no business legislating virtue; indeed, one of the symptoms of totalitarianism is the persistent attempt of the state not just to punish its citizens for wrongdoing, but to change their nature, to make them what its rulers conceive to be good. But patently the state has the obligation to protect the young against the public acts of the vicious.

This means that, in the matter of the sale and display of pornography, the state, the apparatus of the law, should have two effective policies. It should strictly forbid making pornography accessible to the young: "No One Under 18 Admitted." But as for pornography for adults, the law should rest content with a decent hypocrisy: "Keep it out of the marketplace, sell it under the counter, and the law won't bother you."

An assumption underlying such policies is that a certain amount of official hypocrisy is one of the operative principles of a good society. It is hard to imagine that any tolerable society would not disapprove of adultery, for the maintenance of the family as an institution is one of the prime concerns of society, and adultery threatens the family. Yet, on the other hand, imagine living in a country in which the laws against adultery were strictly enforced —the informing that such enforcement would entail, the spying, breaking in upon, denouncing, the regiment of self-righteous teetotalers. What is obviously needed here is what we have: unenforced laws. It is only an all-or-none zealot who cannot tell the difference between the deplorable hypocrisy of a man deceiving his neighbor for his own gain and the salutory hypocrisy of a government recognizing the limits beyond which it should not encroach upon its individual citizens. Another assumption underlying these recommendations is that the censorship of simple pornography for adults will never be very effective. There is a steady demand for it, and it is not important enough to prosecute at much expense. The main function of laws against adult pornography is to express disapproval of it.

A by-product of society's official disapproval is worth mentioning: it is a kindness to those who enjoy pornography. Just as a criminal's status depends upon a line beyond which he has transgressed, the law for him to be outside, so the pleasure of one who enjoys pornography depends upon his act's being thought shameful. It is a pity that some people can enjoy sex only or most when they think that what they are doing is shameful, but since there are such people, it is cruel to deprive them of their shame, just as it is cruel of a parent to withhold from a disobedient child the punishment he has courted. Indeed, it might be socially imprudent so to deprive those who enjoy pornography. Their indulgence in that vice does not demonstrably lead to other antisocial behavior, for they are inturned people whose unpleasant sexual tensions are more or less adequately relieved through pornography. If society has any respect for them, it will sternly assure them that what they are doing is nasty by passing a law against it, and then will pretty much leave them alone.

Clearly the logic of this argument leads to prohibiting certain books and works of art that are now legally available in some parts of the country. For example, in some localities the courts have refused to prohibit the sale of *Fanny Hill.* This refusal seems to me quite irresponsible on any grounds other than a general refusal to censor pornography, for by any meaningful definition *Fanny Hill* is pornographic. Such story as there is in the novel exists for no other purpose than to provide occasions for detailed accounts of sexual encounters, and these accounts are the only passages in the book with power to stir the reader's emotions. The characters are very simple types without intrinsic interest, and Fanny herself is little more than a man's fantasy of female complaisance and sexual competence. The one literary quality which has made the book celebrated is a certain elegance of style; compared to most simple pornography it reads like a masterpiece, but to anyone familiar with eighteenth-century English prose it reads like several other third-rate novels. Surely the world is not in such need of third-rate eighteenth-century English fictional prose as to allow this consideration alone to justify the public sale of a work of sheer pornography. What else would justify its sale is hard to imagine. To deny that the book is pornographic, or to say that its literary value redeems its pornography, is to blur distinctions, and for an august court of law to do so is for the state to abrogate one of its functions. An essential and conservative function of the state is to say "Thou Shalt Not," to formulate society's taboos. Unless I am seriously mistaken, in this instance the court, speaking for the state, has refused to draw a clear line which corresponds to society's actual customs. In our culture the place for nudists is in a nudist colony, not on the city streets, and the way to sell books like *Fanny Hill* is under the counter, not over it. In the name of enlightenment and sexual permissiveness the state is violating an actual taboo, and the counterreaction to many such violations may very well be a resurgence of that savage fanaticism which burns books and closes theaters.

I am going to defer a consideration of the nihilistic use of pornography, which would logically come next, and instead look at certain borderline questions of enforcing censorship. The censorship of unquestionable pornography is of little interest; it pretty directly reflects what decent society considers indecent at a given time; it is custom in action. But the censorship of borderline pornography demands discrimination and philosophy, without which censorship can degenerate into puritanical repressiveness of the kind there has been quite enough of during the past two or three centuries.

Thus far my argument on what to censor and why has led to a legal position which is at least within hailing distance of common practice in the United States now. To purveyors of raw pornography our practice says in effect: Bother your neighbors, especially children, and you will be punished; leave others untroubled by your vice and you will be viewed with disapproval by the law but left alone. This attitude is fine until one gets down to cases, but once it is a matter of wording and enforcing a law, the question must be answered: How is one to distinguish between pornographic and decent art? Still, such lines must be drawn if there are to be laws at all, and they must, in the nature of things, be arbitrary. As I see it, a more manageable form of the question is this: Who should do the censoring? How should the board of censors be constituted? Whatever the answer to this question may be, whatever the best method of censoring, one thing is clear—our present method is unsatisfactory.

As things stand, an object is banned as pornographic on the judgment of some official in customs or the postal service or else by some police officer prodded by a local zealot. In most cases this judgment presents little difficulty: even civil liberty extremists who are opposed to all censorship on principle are apt to blanch when they are confronted with genuine hard-core pornography, the unarguably warped stuff, the bulk of the trade. But sometimes there is the question of assessing the value of a work of art, and for this task the bureaucrats and policemen who are presently empowered to make the day-to-day decisions are unqualified.

Should *Fanny Hill* be offered to the public freely? When society has said No for generations and when judges and literary critics cannot agree, it is wrong to allow a police sergeant to decide the matter. If a duly constituted public authority says "*Fanny Hill* shall not be sold in this state," then the policeman's duty is clear: arrest the man who displays it for sale. But to leave to bureaucrats and policemen the task of making all the delicate discriminations necessary in deciding whether the novel should be censored in the first place, is genuinely irresponsible of society at large and of legislators in particular. To be sure, cases are brought to court, where judge or jury decide. But the laws offer such vague guidance that far too much depends on the quirks of the judge or jury at hand. No censorship might be preferable to what we have now.

In fact, a strong case can be made for removing all censorship of pornography. Here are six arguments for abolishing censorship. The first three seem to me valid. No law can be framed so as to provide a clear and sure guide to bureaucrat, policeman, judge, and jury. It is very hard to demonstrate that pornography does in fact injure many people severely, even adolescents, for if the desire to break taboos is satisfied imaginatively, it is less likely to issue in antisocial acts. The less power the state and the police have the better. There are three further arguments against censorship which are commonly used but which I find less persuasive. Decent citizens can by their very disapproval segregate pornography without assistance from the state. But, in an age as troubled as ours and with so much private indiscipline and theoretical permissiveness in sexual matters, there is little reason to suppose that the moral disapproval of decent citizens would actually limit the public distribution of pornography. It is arguable that some people are rendered socially less dangerous by having their sexual tensions more or less satisfied by pornography, tensions which unrelieved might well lead to much more antisocial acts. But pornography if it is to be of help to those who use it, must be outside the law, must be clearly labeled *shameful*, as a weakly enforced censorship labels it. In the past, censorship has not succeeded in keeping books of literary value from being read but has only attached an unfortunate prurience to the reading of them. But the prurience attached to reading pornography derives less from breaking a law than from violating the taboo which caused the law to come into existence.

There is another argument, more important and more erroneous than these six, which is commonly advanced in favor of abolishing censorship. It hinges on a mistaken liberal doctrine about the nature of sexual taboos. According to this doctrine, sexual taboos, like fashions in dress, are determined by local custom and have as little to do with morality as the kinds of clothes we wear. However—the argument goes—people frequently mistake these sexual taboos for ethical rules, and pass and enforce laws punishing those who violate taboos. The result is a reduction of pleasure in sex and an increase of guilt, with an attendant host of psychological and social ills. The obvious solution is to abolish the taboos and so liberate the human spirit from its chief source of oppression and guilt. At the moment in America, this doctrine finds extensive elaboration in the writings of Paul Goodman and is present to some degree in the writings of many other intellectuals.

It presents a considerable difficulty: by supposing that the potent and obscure emotions surrounding sexual matters derive from unenlightened customs, it holds out the hope that enlightened views can liberate us from those customs so that sex in every form can become healthy and fun for all. This is a cheery, optimistic view, not unlike the sweet hopefulness of the old-fashioned anarchists who thought that all we have to do, in order to attain happiness, is to get rid of governments so we may all express our essentially good nature unrestrained. Such ideas would show to advantage in a museum of charming notions, along with phlogiston and the quarrel about how many angels can dance on the head of a pin, but turned loose in the world they sometimes cause a bit of trouble. Sexual anarchism, like political anarchism before it, is a lovely daydream and does no harm so long as it is recognized as a daydream. But it has come to be a part of fundamental liberalism, and so a part of the body of doctrines accepted by more and more of the rulers of the nation. Conceivably the First Amendment will be taken literally ("Congress shall make no law . . . abridging the freedom of speech or of the press") and many or all legal restraints against pornography may in fact be removed. But I believe that so far from eliminating sexual taboos, such an official undermining of them would only arouse the puritans to strengthen the bulwarks; the taboos would be made more repressive than ever; and many of the goods of liberalism would be wiped out along with and partly because of this Utopian folly. Decent people had better learn how to censor moderately, or the licentiousness released by liberal zealots may arouse their brothers the puritan zealots to censorship by fire.

A civilized method of censoring is feasible. One does not have to imagine a Utopian system of extirpating pornography through some sexual revolution, an Eden of erotic innocence in which prohibitions will be unnecessary because social relations will be as they should be. In our actual, historical United States, in which perversions and pornography flourish, one can imagine a better method of restraining pornography, which is yet within the framework of our customs and procedures. It would operate somewhat as follows:

All decisions about what is legally pornographic in any of the arts is in the custody of boards of censors. Such a board is elected or appointed from each of three general categories of citizens: for example, a judge or lawyer of good repute, a professor of art, literature, or one of the humanities, and a social worker, psychologist, or clergyman. These are not exciting categories; but in them, if anywhere, are likely to be found citizens whose own opinions will reflect decent social opinion and who are also capable of making the various discriminations the task calls for. Obviously it is necessary to keep sexual anarchists off the board; just as a person is, or used to be, disqualified from serving as a juror in a murder case if he were against capital punishment, so one would be disqualified from serving on a board of censors if he were against censoring pornography. A board of censors must never look to a set of rules of thumb for guidance—not, for instance, to the quantity of an actress's body that must be covered. Is a burlesque's dancer's breast indecent from the nipple down or is it the nipple itself that offends? That way foolishness lies. Rather, the censors must look only to their own personal experience with a given work of art for only in such experience can art be judged. For this reason, the censors should be people for whom society's taboos are part of themselves, not something in a code external to them. No photograph, drawing, book, stage show, or moving picture is banned by the police except at the instructions of this board. Its decisions, like those of every quasi-official public agency, are subject to appeal to the courts, but the Supreme Court would do all it could to dodge such cases. The banning is deliberately hypocritical: out of sight out of mind, so long as children are not molested. The aesthetic and moral principles guiding the board are roughly these: distance and effect. At the distance of a movie close-up, a kiss between husband and wife can be pornographic. If a child and an adult were sitting side by side watching a stage performance of a witty Restoration comedy of adultery, they are at altogether different distances from the play, the adult closer than the child; but at a marionette performance of a fairy-tale melodrama they reverse distances, the child closer this time and the adult farther away. As for effect on the spectator, this consideration is only slightly less tricky than distance. The question to be asked is whether a story intrudes on the privacy of its characters in order to give the reader vicarious and perverse sexual excitement or in order to provide him with a sympathetic understanding which he could have got in no other way. These criteria of distance and effect—these rubber yardsticks—apply to the parts as well as to the whole, so that a novel or movie of some aesthetic merit may be judged as censorable in part. In a movie the part is excisable with more or less aesthetic harm to the movie as a whole; with a book, if the board decides the gravity of the offense outweighs such literary excellence as the whole book may possess, the book is banned—not burned, just no longer offered for public sale.

This system is scarcely watertight; it presents plenty of opportunity for contradictions and revisions; it has tensions built into it. But it would not be likely to become troublesome politically; for, without strengthening the state appreciably, it provides a better way than the present one for our society to enforce certain inevitable taboos. Civilization behaves as though men were decent, in full knowledge that they are not.

The last aspect of the subject I am going to deal with is the use of pornography as a weapon of nihilistic destruction, especially by a writer important for so using it, Henry Miller. The term nihilism here signifies a great deal more than it did originally. In Turgenev's *Fathers and Sons*, where the word was given political currency, nihilism was quite idealistic; it held that a given society (Russia, in that case) was so corrupt or wicked that it should be destroyed, but destroyed so that a better society could emerge from its ruins. However, there is a nihilism which is not against this or that unjust society or social injustice but against society as such; its rage is not just political but metaphysical as well; and pornography is one of its weapons.

Of nihilistic fictions, Henry Miller's *Tropic of Cancer* is one of the most widely read and best spoken of. Miller is not only a fairly good writer, but the personality he projects in his book is attractive. When he stands stripped of his civilization—stripped down to his language, that is—the savage that is left is not exactly noble but he is at least honest about himself, self-indulgent, energetic, beauty loving, and interested in the world, not a cold-hearted, torturing pervert. The one overwhelming moral virtue Miller embodies in his book is self-honesty; if you're going to be a whore, he says, be a whore all the way. This honesty is doubtless what most attracted Orwell in Miller's writing, though Orwell was a most fastidious man otherwise. Miller's prose is usually vigorous and sometimes splendid, and he is the best writer of "the character" since Sir Thomas Overbury. Should *Tropic of Cancer* be censored or not? According to the standards for censorship advanced earlier in my argument, it should not be censored for its pornography: as a work of art, it has considerable merit, and it could not achieve its ends without the use of intrinsically pornographic episodes and images. But the conflict of interests in judging this book is acute, for the purpose of Miller's novel is not just aesthetic, it is nihilistic as well. The literary value of the book is enough to redeem its pornography but not enough to make one ignore its destructive intention. *Tropic of Cancer* has no structure and is very verbose; it is, like Miller's other books, an anatomy and a segment of his imaginary autobiography, a string of images and actions. But it does have an unmistakable message: society is intrinsically vile, let us return to the natural man. In effect, this return to nature means as little work as possible and lots of loveless sex. Miller has often been mispraised, for example by Karl Shapiro, for a supposedly pagan rejoicing in sex. Miller himself is honest about his intention. Again and again he represents the sexual antics of his characters as evidence of desperation, lurking behind which is the total despair of meaninglessness. He is what he says he is: an enemy not just of the badness of our society, not just of our specific society, but of society as such. To do what he can to get his readers also to become enemies of society, he assaults with persuasive force taboos, especially sexual taboos, which are intrinsic to social order.

Yet a whole new set of justifications are needed if *Tropic of Cancer* is to be banned, justifications having to do with pornography as a destructive social act. As an act against society, to write, publish, and distribute a book like *Tropic of Cancer* is more serious than to write, publish, and distribute a pamphlet which intellectually advocates the forcible overthrow of the government but less serious than to take arms against the government—about on a par with inciting to rebellion, an act which a secure, free government will watch carefully and disapprove of strongly, but not forbid and punish. In other words, the only plausible argument for suppressing *Tropic of Cancer* would be that its publication is a dangerous political act and not that the book is pornographic, even though its pornography is the main instrument of the book's nihilistic force.

If you want to destroy society—not just write about a character who wants to, but if you want to make your book an instrument for destroying, a weapon—then you need pornography. For since society, at least Western society, is founded on the family as an essential social unit, nihilists and totalitarians must always attack the family as their enemy: conversely those who attack the family as an institution are enemies of our kind of society. The totalitarians would substitute the state for the family; the nihilists would dissolve both the state and the family in the name of unrestricted gratification of natural appetite. To effect this dissolution, nihilists assault taboos, both because taboos restrain appetite and because they are an integral part of civilized order, of society as such. And since of all taboos the sexual ones are much the most important, pornography becomes for the nihilists (as it does not for the totalitarians, who need taboos) important as an instrument of dissolution; obviously a nihilistic representation of people violating taboos will be effective only if the representation itself also violates taboos. The reverse does not hold: pornography is not intrinsically nihilistic; conventional pornography recognizes and needs the rules it disobeys.

Because most pornography is not terribly harmful, and also because of the prevalence of liberal permissiveness in sexual matters, our society is falling down on one of its lesser jobs—the drawing of firm lines about what is decent. Furthermore, it has not sufficiently recognized that indecency can be and sometimes is put to politically dangerous uses. Society should oppose those who proclaim themselves its enemies and who subvert it by every means they know, not least of which is pornography. But violent repressiveness is not the best way for it to oppose them.

If one is for civilization, for being civilized, for even our warped but still possible society in preference to the anarchy that threatens from one side or the totalitarianism from the other, then one must be willing to take a middle way and to pay the price for responsibility. As things stand now, so liberal are we that a professor whose salary is paid by the state can speak out more easily in favor of *Tropic of Cancer* than against it, applauding not just its literary merits but also what he calls its celebration of sensuality and antisocial individualism. These are his honest opinions, and he, no more than the book, should be censored for advancing them. But his colleagues should not allow themselves to be cowed by his scorn of what he calls their bourgeois respectability but should rise in opposition to those opinions. In Miller's own presentation, his sensuality, intended to guard against despair, becomes a way to despair; his individualism is a frenzied endeavor to compose a self in the vacuum of alienation, an alienation which he childishly blames the absolute villain, society, for imposing on him, the absolute victim; he intends his book to be an instrument for persuading his readers to abandon society, abrogate responsibility to their fellowmen, and revert to a parasitic life. He claims that this sensual life is more joyous and fulfilling than any other possible in civilization; but what he describes is not a sensuality which is indeed a fulfillment for adult persons, so much as a would-be consolation for those who aspire to the condition of babies as a remedy to their grown-up woe.

To be civilized, to accept authority, to rule with order, costs deep in the soul, and not least of what it costs is likely to be some of the sensuality of the irresponsible. (In this respect the politically repressed are irresponsibly being denied responsibility. This would help account for the apparently greater sensuality among American Negroes than among American whites, for as a group Negroes have only recently been allowed to assume much social responsibility.) But we Americans, black and white, must be civilized now whether we want to be or not. Perhaps before civilization savages were noble, but, if there is anything we have learned in this vile century, it is that those who regress from civilization become ignoble beyond all toleration. They may aspire to an innocent savagery, but what they achieve is brutality.

At the end of *Tropic of Cancer*, Henry Miller says: "Human beings make a strange flora and fauna. From a distance they appear negligible; close up they are apt to appear ugly and malicious." What Miller says is right enough, but he leaves out what matters most. There is a middle distance from which to look at a man, the flexible distance of decency and art, of civilized society, which defines both a man looking and a man looked at; and from this distance human beings can look pretty good, important, even beautiful sometimes, worthy of respect.

Afternote

I once published a piece on Page 2 of the Sunday *Times Book Review* which began by taking off on Auden's famous line "poetry makes nothing happen." In the piece I called Auden "our wisdom poet," and for this Seymour Krim later accused me of "genocidal pride," even though the second half of the piece elaborated on Shelley's "poets are the unacknowledged legislators of the world." I had made the mistake of having two ideas on the same page, and he had selected only the one he wanted to hate.

I thought that in this essay the doubleness of my opinions on pornography and on censorship would be obvious to anyone who did not have a closed mind. But the first reactions to the appearance of the essay in *Harper's* pretty well set the pattern of response it has since elicited. Nine or so letters supported my general position, a couple of them preparing me for the onslaught to come, and ninety or so attacked me. A few of these said one must not be against pornography since there was no such thing or since it existed only in the eye of a dirty-minded beholder or since anything promoting sex in any way was good. Most, however, censured me for advocating censorship. "That's not what I said! It's not that simple!" I said that I disliked censorship and that by and large it is badly handled, and that the censorship I conceived as possible for pornography would be erratic, inconsistent, hypocritical, and weak. But they did not notice. From these responses I learned, what I had not adequately appreciated before, how belligerently single of mind liberals are on certain subjects, censorship being high on the list (they can also be bigoted about how open-minded they are). Lawyers seem to have less difficulty in detecting my ambivalence than do literary intellectuals. There being very few reputable intellectuals who have spoken against pornography in public, I am asked every so often to appear on panel discussions and such like, but never—thank the lord—to appear as a witness, on either side, in a porno trial.

In one important respect, events have clearly proved me wrong. I assumed a greater coherence of standards about sexual customs and general attitudes toward pornography than apparently existed in 1964, when I wrote the essay, or certainly obtains now in 1971.

On one small point I have changed my opinion, that laws prohibiting pornography are a kindness to those who need it by reassuring them it is nasty. Sigurd Burckhardt, who read the essay in typescript and pretty much agreed with the argument, thought I was being too fancy in using this rather shaky notion to lend support to even a conjectured censorship, and he was right.

Seemingly, I feared too much a resurgence of reactionary oppression, to which the removal of censorship of pornography would make an emotional contribution greater than its actual social importance. The courts have in fact relaxed the old restraints —though the Supreme Court was still uneasy in the Ginzburg trial over the way pornography is offered to the public for sale. As books, magazines, plays and happenings, movies, and works of plastic art have gotten dirtier, the reactionaries have muttered and threatened impeachments and formed societies for the prevention of—but not much more. In this matter, I hope I will continue to be proved wrong, and I hope further that the Danish experiment of removing all censorship whatever proves demonstrably uninjurious and unthreatening, so that we can follow suit. Pornography itself rapidly gets boring, and so does talking about it. But the case is by no means closed as yet. Seventh-grade teacher: "Here, what's the fuss back there?" Chloë: "Jerry took my porno comic, teacher. Make him give it back to me." Jerry: "Here, stupid, it's nothing but another old Hotbox Fergusson, anyway. Take it." Maybe the reason I cannot imagine such a scene's taking place in reality is that I think it shouldn't. Can you? Should it?

To my mind, the most interesting aspect of the controversy is aesthetic, insofar as I can make a distinction between the aesthetic and the moral, especially in fiction. My approach, treating literary and sexual matters as being also within the moral realm, is, whatever else, not *with it*. However, from many little asides picked up along the way, I suspect that my views, old-fashioned though they are, are more widely held than expressed. But they obviously are not very *interesting*—one of the prime categories of Zeitgeist. This was brought home to me vividly, not long ago, after I had been on a program with Leslie Fiedler, who by any criterion is interesting. A woman I had never seen before bustled up, eyes sparkling, and told me she agreed with me completely but she was writing her master's thesis on Mr. Fiedler's criticism—"I just think his ideas are *terrible!*"—and did I have any influence with him, could I get her an interview with him. It's tempting, after a few like that, to decide you'd rather be read than right, especially when you aren't always all that sure how right you are.

The aesthetic issue that interests me here is not the one I have proposed in "Against Pornography." I have not come across any direct challenge to the thesis that "distance" is the key aesthetic question in determining pornography. The issue is a cluster of arguments advanced by Leslie Fiedler, John Barth, and Susan Sontag, among others.

Fiedler's is the most innocent. In his energetic speculations on the myths buried in pop culture, he is indifferent to the moral dimensions of pornography, as to those of the Western, the gangster movie, sci-fi, or popular song lyrics; what people *think* those dimensions are, *that* can be interesting. One cannot fault him for this approach, which does in fact turn up some notions worth considering, illuminates some odd corners. Its dangers are two-fold. First, zestful for the interesting, one can shunt aside the disturbing effect too much pornography may have on adolescents. Second, one can overvalue the aesthetic importance of a myth or archetype which one finds in a pop work; *Tarzan of the Apes,* for example, or *The Wizard of Oz* are aesthetically trivial, whatever interest they may have to a theorist of American culture with a thesis to ride. Enthusiasm for pop of all sorts, not just pornography, produces some astounding judgments; I do not know what else explains how a poet as fastidious as Adrienne Rich could claim that Bob Dylan's pop lyrics vie with John Berryman's dream songs in range and richness of language, above all other contemporary poetic language in the colloquial mode.

Barth's attitude is that fiction as an art is moribund, a mass of work not to be added to or enriched by writers now but for them to pillage and cannibalize. With all traditions discarded, that which tradition despised becomes useful just because it was so despised, and its being offensive, like pornography, is a bonus. Barth also explores, like other postmodernists who turn to pop, the uses of bad taste, boredom ("creative boredom" is his phrase for it), blasphemy, and so on. I had thought Cioran was the ultimate nihilist, but there is a sense in which Barth outdoes him; Cioran still cares that there is Nothing there to connect with, whereas Barth is the disengaged aesthete of nihilism. His endeavor seems merely perverse to me, no more than fun and games—he is the best parodist around. I am willing to be shown, but he has not showed me yet.

Sontag's essay "The Pornographic Imagination" makes the best case I can imagine for the aesthetic possibilities of pornographic fiction. She is contemptuous of most pornography, and she is distressed by its mass availability to the young; she knows what it is. But she makes a valid argument for the perverse seriousness of three pornographic novels; I have read one of them, *The Story of O,* but not the others, both by Georges Bataille. I abominate *The Story of O,* but I cannot dismiss it literarily as I can nearly all the other pornography I have read; it is a novel of some stylistic and structural merit, and to some extent it puts its pornography to the service of an end other than sexual arousal or disgust, as Sade does also, though much more crudely; *The Story of O* is not heavily didactic as Sade's novels are, nor does it try to develop character as novels usually do—pornography is intransigently depersonalizing. It moves, Sontag argues and I think her perception is right, toward a quasi-religious revelation, toward O's transcendence of personality through perverse eroticism, her loss of self through degradation. But there is no gain achieved by this loss of self; O is removed from everyone; nothing but meaningless death can await her now. In my view, this is the erotic nihilism, like Cioran's terrifying theological nihilism, of a balked Christian mystic. I must take on faith Miss Sontag's higher ranking of Bataille's two books, for I shall never read them. In respect of pornography and nihilism, my consciousness has expanded enough. There are things I want not to know.

12

Revolution Instead

One afternoon when I was going on three, my mother took me along to visit a sick friend in the country. Assuring me with a kiss that I would be alone in the car for just a little while, she left me with my favorite toy; but the moment she was out of sight, I was seized by the urgent need to have a bowel movement. It was stifling hot, and I was unable to lower the windows. The Model T's one door, on the passenger's side, was too tight for me to open —or else the handle was too stiff to turn, I can't recall which. I was out of diapers by then, but there was no pot, and deliberately to use the car seat or floor as a toilet would have been such a desecration it did not occur to me as a possibility. Perhaps to keep that temptation out, panic filled my mind. My screams went unanswered. Helplessly, I soiled my pants. *Look what happened to me.*

Twenty years later, exempted from military service in good part because I suffered severe attacks of claustrophobia—I also walked in my sleep—I followed Freud's example and interpreted my dreams for a couple of years, finally sweating out that trauma in the Model T and analyzing it according to what I understood of his principles. For another twenty years, my attacks of claustrophobia, though they did not disappear, diminished in frequency, and none of them were too much for me to handle, as some earlier ones had been, forcing me in mad panic to *get out now*. While that baby misfortune had been lurking in me unacknowledged, it had retained the virulence of a transgression unimaginably horrendous. *See what you made me do.*

My looking at the event plain twenty years later, my thinking about it with humor, drained some of the toxin from it. This is my interpretation. Feeling abandoned by my mother, I had wanted to run to her, in order to punish her for having gone away and also just to be with her; but this urgent desire was balked by the car itself. My double fury stained blind by fear of the consequences, I hurt her as best I could by violating my newest, strongest taboo: I defecated in my clothes like a baby. Back from the house, my mother was distressed by my distress—not by what she called the "little accident" I had had—so she of course did not punish me for what I felt to be a gross transgression. But, since in her eyes my sin was too trivial to merit punishment, it was also so trivial that she did not imagine my massive need of forgiveness. I was just having a childish upset: she soothed me. The soothing sealed *it* in, out of sight; I was stuck with *it* for life.

I am moderately confident of this unraveling, because never have accesses of my claustrophobia been accompanied by the need to move my bowels; if I had blamed the car for my panic, I would have done something bad to it; instead, I soiled the pants which my mother had made for me and which she had ironed fresh that morning. My adult, retrospective (and orthodox) guess is that the core of my impulse to hurt her was rage at her not for having locked me in but for having abandoned me. But the cause of the rage has mattered to me less than the fact that my being shut in so intensified my potent, unacknowledged, destructive emotion that it became unmanageable; now, adult, when I have some potent, unacknowledged, destructive emotion, my feeling of being closed in intensifies it, yes, but also helps me to confine it, contain it, manage it. *Well, at least I can do this with what happened to me.* In any case, now as then, to imagine being stifled to death fills me with an intense, special horror.

The way I know the world, the way I put together what I know of the world, was malformed by that small, ill-timed distress. But perhaps this malformation is not wholly useless, the world being put together the way it is.

The confusion of my political ideas and feelings sometimes becomes so grave that, feverish with rage, contempt, dread, despair, intellectual claustrophobia, I am alarmed by my own instability. Rage: at criminal oppressors, whether slum landlords for their soul-stagnating exploitation of the cowed, or white-sheeted assassins waylaying blacks and civil rights workers, or warmakers. Contempt: the mugwumps and cowardly hypocrites forever; currently, of young self-proclaimed revolutionists who, in the name of exalted ideals, Freedom and Justice, provoke from authority a responsive violence, an illegal force, a tyranny, which must be one of the things they really want—why else would privileged taunters, these new remittance men, throw plastic-bag bombs of urine in cops' faces and call them pigs? Dread: of technology; of our future which, to the extent it can be imagined, can hardly be desired by us as we are; of what science has sanctioned us to do with its potent marvels first in the West and then to all mankind. Despair: of any remedy to our plight; what we most need is an unimaginable change of heart, of a sort no political change could accomplish, only a religious one, and none such seems likely to happen. Intellectual claustrophobia: from onrushes of thinking about all this, trapping myself every time, no matter which way I go, into the mad notion that man himself, the world itself, is mad. The notion is mad both because it is unreal—after all, much of what I know about these matters comes to me through the mass media, that pseudo-reality, not through my own experience—and also because it is unseriously self-contradictory, at once darkly unthinkable and much too fashionable.

The obvious way to deal with an unmanageable problem is to not-think about it. My mother was an adept at not-thinking about unpleasantnesses, and I used to be pretty good at it too; on at least one big matter I still am. I have not-thought about life-after-death so successfully that by now I have neither emotions nor opinions on the subject; it seems to me none of my business. I find the ghost of Hamlet's father good for shivers, but "To be or not to be" a bit of a bore—for God's sake, man, shrug. However, I watched my mother as age and illness broke her down and flattened her out, and I too am so put together that I will grow old for no good reason ("Dear daughter," cried Lear on his knees, "I confess that I am old. Age is unnecessary") and I too may sicken toward death. I worry that, if this happens, non-thoughts about immortality will rise up into and seize my vacating mind, for Mother dying was occupied, hideously, by the lumpen fears and gypsy lusts she had so long not-thought.

But politics, the ways we govern each other, I am unable to not-think about for long. Despite my dread of paradoxing myself into "either the world is mad or I am mad or we are both mad," still not-thinking about politics is worse. For from the stifle of not-thinking there is no relief I know of but death, whereas from the cage of insoluble paradox I know of at least one escape. "O, that way madness lies," said Lear of the wrongness of those heads of state his daughters, "let me shun that." But wrongness permeated everything he saw; he could not shun it. He went that way; he escaped into madness. And so, I think, would I, if I ever stopped writing.

I am not in fact mad—not certifiable at least. And I am fortunate in that, being an orderer of words by vocation, I have use for confusion: it keeps me telling stories.

Moreover, during this past decade, the political disturbances in myself, the institutions I am part of, my country—throughout the whole earth—have not kept me from taking political actions which I see in retrospect as having a certain coherence, and these actions are far more moderate than are most of my political feelings most of the time. I yearn to be an anarchist and tear apart our blatantly wrong society—Yippee!—and I yearn even more to be a dictator and impose my will as law. (Actually I would probably turn into a routine despot in no time. About rather small arrangements, such as hiring, prize-giving, policy-making, firing, punishing, in not very important institutional roles, I have sometimes been empowered to say and I have said: "Let it be" and it was. Great! Nothing like it! Till the morning after. I unhappily suspect that, as autocrat, once I had promulgated a great edict setting many things straight, I would be so riven with doubts that I might very well allow flatterers to surround me, soothing my spirit with unctuous murmurs: "You were not wrong, you did not make a mistake, do not falter for we your people need you, you are right, you are right, you are right.") But, as things stand, when push comes to shove, I settle for that pallid oxymoron *conservative liberal* in order to act at all. I am a libertarian who likes socialism even less than capitalism. I am equally opposed to keeping things the way they are and to progress, to rule by our rich and to salvation through politics, to oppressing you for your own good and to liberating you for your own good. I am a man in between.

Even though my hottest feelings about our society are revulsions—from its corruptions, from the tedium of its processes, from the envy it propagates, its zeal to sully the excellent and bring down the high, its pimping for mediocrity in the name of justice—still, I believe in representative democracy enough to accept our oligarchical version of it. I do not believe in republican government as a Christian who has the wicked devil to hate with half his heart can with the other half adore the one, the just, the good and only-good God, but as a pagan has to put up with the complicated, whimsical gods he was born under. Knowing they are at least as bad as good, wishing he owed allegiance instead to a glamorous One he has heard about in a kingdom over the sea, he performs impatiently—yet he performs—the mostly drab rites they demand of him. I wish I had over me a monarch whose authority was divinely ordained; then, his defects as a man and errors as a governor would be much easier to put up with, being in the nature of things and none of my doing. But in a secular world the office of governor must be authorized by the governed—otherwise, rule by fixed bayonets, with which we are threatened—and the governed must assume more responsibility than most people want—otherwise, rule by money, which we largely have. Finally, I guess, since America is quite secular, democracy must be worth our trouble. Like Kent, I would be happy to find a king, even without a throne, to whom I could say: "You have that in your countenance which I would fain call master." But mad Lear teaches me what I, democrat, am likely to settle for: "A dog's obeyed in office." I wish it had been the gods who put Lyndon Johnson above me; but since I helped in a tiny way to put him there, I also could and did help in a tiny way to restrain him from the tyranny he showed signs of yearning for; and that was worth doing.

In this world generally, but in a republic especially, we must help one another stop in time.

Four married couples.

A man of fifty, high in the esteem of his colleagues, declined into despair. So far from taking his wife with him as he sank, he told her, and he meant it, that he was grateful to her for having helped him keep afloat for several years. When he killed himself, she suffered bitterly for a while. Within two years she remarried.

A chemical engineer in San Diego, where the climate is benign, after several years of working in an armament industry for a high salary, moved on from marijuana to LSD and took his wife with him. "Civilization has failed, America has failed, if you are to save yourself you must get out." He decided to emigrate to the Hudson Bay and survive by hunting, fishing, and serving as a guide. His wife was afraid to go there; she was used to their split-level life, and they had two children under five. But she had gone so far with him already that she no longer knew how to stop even herself, much less him. He packed into a panel truck all the possessions they were keeping; but to get her into it, the morning they drove off, he had to dope her—and she did not stop him from doping her—so heavily that they were a day and a half on the road before she could tend the babies properly. That was three years ago, and their money has nearly run out. They are there still, and they swear they will not return.

A tall, masculine young woman of powerful mind, a somnambulist, after pushing her hand through an eighth-floor window while sleepwalking, went into psychoanalysis. Unfortunately, she espoused a liberal dogma of Adjustment: adjusted women marry and have children. She took as husband a man half a head shorter than she, less well educated, less intelligent, and she had by him a child for whom she did the things the books said loving mothers do. But she was very unhappy. She blamed her husband: he had not fulfilled her, he did not even keep her from lapsing into insanity from time to time. Having striven and failed to cross over into Adjustment, she jumped off a bridge to her death. And (I imagine), even as he had not been able to hold her back, so he could not stop himself from going with her as she had pulled: at any rate, four months later his heart failed to go on beating.

A man who had been a conscientious objector during the war, once divorced, his only son maimed in Vietnam, married a woman who had worked as a legal secretary. She is very feminine, and she has thought hard about Law. She does not oppose the baby emotions which he can not control very steadily and which have cost him many friends; she, who was raised in Manhattan apartments, goes sailing with him though the sea scares her, and they walk through woods and fields naming the plants and birds; he often cannot get to sleep, and she stays up with him till dawn. But when he threatens to bring his senile father to live with them, and when he says that from now on they must make do on a hundred dollars a month because he is going to give the rest of his earnings to poor Negroes whose ancestors his ancestors enslaved, and when he tells her he is going off for the weekend with another woman, she says each time, "If you do that, I will leave you," and that is all she says. Of his fears, that is the deepest one available to her, and she puts it to the service of love. She takes the risk, of course, that *because* she will not give in to him on these demands, he may escalate his threats: "I am going to kill myself, I am going to kill you." If that happens, she should and I think will get out. But that has not happened, for he knows with his heart that she does not want to leave him and with his reason that she is right. For five years, because she goes a way with him but refuses to go too far, he has been stopping in time. May they go on that way.

Just as marriage connects a man and a woman who will mold each other in any of innumerable combinations, so the institution of marriage is the principal mode of intercourse between sex and society, between libido and law, an intercourse essential to the welfare of both. Uninvigorated by libido, law petrifies, becomes too rigidly unyielding in some respects and much too easy to break in others. But the converse of that seems to me no less true and at present more important: unrestrained by law, libido tyrannizes. *To get all you want of it* is less likely to make you connect with or know others, or even one other person, than to make you go for *it* all the time; and metaphorically this is a tyranny. But, worse, like a usurer creating money out of money, you can develop an artificial appetite for sensual satiation, a superappetite itself insatiable, and finally, sapped by insatiety, you may very well yearn for some outside force to restrain you; and this is an open invitation to literal political tyranny.

During the past decade America has been undergoing, for much-discussed reasons and in overadvertised ways, changes in sexual attitudes and customs—what is called "The Sexual Revolution." Contraceptives and abortion, in addition to antibiotics, have made it possible for sexual indulgence to be exempt from the old consequences to a degree and with side effects that our ethics has not yet been able to accommodate; but what, in my opinion, constitutes a political threat is that, in reaction against the excesses and distortions of puritanism, society has taken to condoning sexual indulgence without positively approving it, has de-moralized it. The demonstrable ways in which this is being done are the sanctionings of pornography and of open promiscuity; what matters more is a deepening acceptance of, or at least permissiveness toward, sexual hedonism. This means letting body-health pleasure replace responsible love as the purpose of every kind of sexual action and combination (including coitus, which this hedonism holds to be superior to other varieties of "genital gratification" only if you make it so). The phrase "to make love" has already turned into a mere euphemism, and at the rate things are going it will soon be tossed into the discard pile along with the Biblical "he knew her"; what will replace "to make love" is not yet clear; the expression I hear most often is "to make it," as in "he made it with her." (This is the same *it* Lear used for the fitchew, the small gilded fly, the soiled horse: "To't, luxury, pell-mell! for I lack soldiers.") Add to all this the widespread acceptance of divorce, and our already undermined institution of marriage may come to be so badly subverted that law and libido would lack any good way to benefit each other and we would lose what civilities we have. Troublesome as democracy and marriage both are, tautening to the soul, and despite their presently impaired condition, still we had better conserve them, try to rehabilitate them. I grant that a revolution, especially a figurative one like "The Sexual Revolution," is a lot more fun, the rewards being immediate, as well as a whole lot easier, for it is hard work keeping your balance in a storm. Even so, I am against that easy fun, for I fear that, in reaction to the unmanageable dangers of libidinal anarchy, we would gain instead a concentration-camp despotism no less evil.

The violent passions which turned the French Revolution into a terror were initiated in good part by an ossified monarchy that was both unjust and incompetent, but the course of the Revolution was not toward the limited goal of a less-unjust, competent government. Too many of the revolutionary leaders had limitless aspirations; their actions were sanctioned, were morally authorized, by the *philosophes* of The Enlightenment, especially by Diderot and Rousseau. It is sublimely appropriate that, when that symbol of the Old Regime's tyranny, the Bastille, symbolically fell in the name of Reason, the most important prisoner set free was the Marquis de Sade; for in him The Enlightenment was given a fourth, dark dimension (which would have horrified the proper *philosophes*). "Unchained, natural impulse is good? Very well, *my* strongest impulse is to inflict myself on others," and he did by word and deed.

(Mythically, that is all very fine. The facts are just as good. When the Bastille was opened to the mob, only seven prisoners remained in it to be liberated. Sade, for the safety of his person, had already been moved to Charenton, an insane asylum, and was freed from there some time later. The same Revolution that made a goddess of Reason by crowning a naked chorus girl in the Cathedral of Notre Dame set loose in society the man who gave sadism its name. More than set loose: he was so criminal, mad, and idealistic that the Terror overcame its suspicion of his noble birth and made Citizen Sade an official in Paris. However, this man who wrote the vilest books in the world was sentenced to death because he was not cruel enough; he neglected to turn in political suspects for execution—being also a murderer, he was, reasonably enough, opposed to capital punishment. He escaped guillotining only because, at the last minute, the batch of cannibals who were about to devour him were themselves cannibalized by a fresh batch. When Napoleon had rigidified the new tyranny, Sade was locked up again in the madhouse, where he died. No mythmaker could improve on the timing of his death: it occurred late in 1814 shortly after civility began trying to establish itself in France.)

The French Revolution remains the chief paradigm for modern revolutions generally, and again and again you can see its influence in the way rebellion is sanctioned, even in circumstances which are wildly inappropriate—as "The Black Revolution" is currently in the United States. The blacks cannot possibly take over, as the French people could, and our government is utterly unlike the Old Regime, if only in that it has self-change built into it and is responsive to pressure. Yet, when a radical black such as Eldridge Cleaver speechifies, his ideas derive from and are far more appropriate to the Enlightened revolutions, American, French, Russian, than to the plight of American Negroes now. When Cleaver speaks of what he knows, especially of *what was there* in his criminal days, he can be very eloquent, but his bombastic political writing is also praised extravagantly. Intellectuals descend directly from the *philosophes*, and, though they appear to be politically sophisticated, they enjoy having their tribal buttons pushed like American Legionnaires at a convention. There is nothing they applaud more easily than anarchy in the robes of Justice.

Conversely, these same intellectual radicals are sometimes contemptuous of Martin Luther King, though not quite openly; after all, he failed in a useful way, for his martyrdom did stir up a good deal of rioting, which is at least a step toward revolution; but I have heard a couple of them dismiss that peace-lover as "a Tom." It seems to me that nothing is more expectable from a great nation like America, and less likely to effect a change for the better, than violence. What is radically different from great-nation politics is to press steadily for a nonviolent redress for injustices. Our cops and our violent radicals have far more in common than either has with King—that "notorious liar" (as J. Edgar Hoover called him), that Uncle Tom. Who is less American than a man who will stand up to you but whom you cannot provoke into hurting back at you, who would forgive you if you let him?

Violence, like taxation, should be a legal monopoly of the state. I chanced to be in Times Square one noon as fifty or sixty conventionally dressed, quiet women came two abreast down the sidewalk carrying signs protesting the war in Vietnam. At first my liberal hackles rose to see two policemen accompanying this civil demonstration, but then I saw why. A fortyish man in a rumpled suit, eyes bloodshot, voice raspy, mouth stretched, face lined like Hate in a morality play, was pointing his finger at the head of a gray-haired woman not two feet from his aim, and he was calling her, over and over with various insulting epithets added, a draft dodger. Only force could have stopped him, but he was not quite breaking the law. I am glad the law permits those women to do what they were doing; and, if it does that, it must also permit that man to do what he was doing. But I think the law should make it very very hard, instead of very very easy, for him to get hold of a gun.

A couple of times when my political confusion has become acute, I have turned back to John Stuart Mill's *On Liberty*, especially the first two chapters, and imagined with his help the polity I believe in most.

I have not turned back to Marx, though he is much more important in the world at large and though I have tried him. For a long time he persuaded me that capitalism was the chief source of modern social evil; the greed it sanctions continues to be, next to envy, the ugliest thing I know; but now it seems to me that industrialization was more important than capitalism in shaping the modern world and that competition in a great many social matters, especially in economic affairs, is a positive good. Most of the vices of our capitalists seem to me no more than to be expected of power men, but some of their vices are unnecessary; of these, the one I hold against them most is that they use their vast fortunes so ignobly; the doges and shoguns did better. Moreover, Marx never persuaded me of the beauty of socialism. I read Dostoevsky too, and thought him wiser than Marx; what he said against socialism was true. (To a half-Quaker half-Methodist like me, the One True Church has no reality; the One True Party, the One True State, these are as unreal to me as Pan-Slavism or America First.) Combined with the stultifying standardization natural to industrialism and the envious leveling latent in democracy, socialism triumphant would make a homogenized world I cannot bear to think about. A universal General Motors with Mesdames Defarges disguised as social workers on its board of directors—this would have horrified Marx, though he has helped make it possible. Though I admire his high intelligence and the ferocity of his moral passion, his German-philosopher prose and his determinism throw gravel in my mental works; but what finally sets me against him is antipathy for two of his erroneous premises, one based on an emotion, the other on a dream.

The emotion is hatred of injustice—obviously in itself a good, an emotion without which no man can be said to be all there—but Marx's error is to make it his overriding political passion. I mistrust a dogmatic evil-hater, for his impulses are not just negative, they are doubly negative, and he becomes a zealot. The main thing he will want to do is to destroy: first the evil institutions and men he hates, then also those like me, who, seeing things as more complicated than that, would restrain his zeal to destroy. Even so, without being a Marxist, I know what it feels like to be one, for I have that same double-negative emotion often enough; though I wish I could love Justice more than I hate injustices, in fact I don't.

But about the Enlightenment's dream of paradise attainable in history, translated by Marx into a classless society as the end of progress, I do not have double feelings at all. Next to the nightmare of exterminating mankind, no political dream seems to me more dangerous. As a gimmick in a science-fiction story, it would have been about as useful as rational carrots and time-warps, but as a basis for political thought leading to action, it appalls me.

According to this dream, which I do not pretend here to summarize objectively, man's aggressiveness in nearly all its forms is a serious misfortune and the source of most of the wrongs of the world, but if we rearrange society rationally, our aggressiveness will disappear and we will love everybody. Behind this dream, authorizing it, is a cluster of rationalistic notions that by now are so familiar they no longer seem monstrous; our impulses are natural and therefore good, and society, by restraining them, is the cause of most of our troubles whether individual or collective; aggression is an emotional perversion, a compensation for frustration and inadequacy; totally freed, we would cease to be aggressive, no longer wanting or needing to govern or be governed. Perhaps most dangerous of all, the dream of man's perfectibility, of his improvability, of Progress, sanctions in those who believe in it—Marxists, socialists, progressives—the very sin they most deplore. Feeling themselves justified, they intrude upon you what they are sure is good for you whether you think it is or not, and they do not clearly recognize the offensiveness of this imposition or even, at the extreme, that it is an imposition. We are going to study you and make you clean and prosperous whatever your customs or your gods say. First we will make you dissatisfied with what you have, you poor victims, and then we, who understand these things, will teach you how to reform and rebel. Beside them, even Christian and Moslem pistol-point missionaries don't look so bad; when they set about saving your soul, they grant at least that you have the power to choose to behave wickedly or well, they do not debase you, as progressives do, into an uneducated underprivileged passive victim without a choice, the clay of History, but leave you your self. It seems to me evident that to deny the goods of aggression, or to call them evils, is to pervert the whole impulse hideously.

An irony of progressivism is that its liberal True Believers are convinced they hate imperialism.

The best ones I know, aspiring to be reasonable, are admirably patient and persuasive. But, because their Faith does not appreciate the dark of the will, their understanding of evil is remote and conscious. Institutional evil they identify zealously, but that inward private evil which is a kind of emotional mistranslating they subsume under "maladjustment" or "mental illness," thereby hoping it can be institutionalized away.

A progressive's purest emotion is pity-the-victim, and he sees victims everywhere: children are victimized by their parents, women by men, the colored races by the white, the poor by the rich, the individual by (our of course sick) society; indeed, when the frenzy is on him, he can think of all mankind as being victimized, if only by prehistoric impulses no longer appropriate to our civilized condition. Without bothering to have emotions about it, he *knows* that the oppressed (nearly everyone) should and can be liberated and that the first step toward this liberation is to persuade them they are in at least one important respect blame-free victims who can do something about their condition. (The reasons are not far to seek why Jews are especially drawn to progressivism: they really have been victimized, and their heritage encourages them to "do something" about trouble.) So urgent is the progressive's zeal to reform—he lives in a state of permanent crisis—and so dazzled is he by his own altruism that he sees only the liberation in his act of persuasion. Convinced that justice is attainable, he cannot believe that the painful discontent, the joy-killing doubt, generated in many whom he has stirred out of their acceptance of the way things are may itself be a new form of victimization. Neither, in his impatience, does he worry that perhaps those who are taught to think of themselves as victims must also be taught forgiveness if their vengeful feelings are to be harnessed for justice.

There is another, equally sinister force which he is not wary of releasing, because he does not fathom its labyrinthine darkness: self-pity, the perverter. In the very many who find it easy to indulge in self-pity, there is no more effective way of strengthening the impulse to mistranslate than by persuading them they are victims. But the first upon whom they exercise this power is of course the one nearest at hand, that is, the Enlightened, progressive, victorious liberator himself. In their mistranslation, his "I pity you" becomes "I am better off than you are." "I am here to help you" becomes "I'm taking you over." "Here are medicine and soap" becomes "you are repulsive." "Let me teach your children scientifically" becomes "you have been failures as parents." "Here are contraceptives and legal abortion" becomes "you should never have been born." Victims of liberation who so mistranslate have open to them courses which resemble those taken by many conquered people. They may despise themselves, as being worthless ("backward" or "underdeveloped") in the eyes of their superiors. They may so react against progressivism that they reject the goods of Progress, accepting only the tools, and behave with savage cruelty (the Nigeria-Biafra civil slaughter). In their fawning zeal to share their conquerors' power and prestige, they may pervert the True Faith into grotesque heresies (Stalin and Hitler were lapsed Christians who converted to socialism.) I prefer the old-fashioned, Mark Antony, sword-and-tribute brand of unprincipled imperialist ruler. If you're going to go around spreading self-contempt, hatred, and sycophancy among those you have conquered, you might as well enjoy your domination; no use spoiling your happiness as well as theirs.

Well, Progress—I am here subsuming the capitalist schisms and socialist heresies under the central scientific orthodoxy into one great Faith—is not only the best disguised but also much the most successful imperialism the world has known. The time is overdue for liberal and humane progressives to recognize that they are a new breed of conquerors. This recognition might jar out of them some of the zeal to push Efficiency, Reform, Change, and spur them to search instead for moral principles by which to rule well. But probably not. For this might also entail their accepting the literal superiority of the rulers (themselves) over the ruled (the "victims"), and that would be incompatible with the ideal of equality attainable in this world. *All men are brothers*—isn't that what Progress is aimed at? Think of the rich resources of self-pity available to that most intricate of victims, an egalitarian progressive elevated into authority by those whom he has conquered with liberation. "I'm not above you, really, and even though I am it doesn't mean anything, it's just an accident of history and education, a temporary arrangement, there are so many improvements to be made, all for your own good, I don't know when I'll be finished, I hate all this, if only you would hurry up and learn to do it for yourselves, forward march." Progressives are lords with freedmen's notions: they neither rule nor allow others to rule well.

Back to secular, unprogressive libertarianism and stoic assumptions: because human beings with free (and therefore unpredictable) wills are what matter most in this world, our imperfect impulses need restraining and directing by government; like the welfare of a child in a family, the welfare of a citizen in a free society depends, among other things, on the administration by authority of firm punishment for the violation of clear rules; the many must consent to be governed by the few, who must be responsive to the needs of the many.

Such a libertarianism, with its complexity and stoicism, with the obligation it lays on its citizens to participate in their own government and its refusal to promise lots of freely flowering love after the withering away of the state, has far less appeal in desperate times than revolutionary Marxism with its regular shots of diabolism mixed with paradise-dreaming—Maoism at the moment. Nevertheless, for lack of better, I am going to go on believing in it, for I think that the forms of our government permit civility and also that there are even now enough responsible men left to keep things running, or enough at least to keep things from coming apart completely. May there be more soon.

It is easy to say, and some intellectuals do say, that our social system is so defective that we should not try to stop it from destroying itself. "Doom! Man is an evolutionary mistake! He might as well do himself in now as later!" This sounds to me like self-indulgent not-thinking, a way of saying: "I'm not-thinking very satisfactorily, thank you. You ought to try it my way too." I believe that, if our government collapses for whatever reason, those who are against totalitarianism of any sort (*and* who do not succumb to despair) will work with all their strength to construct another system of government fundamentally like ours now, and probably fail. This is reason enough, it seems to me, to be against destroying our system by revolution or encouraging it to destroy itself, but instead to be for conserving it, for repairing and strengthening it—for increasing its authority over us, since we are babies, as well as our exercise of authority within it, since we are not babies.

Two liberal Jews.

She remembers that one morning her father gave her four million marks with which to buy a notebook and that she lost the money on the way to school. All it would have bought was a little notebook, and by afternoon it would not have bought even that; yet, four million. . . . At eighteen she escaped from Germany with her parents, but two grandparents and three of her six uncles and aunts disappeared never to be heard of again. . . . When she finally was admitted to the United States after the war, she felt happier and safer than she could remember feeling ever before. But after a while it occurred to her that she could not accept the benefits of the American social arrangements, as she was doing, without also accepting a commensurate responsibility for them, as she was not doing and as she had no natural inclination to do. She who had suffered bitterly from racism must not let it go unopposed, much less benefit by it even indirectly. Having experienced anarchy and totalitarianism, she does a certain amount for the civil rights movement—nonviolently, usually though not always legally—that civility may survive.

His parents were prosperous and liberal second-generation New Yorkers, and they had, as was conventional, supplanted their parents' religion with faith in science and a disposition toward socialism. In college, he acquired an ardent faith in the most idealistic anarchism: no government, man is good, science will save us, progress. He became a surgeon. But, though he charged only the going fees and though he did more than the customary amount of charity work, he became rich; he bought a place in the country, cultivated expensive tastes in food and wine, began to acquire paintings and statues. Where was the equality in this? He entered psychoanalysis and came out of it dismayed. He had become a surgeon not only because he wanted to help people but also because he liked to hurt them and even more because he enjoyed playing the dictator in the operating room. He liked his superior status in the social hierarchy. He liked having more money than most people. It made him feel very good that when he said to people *jump* they said *how high?* Moreover, he wasn't about to relinquish any of these bad things he liked so much. He was vile. Man is vile. You can expect anything of anybody, and technology —which used to be our main hope in a hostile world—has given men terrible destructive power. The only way to preserve what there is worth having is with guards. Totalitarianism is inevitable.

. . . The stronger his conviction that The Day he dreads is surely coming, the sourer his impatience with liberal causes and with the very idea of civility, much less that impaired civility of ours which is all he has ever experienced. The last time I saw him, at his house for Thanksgiving dinner, this surgeon tore the drumsticks, thighs, and wings off the turkey with his bare hands.

Partly, young American college radicals, from the crazies to the fellow travelers, are merely conforming to the two-centuries-old Enlightened tradition of how to rebel. (An instance of this. At Syracuse University, during the student uprisings set off by the invasion of Cambodia, the most visible sign of our students' seizure of the campus was the erection and manning of flimsy tangles of wire and lumber at the various entrances, in a 1970 functionless imitation of the real barricades in Paris in 1789. Indeed, early on, some student had spray-painted on an old classroom building of this utterly American university AUX BARRICADES.) But a considerable part of the inappropriateness of the behavior and rhetoric of the most vigorous of them derives, I believe, from their not admitting what they are ultimately opposed to. It is true that they genuinely hate the Vietnam War, racial discrimination, and the pollution of the environment, but I doubt that remedying these evils would appease their intransigence. If you accuse a manifestly flexible government of rigidity, cry out against the evils of a society and deny its goods though one of those goods is your right to cry out, and urge your faction to tear it apart NOW though it is manifestly too strong for you to tear apart, then, no matter whether you are sane or insane, what you really most want must be something other than what you say you want. A true, whole revolution consists of the violent and illegal destruction of a government by a group out of power which then sets up a new government. But our nihilistic anarchists appear to want only the first, destroying, easy half of revolution. They say they are against Injustice and for Freedom. But they do not devote their energies to remedying specific injustices in one of the freest—maybe it would be more accurate as well as more unpleasant to say one of the most permissive—countries in the world; they would destroy this government without having a new system of government to put in its place. This can only mean that what they most profoundly want is to remove every restraint on impulse, to abolish governing itself.

In this, they are being true to their parents in a way their parents did not foresee or intend. Our cry goes up: *What have we done to our children?*

Not having liked a great many of the rules by which we had been reared, we retained the basic ones (Don't touch, it's hot), but then, being Enlightened modern-style, we did not replace the castoffs with clear new moral rules. Rather, we tended to substitute a sympathetic attempt to understand motive for the firm, unargued administration of previously defined punishment; too often, we used psychological talk to evade the exercise of our moral authority as parents; we put a complicated yet easy *why?* where a plain hard *no* would have established for our children that limit within which freedom sings and beyond which it shrieks (Ginsberg's *Howl* is their anthem); we made them skeptical and ingenious. A father whacked his daughter on the bottom for hurting her baby brother, and then proceeded to lecture her on responsibility, sibling rivalry, God knows what all. "Daddy, forgive me," she wailed. "I do forgive you, but . . ." "No, forgive me. *Quit talking about it.*" When a Calvinist child is ordered to his room to "think over" what he has done, he is meant to set his soul in order so that the punishment sure to come will cleanse him. When a psychologized child is sent to think it over, he is meant to improve his future behavior by reasonably understanding the motives for his past behavior; but the dark, tangled, cheating emotions, in need of punishment but being given none, turn back upon "thinking it over" and transform the thinking itself into an unclear kind of punishment. Perhaps this helps account for the slovenliness of moral discrimination which characterizes the "Youth Culture": killing is bad, sex is good, cops are pigs, expand your mind, do your own thing. Contingency? Occasion? Conflict of values? Duty? Blow it, motherfucker. Come on, baby, let's ball. . . . No wonder realistic fiction, the most finely moral form of art, has waned in popularity. It was nice when intelligent people still thought, even if only psychologically. I miss it.

Another error of ours. Much too often we saw our children's

transgressions as no more than evidence of psychic health: rebellion being natural is therefore good. By thus treating much of their early disobedience indulgently, and even applauding it when it was directed against laws we considered to be not rational but merely customary, we surreptitiously sanctioned their later rampaging disaffection. But, having in their parents both confused models of how to rebel and also unclear (sometimes literally absent) authorities to define themselves against, they have rebelled in ways ill defined, evasive, incomplete, often violent, often ugly —at the extreme, nihilistic. The son of divorced, radically permissive parents in high school ate himself into obesity and promiscuously joined every social protest that marched by, and in college, until he dropped out, studied to become a penologist.

In tending toward nihilism, these educated children of educated parents are not unique; anarchic resentment of restraint has always been endemic among us—the feeble because unpopular gun-control laws, for example, or the myth of the frontier. If government in the United States collapses, as could happen, it will do so partly because it does not govern enough but more because so many of its citizens refuse to accept our halfway adequate government, much less to participate in it. Indeed, considering how widespread is the reluctance to exercise or accept authority, beginning in the family, we are being governed now no worse than we deserve and perhaps better.

"Control as such is evil." I heard a man say that. I was on a panel with him. He was an obviously intelligent, apparently sane young man, an associate professor of English, a scholar-critic of good repute. He said that the great merit of Burroughs' *Naked Lunch* was to force upon us an awareness of the true nature of our aggressive urge to control others. He cited as his intellectual authority, as the thinker who had primarily authorized him to assert "control as such is evil," Norman O. Brown, and I think he is right. Marcuse and Goodman are not wild enough for our political utopists now; Brown is the most important proximate authorizer of their nihilistic attitude toward government, even though his message sounds more religious than social. ("The next generation needs to be told that the real fight is not the political fight, but to put an end to politics. From politics to poetry.") One part shaky Freud, one part solid Rousseau, and another part rampaging permissiveness, his thesis is that psychic repression, or inhibition, is the root of human ills—as though the Bastille caused Sade's cruelty. Brown dwells largely on the paradisal benefits of removing sexual controls so that everyone can partake freely and almost sacramentally of conscious sexual joy. The Enlightened young had meanwhile been prepared by other influences to embrace Brown's teaching. If you believe that aggression is a curse and that acceptance is suspiciously unprogressive, passive, downright religious, then both the marvelous male flesh of erotic assertion and the equally marvelous female flesh of erotic acceptance are fundamental threats: assertion and acceptance are built into our very bodies; we can't connect in love without them. How evade this? Unisex costumes, drugs, women's liberation—several devices have evolved for blurring the terrifying difference, but none works better than Brown's jolly polymorphous-perverse sexuality (translated, this means baby sex, lick, diddle, and suck, "if it moves fondle it"). Convinced and grateful, Brown's believers extend to practical politics the master's quasi-mystical teaching about removing restraints. Paradise Now. The fact that the most rudimentary control of all, of mother over baby, patently cannot be removed, being essential to the baby's survival and a source of happiness for the mother, does not faze these zealots. But then, zeal seldom is fazed by plain good sense.

They really mean it. *The New York Times* for 2 August 1969 carried a story about a conventional hippie group in a valley in Oregon—nudity, drugs, repudiation of money, free love. A former money-earner named Big Tree, his wife Little Tree, and their daughter Lotus Tree had found contentment there, despite obstacles and hardships. "Some will stay," the article concludes, "but even those feel they are only beginning their quest. As Big Tree put it one day, pointing to his baby daughter: 'We're waiting for these kids to talk so we can find out the next step. We're waiting for instructions.' "

One has to do something to keep from recognizing the lunacy of notions like that. Drugs are useful. Lotus land.

Drugs as a substitute for government.

Surely a full civility (like a full love) which accepts, controls, rejoices in its aggressive feelings is superior to a politics-as-usual by those who are not all there. The drugged are not all there; they are on a nowhere trip.

When I transgress against you, don't just go away and leave me there, get angry with me, punish me, forgive me, that I may be truly purged of my guilt.

The best to be hoped for from the de-aggressioned is Beatles music, and that is not good enough.

Without aggression there would have been no Venice, Byzantium, or Kyoto, those most beautiful of cities, for the engine that drove the builders was powerful men's competition for glory. Individually to each other: "Look how glorious I am!" Collectively to their neighbors: "Look how much more glorious our city is than yours!" Without aggression, no desire to excel; without the fruits of excelling, men would not have much worth having.

Obviously, uncontrolled aggression is terrifying, destructive, a source of evil (as is uncontrolled libido). When old Lear abrogated his authority, transferred his power to the wrong people in the wrong way, the civil controls were wrecked, and aggression and libido were set loose. Some turned into lustful fiends, some went mad and were swirled about by thunderous winds, and very many were murdered before a control was restored. This, the strongest of plays, has as its central theme what happens when authority is transferred wrongly or abrogates, for there is no more important concern in the city of this earth. To be able to imagine those forces released and yet to control them in forms adequate to their power, as Shakespeare did in *King Lear*, is to make what surely is as great a thing as any man ever made. Civility, like high art, orders aggression well.

If a society wants the fruits of excellence, it must encourage competition. What can be done about the sadness of those who enter the competition and lose?

One way of handling this problem is to insist on subordination as in the nature of things. Some men are stronger than others, some make better temples, some have more money, more intelligence, better health, more luck, higher status, and there is nothing to be done about the fact of these inequalities, though perhaps something can be done about specific ones. You do not have to enter the competition. If you do what is appropriate to your station in life, you will then be free to admire the fruits of those who have competed and, gifted and fortunate, have excelled. If you enter the competition and do only modestly, yet you have done something well, worthy of some admiration. If you enter and fail entirely, you will surely suffer but you are not necessarily despicable; you may only have made the mistake of thinking you could compete when in fact you lacked the ability, a forgivable error, or you may have been unlucky. The advantage of this system, which is the dream of aristocracy, is that it encourages admiration of genuine excellence and reduces envy. An aristocratic society has a strong affinity for artists, for art is by its nature hierarchical —some works of art really are better than others, as artists know best of all. An architect is more likely to design something superb if a proud shogun says, "You are the best, make me a magnificent palace," than if the city planning board commissions him as one of a "team" to collaborate on a housing project. His political views may tell him that housing common people is better than glorifying the great; his ambition tells him otherwise; and an artist's ambition is far more intimately connected with his creative imagination than is his political philosophy. Socialism has produced no supreme art and, I think, will produce none—neither the free, just, equal, reasonable socialism of the dream nor the totalitarian socialism of the communist reality. Egalitarianism, by making it shameful to have too much or too little money, robs the poor of the dignity of status and takes all magnificence from the ostentation natural to the rich, thereby vulgarizing both rich and poor. Whether aristocracy has ever worked very well I do not know; it hasn't a chance now, not among us; but it was a fine dream and out of it came many if not most of the marvels of art.

Egalitarianism has been ever-increasing in the modernist period, and because it denies that subordination is natural and a social good, it has no adequate way to handle the problem of those who compete but fail to excel. In such limited areas as sports and musical performance, subordination cannot sanely be denied (this doubtless has much to do with their popularity among us, for we need an occasional jolt of flagrant competitive excellence as antidote to the lies of equality). But in social arrangements subordination can be and is subverted. "It's just a matter of opinion, and mine's as good as yours." "He thinks he's so great, but he's no better than I am." Vox populi Americani.

Of all the noble social ideals, equality is the most dangerous. The Christian ideal that all men are equal in the eyes of God at least gives comfort to the sufferers who believe it is true, though about the only thing in human experience that supports it is the awe one feels in the presence of the dying. But the secular—and valuable—ideal that all men should be equal before the law has spread to areas of concern where it is not only inappropriate but harmful. Because equality came to be inextricably associated with justice, every kind of subordination, even the most natural, came to be felt as unjust, and this sanctioned envy. (I will not forget the teeth in the smile on the bland face of the failed poet who first denied that X's poetry was any good and then uttered these words: "It isn't *fair* that some people are more gifted than others.") The ideal of equality doubtless originated in reaction against the cruel inequities of tyrannical privilege. But instead of stopping in time, saying *everyone has the right to a fair trial*, the rational zealots went on to say *all men are born equal.* Once a decade this is absolutely true, when the census is taken, and every couple of years, in the voting booth, it is sort of true. At nearly all other times and in nearly all other respects, it is untrue, as anyone can see who takes off his Enlightened spectacles and looks. A rich young senator with martyred brothers, and a poor stupid friendless alcoholic old housebreaker with a criminal record, are not equal, either in the hands of the police or in the matter of hiring lawyers or in the dock before judge and jury (any more than they are in the matter of obtaining medical care), and it is impossible sanely to imagine a society with actual, functioning people in it which would not contain similar inequities. Still, an ideal does not have to be realizable to be of value. The ideal of equality before the law provides support for opposition to those Star Chamber and secret police methods by which the powerful are always tempted; it sets a sound limit to how much they can get away with short of brute force. Similarly, the ideal of equality of opportunity encourages the practical good of making education freely available for all. But such genuine benefits as these are almost wiped out by the maladies of egalitarianism: holding subordination to be a social evil, it tries to not-think it out of the nature of things, whence frenzy of the belly and members, lassitude of the mind, and heart strain.

Egalitarianism tells you that "everyone has an equal chance" and so encourages you to enter some competition or other. (In this respect black Americans are luckier than white: all they need in order to keep that lie off is a horselaugh, whereas a lot of whites spend most of their lives toiling in it.) But most who compete fail, and failure hurts. A natural thing to do with this pain is to turn it into vengeful envy of those who win. It is one of the chief jobs of religion, ethics, law, custom, to help the losers not do this. Egalitarian materialistic democracy, so far from helping them refrain from envy, further exacerbates their misery; having urged them to compete no matter what, it then makes the rewards of winning too often worthy of only a debased admiration. Two examples. In the middle reaches of the literary world, there is a widespread disposition to assume that a best-selling novel must be spurious. There, success, so far from being the reward of merit, is the proof of phoniness. For the other, less sophisticated side of the coin, consider Twiggy. An unattractive, untalented fashion model whose success was publicitously manufactured, she was able to do, and she did, nothing for her wealth and celebrity. Such success is an intricate perversion of our need to admire another for having done something worth doing. It is envy's egalitarian revenge on excellence.

Envy is the chief reason why, though I believe in republican democracy, I do not like it much. Coriolanus in Shakespeare's play is wrong, but I am on his side every time and against the citizens, for they are both wrong and ugly. There is no one I revere more than Socrates: he upheld the very laws which his inferior fellow citizens misused to kill him with.

Many intellectuals believe that the two Kennedys and Martin Luther King were the victims of as-yet-undiscovered conspiracies. That is too rational for me. Envy assassinated them. What better reason for a failed American to shoot a man than that he is rich, handsome, fortunate, and powerful, or, most intolerable of all, good?

But the cure for the ailments of egalitarianism and envy is not a revolution—a violent overthrow of *this* government and setting up *that* one in its stead. Indeed, most of the revolutionaries around, being socialists of one kind or another, would only exacerbate egalitarianism without showing the slightest understanding that, though the greed of the capitalists would thereby be extirpated, the envy of the masses would be inflamed hideously.

There is at least this to be said for democracy: it makes it all but impossible for anyone to attain great political power if he is without visible baseness. As a result, we are not likely to be threatened by the rise of some perfectibilitarian who, like Shakespeare's Brutus, is himself so noble that he imagines society can be cleansed of its imperfections (such as the ambitiousness of rulers) and that he is pure enough to do the job. A gangster in office does less harm to society; but so admirable and so rare is a Brutus, in all the visible ways, that nothing but our propensity to envy would keep us from electing him to office.

I know of only one egalitarian solution to the problem of what to do about aggression, competition, envy, which is at all likely to work: drugs, the greatest leveler next to death. The young anarchists in Chicago during the Democratic convention in 1968, despite a broad streak of nihilism and drugs, were at least combative and aggressive; to provoke the police, for whatever reason is an action still visible on the political spectrum. But the uncompetitive, stoned hedonists at Woodstock, all aggression stunned, and their indulgent cops, solicitous as caretakers in a tranquilized ward—there is an image of egalitarianism rampant. Better they should live themselves to death, envy and all.

I don't think it is accidental that this image parodies a concentration camp. If a clever despot seized power in America, he might well "liberate" drugs from the repression of law and perhaps even hand them out free. They are cheaper than secret police and tear gas and tanks and the like, and it is our egalitarian rebellious young who use them most. He would do this, of course, as they themselves would, in the name of Liberty Equality Fraternity.

I am assuming that, although the orthodoxy of rebelliousness is about as advanced in the United States as, say, in China, our young rebels are less disciplined than the Chinese. In the mid-sixties, Chairman Mao, wishing both to shake up the bureaucracy and to strengthen the allegiance of the young to rebellious Marxism, sanctioned and directed their natural restiveness—the "Cultural Revolution." Surely he is the most intricate of rulers. Who else has ever been so confident of being obeyed that he dared command insurrection against his own government, so confident he knew where progress was headed that he dared make riot and discontent part of his subjects' training? But among our young, government-authorized rebellion would not be possible; they are so ill disciplined that not even a Mao could direct their rage or stop them in time. Any despot of ours, unless he were a true anarch, would be much better advised to substitute drug's delusion of spiritual vitality, drug's cancer of the will, for true rebellion and true obedience, thereby affording his more troublesome subjects both happiness (in parody) and equality (the equality of razed aspirations and blurred differences).

One evening in the spring of 1969 as I was driving to a nearby university to take part in a literary symposium the next day, I heard on the car radio that the students were in process of liberating the administration building. (Good Americans following the example of their fathers who in occupied countries during World War II said they liberated farmers' chickens when they stole them, our student activists liberate a building when they seize it.) According to the announcer, they were doing this as a double protest: against contractors who were constructing new university buildings for discriminating against black workers and also against the city police for brutally dragging a student out of a church where he had taken sanctuary. The action they were taking to protest the racial discrimination seemed in a muddled sort of way commensurate to the magnitude of the injustice itself—*this* specific political action against *that* specific social evil (though unions are more guilty than employers of the racism in the building trades and though the university had only discriminatory contractors to choose among). But sanctuary? Not only did sanctuary fall into desuetude hundreds of years ago in Europe, before Christian America got started, but the young man, though he was not a Christian, had taken asylum in a Unitarian Church—and the Unitarians themselves are in doubt how Christian they are. It sounded like a parody: instead of a Christian subject's taking refuge in a Christian church from a Christian king's soldiers, a non-Christian citizen in a dubiously Christian church was claiming immunity from arrest by a secular democracy's cops, though he lacked custom to support him and though they lacked fear of sacrilege to give them pause. This must be a put-on, but who was trying to put on what?

When I got to the home of a professor friend, I learned three more things. The first was that an important part of the reason the young man had been treated harshly was that he used and advocated the use of drugs; the cops who had hauled him in were from the narcotics squad. The second was that the chief of this squad was commonly thought to be under the direction of, and possibly a member of, the Mafia. The third was that another professor's son, a freshman, had telephoned his mother a little before seven to say he wouldn't be home for dinner because he was liberating the administration building. When she began to expostulate, he said he had to hang up, there were twenty other boys and girls lined up at the pay phone waiting to call their mothers. He got home by midnight, and even while scolding him, she filled him with hot chocolate and toasted cheese sandwiches—his real mother thereby supporting his transgression against his Alma Mater.

The president of the university obtained authority to order in the police when he thought the time right, and then, having consulted with the executive committee of the university senate, he sent into the occupied building professors whom the students were known to find congenial. They talked all night in relays. By seven in the morning, most of the students had gone home and the rest were tired. When the president told the holdouts that, if they did not peaceably evacuate the building, the police would go in and arrest them, they came out with their hands on their heads.

I witnessed two events. Shortly before two in the afternoon, going from one half of our wan symposium to the other, we passed through the central plaza of the campus. There, on a dry fountain, stood the leader of the uprising, exhorting a ring of two or three hundred students. In the hoarse voice of demagogic rage, his face a mask of Hate, he was speaking of the captain of the narcotics squad. "This man is not a human being. He must be exterminated on sight."

In the symposium hall, we had barely started when sixty or seventy rebels filed in shouting and waving placards. They urged the audience to join them or at least to come at four o'clock to the men's gym where "the people will take over." After a while they serpentined out, and we continued. Presently, as one of the panelists was in the midst of his talk, a skinny sansculotte with long sideburns and granny glasses got up from the front row and began writing on the blackboard behind us. Someone had previously printed CONCERNED STUDENTS JOIN US, and he was scrawling over it the indispensable NOW. When we professor-participants glared around to see what he was doing, he scurried for the door muttering apologetically, "I'm sorry, the chalk squeaked."

At four in the gym the people did not show up, much less take over, and the whole thing fizzled out.

That evening I learned that the leader of this insurrection had recently dropped out of school, just six weeks before he was to get his A.B. with honors. He was one of the best English majors, his professors agreed; he had written that winter an especially fine paper on Diderot. One professor who had spent long hours that night talking the rebels out of further violence said that he was in favor of giving that budding intellectual his degree anyway, certifying him not for what he had accomplished but for what he *was*, and a couple of other professors agreed it would be a good idea. (Nothing came of this. One can imagine what the president of that university would have done had such a proposal reached his desk: he was a man who accepted and exercised the authority of his office; *in loco parentis*, he did what a parent should.)

I also learned that the enthusiasm for drugs on that campus was extensive. A couple of weeks before, there had been a symposium on drugs which had filled the gym to overflowing. At one point, a man got up on the stage to say that, after several years in prison, he had given up all drugs. Timothy Leary, the former intellectual, now guru, who took over from Aldous Huxley the role of sanctioning the use of drugs, said to this man, "If you mean it, take your clothes off." The man stripped, and went on speaking. The panelist on the stage who was disturbed most by this sincere nudity was the Black Panther, who kept saying, "Man, get dressed. Come on, man, put 'em back on." But then, it isn't Paradise or lotus land the Panthers want now, it is a fair share of the earth; however confused with Enlightened fantasies, they are still in politics; there is at least an off chance that, if they refrain from mass martyrdom and get what they say they want, they would stop. . . .

Not enough that a lot of these would-be revolutionaries should be kids with tin soldiers. Not enough that their leader should be a student of literary art mouthing murderous clichés. Not enough that the most important police officer involved should perhaps be a shield for criminals and himself a criminal. Not even enough that an intellectual professor who counseled restraint and legality at one time should recommend at another that the leader of this insurrection be given a degree he had neither earned nor asked for, thereby rewarding him rather than punishing him for his violent words and illegal acts. Worst of all, the crown of my confusion, was this: what the students were most enraged at, far more than at the evil of racial discrimination in the building trades, was that the police were making it hard for them to get all the drugs they wanted.

That episode generated more turmoil in me than I could keep down with laughter. "I won't be home for supper, Mom," and "I'm sorry, it squeaked," these were not enough. I felt like killing somebody; anybody; lots of people.

Twenty years after the war, at a time when my daughter was enrolled in my Alma Mater, my mother died. The morning of the funeral was very hot. After the service in the funeral parlor, eight of us in the immediate family got into a powder-blue Cadillac limousine, in which we were to follow the powder-blue Cadillac hearse. But our chauffeur had misplaced the key. The car had been sitting in the sun for a while, and since the motor was not running, the air conditioning was off. I was on a jump seat in back. Suddenly I felt the need to get out. I told myself with rational lucidity not to be phobic, this situation was merely recapitulating that long dug-up trauma in the Model T. For all the good this did me, I might as well have been reciting the Lord's Prayer or the Pledge of Allegiance. "Forgive us our trespasses as we forgive those who trespass against us one nation indivisible with liberty and justice for all." The need swelled toward panic and I reached for the door. There were no handles of any kind on the inside of the rear doors; the doors had to be opened from outside, and the windows could be lowered only by buttons on the driver's door when the ignition was on. I asked my brother in the front seat to get out *quick* and open the door for me. He did. Presently the chauffeur returned. I traded seats with my brother, and rode to the cemetery with my fingers on the door handle.

Since then, my claustrophobia has returned full force. But the most acute attacks do not seem to be provoked by my being literally caught in a boxlike place. The worst panics come when I have just lain down in bed. The feeling swells in me: *I have to get out NOW*. But it is not the bed, or the bedroom, or the house I have to get out of; it is my own body. So far, in fifteen or twenty minutes the feeling has faded away. I do not know why it fades, any more than I know what to do about it while it is there, except to contain it rigidly—the concentration camp of myself.

Lear to his two cruel daughters:

> I will have such revenges on you both
> That all the world shall—I will do such things—
> What they are yet, I know not; but they shall be
> The terrors of the earth!

But he did not do such things, because he could not. Then toward the end, to his gentle daughter:

Come, let's away to prison.
We two alone will sing like birds i' th' cage.
When thou dost ask me blessing, I'll kneel down
And ask of thee forgiveness.

But that didn't work either: she was murdered in the prison, and his heart broke. Perhaps Shakespeare himself found what to do? I think of him in the words he put in Lear's mouth: he took upon himself the mystery of things, as if he were God's spy. No one ever spied for, and on, God better than Shakespeare, and he wrought as well as any man ever did. Yet that didn't work either, neither for the world at large nor for us who admire him above all other writers. Here we are anyway. (Maybe it didn't work even for him: he practically disinherited one of his two daughters, leaving nearly all his property to the other.)

When I hear a revolutionary proclaim *All men are brothers*, I wonder "Who's the father?" and I can't help thinking of Cain and Abel, and the children of Oedipus and of Lear, and my own families, both the one I was born into and the one I have helped make. Being hypersensitive to sentimental metaphors, I object: "Isn't it enough for all men to aspire to be fellow citizens?" Nothing seems to me more dangerous than to model the city of Man on the city of God. In the city of God there is the perfect father and all men can indeed love one another as brothers should (and as they seldom, in this world, do). But in the fatherless city of Man, there is government, and—let's get right down to rock bottom—government is grounded on fear and domination.

The prime reason I have seldom disobeyed the law is fear of punishment if I am caught. I like to speed on the highway. The reason I no longer speed has little to do with the brotherhood of man or any other kind of love, and only a little to do with my own safety. It is because I have been caught twice by the cops and will lose my license if they catch me a third time and because they forced me to go to a class where a firm, gentle former truck driver scared me with statistics and movies. Once when I was a bureaucrat for the National War Labor Board, I was offered the opportunity to make some money by graft. The immediate and strongest reason I refused was that I had a neighbor—as good a man as I—who had recently spent a year in prison because he was caught embezzling. In us who are less than saints, fear has incomparably more to do with civic virtue than does love; as citizens we do good much less actively than we avoid getting caught doing wrong (and the obvious way to avoid getting caught is not to do wrong).

Likewise, in most of us domination is a source of strength and gratification. The family I came from was well below the middle of society in status, wealth, and influence, though by no means at the bottom; and I am now, in those same respects, well above the middle, though by no means at the top. I like it better up, not least because here I suffer less from envy. When I was fairly low, I was, after my father, a sort of Quaker; Quakerism encourages you to aspire to saintliness, and Quaker saintliness is a spiritual condition which, unlike Dante's hierarchical paradise, knows neither more nor less. I masked my envy for the high with pity: the poor-little-rich-boy syndrome. Now that I am fairly high, having little of the Buddha, the St. Francis, the Gandhi in me, I am not going to renounce what I have and descend in the scale if I can help it. Moreover, though I oppose the extremes of dictatorship versus slavery, of destitution versus untaxed, unearned, unreciprocated superwealth, and though I detest a scale which locates people in good part because of their religion or color, I am not going to try to abolish social hierarchy as such: it can't be done.

Aren't you glad that fear restrains the nuclear powers from using their bombs, and do you really believe that anything else ever will restrain them but fear, whether of each other or each of its own potential for evil? Do you blame Augustine for being a bishop for thirty-five years, or Joe Louis for slugging his way to the top, or Shakespeare, on the evidence of the sonnets, for feeling fine to be the best poet around, or Hirohito for assuming the throne that was his by right of birth and social consent?

What goads me to say such obvious things? Reaction to those who, appalled by the nightmare which the American dream has turned into and fuddled by the lie of egalitarianism and also enraged by the tedious imperfections of parliamentary reform, proclaim that fear and domination are evils which can be extirpated by altering the social order: *Liberty Equality Fraternity, NOW!* No. Fear and domination are givens; we are loaded with them. To suppress them is to make them evil indeed, and one of the highest benefits of government is to put them to good use. If my fear goes unaccommodated, will it not pollute my love? If my drive to excel, rise, dominate, is not harnessed and made responsible but is rather contemned, outlawed, and even denied, what is to prevent it from turning me into a cringing bully?

I am sure it is not admirable to be the way I am in these respects, but I am just as sure that it has very little to do with my nationality, religion, or race. This way I am is probably pretty much the way you are whoever you are, and society, for its good and ours, had better incorporate our tendencies somehow or other, not just lock them up till they burst out mad.

Let me take you for a few paragraphs into the labyrinth in which I cannot help enreasoning myself from time to time. I shall keep the pressure down as well as I can and the sentences straight. I do not think I alone am lost in there; without having actually met anyone else in there, still I keep sensing the presence of others. That is, though I am quicker than most to feel trapped and though I may even, out of some perverse impulse, have constructed this mental labyrinth in order to feel trapped in it, yet I believe I made it that way less because of irrationalities in my personality than because of the nature of man's reason, as evidenced in history and in common experience.

To begin with, I take it as given that scientism is the active faith of most men today. One bald instance. President Nixon is both a professing Christian and a true believer in 100 percent Americanism; yet his memorable comment on the first moon-landing was a tribute to science: "this is the greatest week in the history of the world since the Creation." His overlooking the Crucifixion only emphasized the sincerity of his gratitude to science for its visible gifts. The hidden emotional logic goes something like: "Science may not have created the world as God did, but it gives mankind the power to rearrange things better, which is more than *He* did for us—at least in this life, which is the one we know we have."

It seems to me that the most marvelous collective work of man is pure science—revealing The Truth by observing and symbolically explaining how things move and are related. Any pettiness of motive that may be involved in leading a man toward The Truth is absolved by his attaining it, and however painful the consequences of knowing The Truth we must not flinch from them. But there is no need for me to recite here the litany of praise for science; everyone knows it.

But, equally, it seems to me that the applications of science have often been dubious and by now are far more harmful than beneficial. Overpopulation, from medicine and hygiene; totalitarianism, impossible without electronic communications; pollution of the environment and of our own bodies; electronic mind control; overkill. But everyone knows the antilitany too. (I have only one contribution to make to it, a quirk of my own. I think that television as a social force is utterly pernicious: it has become as essential as the press to our politics; yet everything it transmits is transformed into numb entertainment. What we surely must need is a change of heart, but television subverts the very possibility. It is a toss-up which was the better show, the first moon-landing or the Kennedy-Oswald weekend. If the Crucifixion had been televised, Paul would not have converted the world but billy-grahamed it.)

Einstein seems to me a figure of Sophoclean grandeur. Purely seeking to understand the preestablished harmony of things, Spinoza-like, he had such thoughts as are the admiration of everyone who values truth and can think at all, and the energy those thoughts released in the world is the amazement of mankind. Yet when he offered to President Roosevelt his knowledge that an atomic bomb could probably be constructed, he released into the social world evils far more pervasive than those released by that claustrophobic conqueror—Lebensraum, Tomorrow the World—who exterminated peoples and to defeat whom was Einstein's motive for offering his knowledge to Roosevelt. Because Einstein thought more beautifully than anyone else of the era, all men are and will forever be subject to a strange anxiety which no previous men could have suffered. He helped technology, obedient to two masters, translate some of his thoughts into a monstrous new thing which the physicist had not intended but for which the citizen accepted responsibility.

Where is the fault?

The governors and generals are blamed, and are blameworthy, for using cruelly the weapons science and technology have given them. But it seems to me the scientists, including the technologists, are at least as much to blame, first for having constructed those weapons and then for having given them over. Scientists collectively are more intelligent than power men; they are trained to make decisions dispassionately; they devote their lives to the truth; because knowledge converts into power so readily, they have laid upon themselves the obligation to be wise. (This does not ignore but is over and above any plain ambitiousness that may also drive them individually.) Everyone can see, in history and in the world about us, what sort of men want to, and do, get power as rulers and soldiers. Could not thinking men foresee what it would mean to give power men limitless means of destruction? Only their faith could have blinded them to such evil.

It seems to me that intellectuals raged almost pathologically against President Johnson and "the military-industrial complex" for the Vietnam War, partly as a way to keep from facing the responsibility of their faith (science) for the atrocities of modern warfare. It was, for example, not a capitalist or a politician but *one of ours*, an honored and conscience-clear professor of science at Harvard, L. F. Fieser, who during World War II directed the "team" that developed napalm. (In an article in the *New York Review of Books* for 2 July 1970, George Wald does not mention this fact, though he is also a Harvard professor of science. Instead, he suggests that executives of a corporation such as Dow Chemical which manufactures napalm might well be brought to court as war criminals, because they have participated in a "crime against humanity.") Science authorizes intellectuals to question everything (except, perhaps, the value of reason itself). But their emotions tell them when they look at modern war: *This that science has done is dreadful.* They do not recognize the authority of emotion, and they have doubted all moral foundations to bits. So, in order not to doubt science away too, they blame this or that power man for even more than he is guilty of, or they blame this or that government, or, at the extreme, they blame government as such. And intellectuals as a class are far more important than their numbers: they counsel the great and teach the young.

Some societies have severely limited the spread of destructive knowledge. The Byzantines, for example, had a weapon called Greek fire which gave them an enormous military advantage against all enemies, and, though they were ruled by cruel, subtle men, they guarded the secret of this weapon so jealously that they kept it not only from their enemies but also, in a sense, from themselves: it is believed that no one man knew how to compound Greek fire. Perhaps several brought the components together, each ignorant of what the others knew, to be mixed by a man who knew proportions but not what he was mixing. In such a society, it would cost a man his head to invent napalm. In our society, it cost the Rosenbergs their lives to transmit to others (if in fact they did it) a few tiny secrets of A-bomb construction, even though the big "secrets" that really mattered were already available throughout the world in scientific publications.

Our rulers blame and punish technician "traitors" for our having monstrous weapons; with equal zeal, many of our radical intellectuals blame and would like to punish manufacturers for those weapons; and of course rulers (Spiro Agnew) and intellectuals (Paul Goodman) blame each other; but, until recently, neither has blamed the scientists much. As I half-blame them, though half I see them as trapped by reason itself. As you may be blaming me for blaming them. No end to this.

The original fault, as I see it, is limitlessness, not stopping in time. When reason was granted the godlike privilege of asking any question and publishing every answer, then science became possible (and industrialism, and the Enlightenment, and the suicide of Man). Religion and ethics both had always counseled obedience to law; for it is obviously in man's nature to rebel against restrictions. Then why was reason exempted, allowed to go too far?

It seems to me that reason was permitted—or wrested permission—to proceed limitlessly because of the very nature of it, us, the world. It provided men with incomparably the best safeguards against the material dangers of the world and much the best remedies for the anxieties of superstition and ignorance. It increased men's strength in most ways. Gradually they learned to trust it. "Well," said reason, "clearly we cannot know everything, so why don't we try to know as much as we can? God's will is mysterious, but the more we know of it the better we can praise Him." This seemed irreproachable. So far from denying limit, reason was seeking to establish it. But what you can prove rationally you do not *believe in*, as I do not *believe in* this pen in my hand. The rational proof of the existence of God began His de-substancing, and by The Enlightenment he was either everywhere or nowhere—small matter which, if he wasn't *there*—and Reason was strong as a giant. "Come on, let's look for new limits, in nature and in man." In other words, science, and men like gods. And in our as yet unnamed, postmodernist world, Nature and Man are attenuating as the Jewish-Christian God has already done.

Now that it is perhaps too late to do much about it, we can see that, as a horseman should accept the limits of his horse, so reason should have consented to be limited by the emotions. *To know more of the truth than you can feel is death to the spirit.* But how could that have been known ahead of time? How can you tell the limit to what you can feeling-know until you have gone beyond it?

Without roots secured in the irrational, no sanity is possible. We must have such roots even though they can also feed great madnesses, for the greatest irrationality of all is to purify reason and then turn it loose on the emotions or them loose on it.

Because our intellects made it possible for us to cause The End, we no longer just fear it, as men have always done; we now, like fallen angels can desire The End too. (Men always desire to do what they know they can do.) But this mind-made desire, this actualized fantasy, can hardly be admitted in full sanity. Both that inadmissible desire and guilt because of it add to the anxiety pervading mankind.

One way to deal with anxiety is to elude it. This as much as anything else I can think of—boredom, breakdown of sanctions, curiosity—accounts for the popularity of drug-taking among the young. It also helps account for their vagueness, their indifference to making arrangements for the future.

Men aggressive enough to become rulers cannot restrain themselves from employing the available weapons, unless faith makes them. Science is our faith, and whatever moderation scientists as moralists and citizens may counsel, the great, enviable power of science sets the example of limitlessness, of respecting no limit as fixed, much less sacred. The president of M.I.T put it neatly: "The solution to science is more science."

Moreover, it is tempting to use the example of science as a sanction for limitless egalitarianism: to pure science, every fact is intrinsically equal to every other fact, no question should be suppressed, no problem unsolved, no answer withheld.

Man is so made that to use his truth-seeking faculty as well as he can is to destroy himself. But this is mad. Therefore, man must be by nature mad. But how then can I, a man, know that "sane" is other than a mad illusion?

What can I do about this labyrinth except to not-think about it? But I live in the world. I can't not-think about it for long at a time. Even if I were a savage in a stone-age jungle in darkest New Guinea, the anthropologists and engineers and doctors are advancing all over me ready or not.

Perhaps there is some saving idea waiting to be thought. I do not have mind enough to think it first, but enough to think it if someone else explains it to me. Perhaps there is no such idea, but I hope there is something somewhere, for I need to change.

Meanwhile, just as I read and trust *The New York Times* more than any other newspaper, dull as it is, hidebound in its liberalism, so when I *have* to do something politically I continue to turn to representative democracy. So far as I can tell, it is the best of its kind available, though I am dead certain it is not enough.

But if the social tensions get much worse—the blaming, the evasions, the neglect of ruling and the refusal to be ruled, the wrong violences—I will be tempted by revolution instead. It would be *instead*, too, for I do not really believe that any revolution could do now what needs to be done. Even as romantic love, so exciting, so all-absorbing, so unconditional, can seem to a married person the cure to the strains of marriage but does not cure them, so revolution with many of us now: *a new start.* No. Yet I might yield to it. For, oh, it would feel very good not to have timorous, self-serving, envious, sort of decent people to put up with, but to have devils to kill and then to kill some of them. I might do it though I know ahead of time that, if I survived even halfway sane, I would be full of inexpiable remorse for my self-indulgence, my infidelity. Yet, there is so much *as if* to civility: *as if* men were decent, *as if* we were not suicidal, *as if* the social order were going to last. It would be wonderful to feel absolutely convinced that *this is what must be done,* as a citizen who is trying to hold things together never does but as a man with a gun in his hand can. I imagine that, if I were holding a rifle aimed at some only-rational counselor, some Machiavellian corrupter of power, *I would know what to do* and do it, and be wrong.

13

Never *Nothing*

The nothing to which nihilism aspires is a pure idea—like absolute zero, a limit which can never be attained. All particles, as they approach absolute zero, quit moving; cease to be knowable; lie as they were, like twigs in ice, mutually disconnected. Yet, even in that region of the negligible, they continue to exist, at least potentially; they continue to be related, at least in the eye of one who has observed where they stop moving. Nihilism is a philosophy of rage, for it can never attain what it wants, can be neither fulfilled nor permanently relieved. Its fulfillment would be to have all things cease to exist, the Void; failing that, its relief would be total lack of order in the motions of things, Chaos. But no matter what nihilism does, almost all things keep on moving describably almost all the time. It must substitute a relief which is occasional, fragile, and only sometimes permanent: disconnection.

To one like me, who has felt his own person pulled toward nihilism as a usable ideal, as a dissolver of doubt and a fixed point in shifting worlds, disconnection does not dwindle into familiarity, but retains its own full dreadfulness; and I see in nihilism the sufficient contour of the adversary. Potent as he is, some of his show turns out to be brag and threat: not he but we effect our disconnections. But he can make disconnection seem desirable; he encourages us to it; he can arrange things so that cold hatred seems good and moving love impossible, so that falling out of communion takes no more than indifference but entering into communion is difficult and risky. He tempts me, and I fear him.

The summer I was thirteen, I contained the ingredients needful to become a nihilist, except for a deficiency of rage. First of all, I had an absolutist cast to my Protestant mind; moreover, I could think abstractly, which is to say that my emotions could be as excited by the idea of a word as by its sound or by the image it evoked. I felt a metaphysical certitude that there was a right order hidden in things, not to be tampered with. Take the heavens.

We lived in the Southern California desert twelve miles west of March Field, a military air base. In those days airplanes were few, slow, and small, and even when one came fairly close overhead I was able to compare it to something I had seen in nature, as I cannot a supersonic jet. Most evenings the sky was clear, and often as the family would sit out in front of the house after supper, we would chat about the stars. One evening, to our amazement, great poles of light appeared on the eastern horizon and began tilting about the sky, now one, now another, sometimes three or four at a time, nine in all. We hadn't the vaguest notion what they were for. When they disappeared, the stars seemed brighter.

The lights appeared every evening. A neighbor who could afford to buy a paper on Sundays told us he'd read that war games were being held at March Field. War games? As long as they were games, Mother could ignore their purpose. As long as it was war, Father doubted what games they could be. We kept watching. Sometimes in one of the poles of light a spot brighter than any star would leap into being. Another pole would lean over to it then, and they would keep that bright spot in their intersection, following it. "Isn't it pretty!" cried Mother, and all of us except Father agreed. He had the habit, when he thought of something extremely disgusting, of dislodging both his upper and lower false teeth, pushing them forward between his lips, and clacking them, at the same time making an unvoiced *chrrr* in his throat. He did it now, and I listened attentively to whatever he would say, hoping he could make sense of that actual fantasy in the eastern sky. But all I heard him grumble was "a travesty," a word which I feared the dictionary would not help me understand.

"Daddy," I said, "did God make airplanes and searchlights?"

"I should say not," he answered. "The devil, more likely."

"Oh now," said Mother, "they make them in factories like so many other things."

"Well," I said, "did God want them to be made?"

Dad snorted. "The last thing in the world He wanted."

"Oh goodness," said Mother, "He can't do anything bad, and when anybody does do a bad thing, He won't let them go too far with it. There isn't anything *so* bad about airplanes. It's war that's bad, and people've always made war. So."

Dad spat.

Among the preconditions of nihilism, one of the most important is to be sure not only that there is a preordained order to things but that this order is worthwhile and means something and that what it means is Christian. The philosophical and emotional ingredients of nihilism are universal enough; but the special configuration of ideas and feelings which produced the word, and the need for the word, "nihilism" did not occur until late in the eighteenth century, after rationalism's full-scale assault on Christian belief. Zen Buddhism, as I understand it, is in one respect exactly the opposite of Christianity; the satori which is the goal of its stern discipline is sudden enlightenment, an essential part of which is realization of the ultimate nothingness of the world; after and only after such awareness, according to Zen teachers, can one return to one's ordinary self there to live in peace, as it were blest.

Even for a Christian writer, direct experience of the void does not have to drive toward nihilism but may seek a purely aesthetic expression; Mallarmé is the laureate of such experience. Nihilism, as I conceive the matter, is an ethical impulse: it is fed by, expresses, justifies the rage of some whom rationalism has unchristianed. It is the dark side of the Enlightenment. When science secularized the universe, some could not get over a sense of having been betrayed: divinity had been the meaning of things, Christ had been love and hope, limit and vengeance had been God's, there was something to die into. Hume shook them, and Voltaire laughed at them in their shaking. They took vengeance to themselves. Nihilistic writers are less interested in expressing their views, aesthetically, than in impressing these views on their readers, morally. They do not cringe in apathy from the tempter's logical whisper, "There is no meaning to the world, so nothing matters." Nor do they give the Zen answer, "Nothing doesn't matter at all." They cry in response, "Oh, nothing matters in the highest, nothing matters more than anything." But they are unsure, being absolutists, whether what they are saying makes good sense; so they shout louder and louder, to cover up their doubt.

The winter before the war games, on the school bus, I had made friends with my first atheists, the Babcock brothers. When I told my parents this, they did not outright forbid me to see the Babcocks. Mother gave me to understand that they were not nice people. But I had been to their house for supper, and the Babcocks were a whole lot better mannered, more thoughtful, and more fun to play with than any of the lunks I'd met in Sunday school. Mother was wrong, but maybe Father was right. He said you couldn't trust appearances. But if the Babcocks had not gravely told me they believed there was no God, I would never have guessed it. How could anybody, especially a family as nice as the Babcocks, not believe in Him? Father was wrong too: I could not distrust their appearance of sincerity. I was especially perplexed by their calmness about it; but the very conception of third- and fourth-generation atheists was beyond me then. I quit stopping by their house on the way home from school, but I also quit going to Sunday school, unless Mother made an issue of it.

In my disturbance, I actually read the poem on a faded old sampler that had been on the kitchen wall as long as I could remember. "Things are not what they seem," one line read.

"Mother," I said, "why is that there?"

"Great-Aunt Hattie made it and gave it to Mama before I was born," said Mother beaming. "Isn't it pretty?"

"Yes, but look at what it says."

"Such a sweet little poem. Longfellow." She chose another line: " 'Life is real, life is earnest.' "

"Yes, but," I quoted meekly, " 'Life is but an empty dream.' "

That made her dig in her ear with her little finger. She gave me a somewhat haughty glance and told me to quit picking at myself all the time. I smiled inwardly, a surreptitious rebel congratulating himself for striking a blow for freedom when all he's done is to give the rug under Mama a little jerk.

My confusion became quite desperate, and I yearned to be rescued. Here I was with a John Bunyan farmer for a father and a Queen Victoria housewife for a mother. But this was the 1930s! Surely something marvelous must be right around the corner waiting to rescue me. But what was it? I began having again the recurrent dream I'd not had for three or four years, about the end of the world. Trouble swarmed me.

There was sex. I was thirteen, and for some time I had been churned to a helpless and buried alarm by unexplained alterations in my body; they had set me rummaging through dictionaries and encyclopedias, from which I'd got a new word at least, puberty. I was ready to be got at by sexology, whose zeal it is to divorce sex from love, leaving it up to you to remarry them if you can.

And there was success. That year, I read a popular book called *The Psychology of Success,* and I watched my father. Success was of the spirit, I had no doubt, certainly not of material goods; it was sort of the way you knew you were tuned in right on Progress; above all, it was not of money. Father scornfully referred to money as "the Almighty dollar," though sometimes he would talk glowingly about what he was going to do when his ship came in. Meanwhile, we did not have enough to live on—this was the depth of Depression—and his face would contort when he had to appeal to an old maid cousin of my mother for money. There were two terrible days when he lay on what he announced must be his deathbed, sometimes moaning, out of his head, "A failure, I'm a failure." Thirty-five years later when he actually died, he didn't have a dollar to his name—he was that kind of failure. But he was attended by his children, who mourned for him—not that other kind. Though I am not likely to doubt my failure if it comes, I could never be certain of my success: having lost every shred of faith in Progress, I don't know what success is if it is.

But of all the qualities which contribute to a man's driving toward nil, I was perhaps best provided with ignorance and impotence. I was so ignorant of the stars, for example, that I knew almost none of their names, much less what astronomy said they really were; knew almost none of the ways in which they moved, much less the laws of their motions. I knew enough, however, to realize that my ignorance was greater than it seemed, for most stars, I had heard, were invisible to the naked eye and even of those I could see most had no names. In my political ignorance, I held in disrespect any customs or laws which had not been commanded by God, that is to say, most of them. I recognized God-and-me and you-and-me. But the network of connections which I now call society and the state was a vague, troubling thing in Washington called the Government; it had been ordained for the good of us all by our Founding Fathers, yet somehow it was also a fraud. Increasingly, as time went on, it got between God and me and between you and me. As for my impotence, it was massive. What could I do to set things straight? War games, the hard times that were making my father miserable, atheism, fraud, puberty—there was only one thing I could do much about, my own ignorance. But such was my frame of mind that every step forward made me realize not how far I had come in knowledge, but how very far I had yet to go in order to get there, and finally to realize there was no *there* to get to, learning was a way without end. The awareness that there is no end to learning did not fill me with joy at the prospect of inexhaustible riches ahead, but with a heavy sense of inadequacy. What kept me going was pleasure in the going—I just liked to learn.

Ignorance, yes; impotence, yes; but raging hatred, not so much. In part I lacked it because in my half-Quaker, half-Methodist family no taboo was stronger than the prohibition against anger and I had not been endowed with more of it than I could contain. However, the younger of my two brothers, when he was two, occasionally took to crying so hard that he held his breath till his body arched taut as a bow and he turned white about the mouth, then passed out. He did not perform this alarming action for any obvious reason; only once or twice, for example, did he do it after being punished for disobedience. Mother attributed it to green apricots, Father to an ornery streak in his character, but they agreed on calling it a seizure. Cats had *fits*, and *seizure* vaguely implied that he had been invaded—I must say his strumming body looked seized, possessed, by something outside himself. *Temper tantrum*, which they rejected, allowed for the notion of an anger so great you might obliterate yourself with it. Why should, *how could*, their baby be that angry? As for myself, it is only now in my post-Quaker, post-Methodist, relativized middle age that enough rage has been released in me to stain my vision from time to time. But in part my rage then continued deficient for lack of food; helpless as a cave man surrounded by mastodons, it was starved by the very enormity of my complaints. What I saw as wrong was so vast there could be no one worth blaming for it but God. How blame God? Perhaps if someone had tempted me to, I would have tried to blame Him. In fact, as close as I came to it was during the winter after the war games. I was standing one day in an aisle in the public library, thumbing through a fat, blue book entitled *Adolescence*, extending my ignorance of sex. A fellow came up whom I had been avoiding on the school bus because once he had nagged at me all the way to my stop that the Bible said the earth was flat so why did I think it was round. Now, staring at a cross section of the female organs of reproduction—the diagram, for all it meant to me, had as well been of the *begats* from Abraham to Noah—when that fellow accosted me in the library I felt caught in a surreptitious act; but he did not so much as glance at *Adolescence*. He was five years older than I, he had borrowed a nickel from me once and never paid me back, he belonged to the Epworth League, he was a born used-car salesman. He asked me, his fat eyes puckering, his voice sticking so that he had to clear his throat, whether God existed. I half turned, said yes of course, and put the book back on the shelf. He asked me what made me think so. I said I didn't know. My discomfort was so intense that my responses dribbled off into mutters, and he went away. What right did he have to ask me that question? Who was I to say whether the earth was round and God existed? I could not imagine that the world could exist without God to make it and keep it going; that prank of pure reason, "maybe the world isn't," illusion without reality, had not occurred to me yet. It had also not occurred to me yet that God might not be good—evil was our doing, that seemed clear enough. God could not not be, God could not not be good, so why did He let half-baked used-car salesmen who weren't dry behind the ears yet ask me whether He existed? Without knowing it, I was ready to hate Him and even to cry He did not exist. Instead, there chancing to be no nihilists about to tempt me, to authorize rage for me, I neither looked straight at the whole confusion I was in nor went away from it, but messed around, avoiding.

A Christian's cry *There is no God* reaches back to the baby's ultimate horror: not of dying, which is beyond his imagining, but of his parents' abandoning him, which he can imagine every night when he is put to bed. But the crier is also an older child brooding: What evil made them do it? What is wrong with me that they can get along without me? Now suppose a child of heroic aggressiveness, vitality, and imagination, who fantasies every leave-taking as an abandonment. He does not rest content, like a normal child, with giving his parents when they return a few punishing, safe blows; he wants to beat them savagely for having refused to fulfill his fantasies by really abandoning him. It comes to seem to him that the pain of actual abandonment would be a relief from the horror of fantasied abandonment, that the absolute knowledge of their vileness would not be as agonizing as the unconfirmed suspicion of it. Wanting most what he most dreads, he dare not hurt them directly, for then he would have to admit that he *cannot* make them abandon him. Instead, he blurs things over by saying how vile they are and how vile he is, and he becomes obsessed with vengeful fantasies. Contorted by horror and guilt, cancerous with unacknowledged wishes, almost the only relief, even temporary, he can find from this fearful tangle is to deny connection: these cannot be my true parents, I must be a foundling. *There is no God*, the nihilist howls, *there never has been One, and anyway He is dead.*

Nihilists are a missionary sect. Believing in nothing, doubting everything except their own doubt, they also want you to believe in nothing, at least to doubt everything. There are a few, to be sure, who do not proselytize, solipsists like Kirilov in Dostoevsky's *The Possessed.* Believing that the only reality was what he knew, he was able to cause everything to cease to exist by ceasing to know. He shot himself. But few go that far out on the scale of solipsism—another approach to absolute zero. Most nihilists and all nihilistic writers, ground in the jaws of contradiction, believe in nothingness and disconnection but need company. They are so offended by your existence, to say nothing of any sign you may show of conscious and moving love, that they set out to do what they can to pollute you; but to do that, they have to connect with you at least a little. If they get you to undermine and subvert as they are doing, you may not have joined them exactly, but you will at least be disconnected in the same region with them, close enough so that there are others to be torn apart from.

Most of my life I have earned my living teaching college English. It is a cardinal point of the profession that we must stir up the students, especially the freshmen, ask them provocative questions, challenge their assumptions. When I was forty and had thoroughly mastered the pedagogy of undercutting, I was teaching at Barnard (the girls' college of Columbia where intellectual subversion is even more orthodox than it had been at Berkeley where I got my degree). One day in midterm, a girl in a freshman class, tossing her head in evident pain, asked me, "What are you trying to do to us?" "Shake you up." "Well, you're not shaking me up," she said, "you're breaking me down." Her hands were trembling, her eyes looked askew, when she lowered her head, her hair straggled over her face unkempt. The word had become flesh—my words, her flesh—in a way I had not foreseen. I began wondering what other words of mine had been doing, invisibly to me, once they got into young people, and I have taken greater care with them since that day.

"A nihilist," said Arkady in *Fathers and Sons,* and he ought to know since the word came into circulation chiefly as Turgenev's name for him and Bazarov his mentor, "a nihilist is a man who does not bow down before any authority, who does not take any principle on faith, whatever reverence that principle may be inshrined in." Stephen Dedalus in *Portrait of the Artist as a Young Man* held as a secret motto Lucifer's formula of defiance: *Non serviam.* Back in the days when the West was still in the process of declining, sentiments like Arkady's and Stephen's looked pretty horrific, established a kind of ultimate, a limit. But, to us who come after Stalin and Hitler, those romantic nihilists seem high-minded dandies: like Satanists at a black mass, they strike attitudes which are never quite free of the ludicrous. You won't serve, eh. What will you do then? "Forge on the smithy of my soul," said Stephen, "the uncreated conscience of my race." How gorgeous! And how empty. And how very dangerous: the moment you convince yourself that your race has not already created its own conscience, for better or worse, you are free to impose your will on it like an ideological despot. Joyce doubted himself into a palsy. Shaking with uncertainty, marching under gorgeous, blank banners, he sought relief by destroying and by imposing his will on you through words: the Lenin of literature. *Because nothing matters, only I matter; because words matter to me most, I shall tear out their meat and make handsome designs of their shells. To read me at all you must submit to me.* He made of art a reversed religion, and his greatest accomplishment was to make of himself a travesty of a saint, make of his own life a parodic work of great art. For my part, I value Richard Ellmann's unimposing biography of Joyce above any of his own imposing books.

Romantic nihilists generally, not being of Joyce's heroic proportions, were not steadfast in what they wanted; often they wobbled into the simplicity of merely hating. The trouble was, they could not help hating many things worthy of hatred—injustice, hypocrisy, abuse of power, false ideals. So, which side were they on? Both sides; a dilemma. They desired to heal the social wounds, but saw these as so extensive that they despaired of accomplishing this desire. To escape the dilemma, they would bring injustices to an end, not by establishing a better order, but by wrecking the social order which created the injustices—by every means, from political murder to intellectual subversion. All the same, to us who have seen in Germany a great nation parody-ruled by a sect of fundamentalist nihilists denying the good and loving everything vile, romantic nihilists seem archaic and almost congenial: somehow, they dream, somehow, if we just destroy zealously enough, somehow love and community and the good will manifest themselves in history. Myself, I no longer believe in that phoenix much, but I feel a certain kinship to those who do. In a world whose chairmen are ready, for so stunted a reason as national rivalry, to reduce the earth to polluted ashes from which no phoenix could rise, thereby parodying nihilism itself, malice putrefied into slobbery, evil as stupidity—to us, in such a world, even the most assertive nihilism repays looking at, it is majestic, it has character, definition. I would rather contemplate the king of hell than the pro tem committee to homogenize the world. He is my adversary, whom I shall not become; mediocrity dissolves me.

In this America we have made where it is hard to love, if you love anything bigger than the house on your back you very likely also hate our society—unjust, ugly, violent, more hypocritical than it need be, disturbed by lying dreams, using money to measure worth, all the time measuring worth, distracted and addicted to distraction. Indeed, so strong is the revulsion against the world we have made (not only in America but throughout the West) that literary nihilism can and does justify itself as being able to express this emotion. Our world is disordered? Very well, a true expression of this experience of disorder must itself be disordered; some novelists allow chance to enter into or even control the sequence in which their pages are assembled for publication. Our world is vile? Only vile words, chant The Fugs, among many, can express its vileness adequately. Senseless? Let the poem be one word printed as many times as the page will hold—a device first used by a dadaist and since adopted by advertisers.

There is a certain force to this line of argument, and it helps explain why nihilism has become chic in recent years. If you can't understand a play, for example, *Tiny Alice*, in which playwright and producers show every sign of confidence that they know what they're up to, then your confusion itself must be the end they are after. If the play seems to mean something and finally denies meaning both within itself and in its subject, that is because the world only seems to mean but really doesn't. Relax and enjoy. Confusion, false promises, sleaziness, and blasphemy can be quite charming when nothing is at stake. Albee accommodates himself to fashion: he muffles the play's nastiest insult in argot, a snigger for the *in* crowd ("tiny alice" is buggerese for "tight asshole"). Genet is a rougher type entirely; but though he openly sets himself against the audience, fashion has nevertheless been able to accommodate to him. Do the characters in *The Blacks* seem to assault the audience? Not really, says fashion, what they are really doing is expressing their hostility—and how deliciously they do it. Myself, I share serious nihilism's respect for the power of art: I find genuinely nihilistic art troubling and dangerous and in no way delicious. At a tense moment of Genet's play, in the performance I attended, a black actor pointed his accusing finger at my white face; I felt the anger at him and at Genet which, I believe, Genet intended me to feel, and I did not enjoy feeling it, as Genet intended me not to. Expressing is only part of what art does; arson may be the firebug's mode of expressing himself, but that's the least of my concerns when I find my house on fire.

If the chic aesthetes identify expression with communication, the moral bigots, the book-burners, go to the other extreme by identifying impression with communication. In my view, things are more complicated than this either/or allows for. A play well performed expresses something of its playwright and its age, and if it is great enough it will express something important in actors and audience of any age; but it is also a new thing in the world with power to impress itself on its audience, to affect them, to change for a while the way they see, or even what they see. Attitudes control actions to some degree, and ideas can modify attitudes in those who are vulnerable to ideas. I have seen a student's pupils dilate to a new idea as to belladonna. What about those who are vulnerable to poetry, as I am? How can I not believe it has power to modify my attitudes when I have known it to change me directly? While taking a deep, unsteady breath after reading *The Rime of the Ancient Mariner* the winter I was twelve, I realized that what I was going to do in life was to write stories and poems. Coleridge, not intending anything of the kind, expressing who cares what?, altered the way I breathed and moved. So, a few years later, did Kafka in *The Castle*—that unfinishable tale of incomplete connections. What about writers who intend to use their force to alter the way I see, love, shall die? How can I not take their intention seriously?

Recently a good deal of favorable attention has been paid to some fictions which jerk themselves up to a certain vigor whenever they describe acts of sex or violence, or best of all sexual violence. The most substantial such book I have read is *Naked Lunch* by William Burroughs. By breaking down narrative coherence and syntax, he aims both to disgust and to confuse his reader. He pushes the rhetorical disintegration so far that only an effort of will could slog me from one sentence—one word-clump—to the next. It is a very modern book: in the democratized West generally and in America especially, the idea of subordination as a good has been so spoken against that even the elemental authority, that of parents over children, has been shaken, and no book assaults subordination more vigorously than this one, narratively, ethically, grammatically. Presumably, Burroughs does this as a form of insubordinate rebellion, but so wholesale is he that, there being no sense of subordination left, insubordination has no meaning either; having leveled authority, he rebels against difference; blur is left. There are people, worthy of respect both literally and morally, who think this shattered fiction expresses the age profoundly. Though I think otherwise—what appalls me about our age is the grinding clashes of monstrous superorders—I can sympathize with that position. Burroughs's destructiveness, disgust, and confusion are embodied in shards of images, broken rhythms, felicitous phrases, and spasmodic actions, so powerfully that I can see how some, having in themselves similar feelings, are grateful to him for finding ways to express those feelings. But to call the book's chaotic vividness high moral order, great satire, is like saying that, because plants must be fertilized, mulch is as fine as flowers. Satire addresses itself morally to the understanding, whereas *Naked Lunch* subverts understanding. When a would-be satirist immerses himself for too long in the ugliness he loathes, that ugliness will become part of him; as in a prurient censor at a dirty movie, behind his zeal to destroy ugliness lurks avidity for it; the satire which he intends to be cleansing, instead adds to the world's ugliness. Such a book does not just express the author's disgust and confusion; even more important, whatever he may announce elsewhere about his intentions, the book releases disgust and confusion in the reader, without containing it within the forms of art. When I read with such revulsion, the fellow feeling is blurred from my pity till all that is left is that sense of superiority which makes pity so tricky an emotion at best. "At least I'm nowhere near as bad off as they are."

Literarily, the only nihilists of our age that amount to much are Beckett in his plays and Genet in his autobiographical writings.

Beckett's fiction inverts toward solipsism, carrying parody as far as it will go on its own power, to its deadest end. *How It Is* consists of the ruminations of a consciousness, presumably human, crawling blindly through mud. Beyond that is parody pure, words selected and arranged by a computer programmed to a table of random numbers. Then comes the antibook itself, a boxful of blank pages. But there is a contradiction built into any finally nihilistic parody of art—a concert or play consisting of a half hour of silence on an empty stage, a black rectangle hung on a museum wall, a lump of ice melting on a pedestal. Since they don't communicate anything in themselves, you have to have explained to you how they are supposed to communicate nothing. What they get across is the extraneous meaning which their makers or exegetes tack onto them. They are vacuous icons; pretending to be images of nothingness, they are signs pointing toward a concept of nothingness. An extreme parodist is really a metaphysician using his work of antiart as a club to beat you with.

But Beckett's plays, especially *Waiting for Godot*, which is no parody, must surely be the handsomest work of literature making a nihilistic statement. The very handsomeness subverts the message. "The world is without meaning and hope." Really? Then why does saying it elegantly matter so much? Besides, the characters in his plays are marvelously connected with each other and with us. Maybe we are abandoned in a world that doesn't mean anything ultimately, but Beckett has made a bit of it mean something to a good many of us. I can think of more nihilistic things to do than that.

I believe that Nazism, by figuring nihilism forth so brutally *out there*, altered the nature of subsequent nihilistic writing. Once a fantasy has been realized in inescapable fact, it cannot thereafter be written about seriously in the same way. After the Nazis, either nihilistic writers descend into and stay in the muck like Burroughs—worse, into the chic like Albee—or else they must be honest writers when they put pen to paper, like Beckett and Genet.

Genet's fiction and drama, though powerful, fail to satisfy formally, but his autobiographies, especially *The Thief's Journal*, do not have to offer structural satisfaction, since a flaw of the part does not much weaken the whole; they chronicle the spiritual life of a nihilist superbly. What Genet found as he approached the dead center of his self was what Dante found as he approached his moral center, fraud in its purest form, betrayal. But whatever Genet the man in history may have done and aspired to do, the character in this confession knows when he lies, and the writer of it tries not to lie. Maybe he does it out of Satanlike pride, as he claims. "It is perhaps their moral solitude—to which I aspire—that makes me admire traitors and love them—this taste for solitude being the sign of my pride, and pride the manifestation of my strength, the employment and proof of this strength. For I shall have broken the stoutest of bonds, the bonds of love." But he is not totally given over to solitary pride. "And I so need love from which to draw vigor enough to destroy it!" Evil yearns to parody love to extinction—knowing that this cannot be done. Genet refers to his book as the "pursuit of the impossible Nothingness," and he is right. For by its very excellence the book denies nothingness. For a poet, whatever has a name exists: never *nothing*. As a literary nihilist Genet has two fatal flaws—he loves the beautiful, finding it especially in perverse forms but also in undisguised openness, and he is usually as honest as he can be. (His grandiloquence and glittery paradox can be mostly attributed to French prose. "I shall impose a candid vision of evil, even though I lose my life, my honor and my glory in this quest." Every competent proseur flashes out sentences like this by the gross.) But literary honesty, being a form of communion, threatens that solitude, that disconnection, of which Genet boasts. "By the gravity of the means and the splendor of the materials which the poet used to draw near to men, I measure the distance that separated him from them. . . . If the work is of great beauty, requiring the vigor of the deepest despair, the poet had to love men to undertake such an effort. And he had to succeed. It is right for men to shun a profound work if it is the cry of a man monstrously engulfed within himself." Genet as writer did not stay at the dead center which he says he strove for as character. (The tension between Genet-writer and Genet-character is the strangest I know, stranger even than that in Boswell.) Genet betrayed his betrayal by writing a book which is at once against and with us. It lays bare the moral nature of a nihilist without itself being an instrument of nihilism. Why? Because he went to Germany in the thirties. At first he was "excited at being free amidst an entire people that had been placed on the index." Then he thought to himself, "If I steal here, I perform no singular deed that might fulfill me. I obey the customary order; I do not destroy it." And before long what he "desired above all was to return to a country where the laws of ordinary morality were revered, were laws on which life was based." After that, he knew that he was defined by disobeying our law as certainly as we are by obeying it, that criminal and citizen are bound together by the law which separates them and which both of them need. After that, moreover, he knew that he needed moral words, the language of Christianity in which he had been reared. When he says "evil" he does not mean something else as Sade sometimes does, nor does he try to confuse you into thinking "evil" has no meaning, nor does he mean by it something personified by the devil. He is an intellectual: he does not worship a person, Satan; he loves an idea, evil; and when he says he loves evil, he means what he says as exactly as Milton's Satan, who was also an intellectual of sorts, meant it when he said "Evil, be thou my good." His experience of Germany in the thirties marked the moment after which nihilism could no longer be as it had been: thereafter, because the bad dream had been incarnated in an actual society, because the madness had been everted into totalitarianism, because, for one whose need is to disobey, having no legitimate authority to disobey is to lose all shape, thereafter whenever a nihilistic writer who could think well enough to write well enough to be worth reading sat down to write as authentically as he could, he would have to go straight and by just so much cease to be nihilistic.

Even in college I did not get into nihilism over my knees. We Berkeley radicals just before the war were all for manning barricades which we knew would almost certainly not be raised, all for no state and no war; but as soon as the Nazis began conquering, we were also all for strengthening our state in order to fight this war. A few months after Pearl Harbor, I was doing war work for the government. I made acquaintance with criminals, and dabbled in felony a couple of times. I declared there was no God. Yet I wouldn't take the whole plunge.

I continued to be deficient in anger. It did not occur to me to rage against God, since He did not exist; and though I was as adept as the next man at blaming society for people's ills, I could never quite get it out of my head that, even if the state was evil, it was people who made it evil—not just a conspiracy of Wall Street capitalists, Kremlin commissars, or Nazi gangsters, but the rest of us taxpayers too. There had not been planted in me early enough that root of permanent rage, contempt for authority, the set of disobedience. In the pre-Enlightenment of my childhood, obedience was an unquestioned good. We children usually obeyed: our mother because we should and our father also because he had a personal authority that made us want to obey him. In this world still, there is nothing I want more than to have over me authority I can respect and to exercise such authority over those beneath me. It is hard to have the one without the other. Under the presidents and congresses and governors of my life, I have learned contempt for most authorities, all right, but, because of my father, I have not learned to enjoy it as a good nihilist must.

More secretly, I suffered the shame of inadequacy: I could conceive more than I could imagine; for example, the end of the world. My father believed that the Bible prophesied it for the year 2000. My childhood dreams of the end of the world had been nightmares with power to wake me up crying, but their climaxes had always been an image—roiling clouds, a clap of thunder, a stump upside down in the sky inscribed with the words *The End.* The dream-image would represent the moment just before the end. Once I came to realize that I never, even in a dream, reached the end beyond images, I feared and knew I feared to go farther. Suppose that at the end there really was nothing? It was thinkable but unimaginable. The closest I have come to imagining nothing is to build on a childhood memory of shutting myself in a dark closet and squatting among the galoshes, wishing that the Old Hag of the House (my great-grandmother) would die horribly; I dared put the wish into words only in a place where I could not be seen, but not even there did I dare say the words aloud for they could be heard, by myself. By subtracting the wish and the galoshes and then adding the cold silence of a cave I once stayed still in for a few minutes, I lean as far into Nothing as I can reach. But this image, being so negative, so subtractive, provides a less satisfactory metaphor for Nothing than does one of physics' stark concepts: an antineutrino in the vacuum of furthermost space, an almost no-thing under normal circumstances, but, there in the unimaginable void, an almost no-thing lacking even energy, unlocatable, negligible.

But that is rather grand. Maybe it is just that I have always been too impatient to be a good nihilist. When I spoiled other people's pleasure or tranquillity, I wanted to be there to get the good of it. Sometimes, I would provoke my next younger brother into wrestling with me, so that I could get him down and lie spread-eagle on him till he beat his head on the ground in frustration. Once I wrote bad words on the wall of the school outhouse, in the clumsy block letters of the school bully. I never told anybody I had done this, but I was there when he was punished for what he had not done, there congratulating myself for having rectified an injustice—think of all the bad things he had done without being caught. I lacked the pure nihilistic zeal to spoil for the sake of spoiling. I once chanced to see a boy urinate on a box of apples which he had just picked and which were about to be taken to town for sale. He did not know I saw him; he would never know who bought the apples; those who ate them would not know the apples had been polluted; he would never know, in all likelihood, how or even whether the eaters would be damaged by what he had done. As I watched him, the expression on his face was serious, gloomy; his eyes did not dart about anxiously; he was not gleeful with naughtiness. I was outclassed, and slunk away.

I had a zeal for connection, and I was lucky in that there were no theories working against my need for friendship. Sexological instruction was viewed in those days, at least in the world I inhabited, as a form of pornography, titillating and shameful. There seems to me even less to be said for sexology than for the blind prudery that came before it. In sexology's glare, mystery shrivels, but for us it at least had dirt to survive in, the teeming filth of prurience. What do the young do now, for whom sex has been not only klieg-lighted but sterilized, who are so clear about the sixty-nine positions of sex that the infinite ways of love seem to them a fearsome labyrinth? Imagine being a young person skilled in operating your sexual feedback system, usually but not necessarily in adjunction to a self-regulating servomechanism of the opposite sex—all this before you are experienced in, much less committed to, that dark other-fucking by which and in which but not for which love is made. I would sooner kill someone with my bare hands, in that intense connection which natural fury drives us to, than fall into the habit of performing sexology's bright clear travesty of love which divorces body from spirit as cruelly as puritanism ever did. Believing that man is by nature a maker of taboos, I see the obscure, ambiguous sexual energies as being so powerful that they must surely generate in us some taboos, and when these taboos are detached from sex till it becomes simply pleasure, they do not just disappear but attach instead to love—*post coitum nihil.* I see the sleek body of aesthetic sex as encapsulating the spirit within it in a furious stasis, a tense, septic passivity like riding in a jet bomber seven miles off the earth where it's 80° below zero even on a summer day, an antiemotion with death in it, button-pushing remote-controlled unsurvivable death.

There are those from whom not even death has been able to disconnect me, especially my father. He was eighty when he lay dying, and he had suffered heart trouble for a long time; I was forty-eight by then and had been father in my own family for a long time. His left foot died two or three days before his heart stopped beating; it was hot summer, and the nurses left the sheet off him; we watched the dark-purple death mount his left leg and begin to mottle his right foot and leg; then his hands; then his arms. His toenails were long untrimmed, and the horny nail on his right big toe had scraped an oozing wound on the side of his left foot—perhaps it had itched as it was dying. The last time I stood by his bed, I held his purpling hand; it was cold and did not respond to my touch. For several weeks afterward, I could not readily fall asleep, as I had usually done, and I hardly trimmed my toenails. I do not know how long my father's dying would have continued to live in me had chance not exorcised it by bringing three events together late that fall. In the same week, two old friends of mine killed themselves; once, we had all three been very close; I dreaded what might happen if those self-destructions got down into me where my father's death still lived. But shortly before those suicides, it happened that I, the oldest of four children, had been appointed head of a committee of four to search for a new chairman of our English department. Never in my life have I undertaken an ordinary task in the line of duty with such intensity—an intensity which from here looks mildly comic—for it was more than a department chairman I needed to find. Before long, my left foot ceased to be so cold when I went to bed, and I ceased to be occupied by the insomniac fear that if I dropped off I might scrape my left foot with my right big toenail, which I took to keeping trimmed short. What survives in me now of my father was him alive, for in that appointed search and finding his death died in me.

At the bottom of hell, walking through murk toward the center of all things, Dante and Virgil cross a frozen plain, and here in the innermost region of windy cold, they find traitors totally immersed in ice haphazard as they fell, "like straws in glass," immobile, cut off from God and from one another. Here is disconnection pure. But in the murk at the center of the moral universe it is not nothing Dante finds; it is the huge, gloomy figure of traitorous Satan, the perfect rebel who dared refuse the perfect authority, the ultimately proud one who does not submit even in defeat but rears in ceaseless torment, weeping, raging, slavering, in his three mouths chewing the three greatest of human betrayers.

Nihilism has a comparable human figure, the Marquis de Sade, that three-faced absolutist. A need for coherence and honesty does not redeem his writing up into valuable literature. His books are like the hideous wings of Dante's Satan beating forth a freezing wind: their only virtue is power. With one of his faces Sade rages against God for having permitted evil in the universe, for having granted him the freedom to disobey. With another face he denies: denies that men have a common nature (which is vile in any case), denies that God exists (Who is to blame for everything wrong), contemns all custom as not being a sure reflection of the moral law (which does not exist either), asserts that we can be certain of nothing beyond our sensations and our egoes (thereby reducing value to *what I want*, for which there are two fundamental satisfactions, the orgasm and the imposition of will, me over you). But with his third face, Sade—the man more than the writer—shows melancholy vestiges of a love so strong that not even he could wholly pervert it: for example, as a functionary during the First Republic, he was imprisoned for lack of zeal in accusing and turning in for execution victims suspected by the Terror. Perhaps he was not moved to that action by love so much as by one of love's facsimiles, hatred of injustice—a risky passion for a nihilist, being easily mistaken for love and indeed sometimes engendering love. However that may be, it seems clear enough that the freedom sought by the cruel, powerful criminals of Sade's novels has nothing to do with justice, only with force; it is for themselves only. They have the bodies of men and the brains of *philosophes*, but they are conscienceless, being, emotionally, devouring babies.

But how is a writer to make his books into instruments of nihilism? Practically, how can a philosophical storyteller be compared to a bloody tyrant, Sade to Marat? What can even that most noxious of books, *The 120 Days of Sodom*, boast of comparable to the harm done by one of Stalin's secret police in the performance of one day's duties? What is a war game beside war itself? Perhaps doubt of this kind provided food for Sade's rage; perhaps overcoming that doubt, having to substitute mental defilement for physical destruction, increased his missionary fervor to insatiable frenzy. In any case, by the world at large these books are not considered symptoms of a mental disease so much as carriers of a moral one; it matters less that they can be considered expressions of a disordered mind than that they are intended to, and can, disrupt the mind on which they make their impression. To be sure, there are no corpses to point to which would demonstrate the power of Sade's novels to produce direct results. But their being banned in nearly every civilized country except ours, at least in the language of the country, attests to the power they are usually thought to have to shape people's attitudes.

The force of Sade's fiction is both general and specific. Generally, I believe, he and his descendants have made two radical contributions to the unfinished revolution that began with the *philosophes* his fathers. The *Sadistes*—not the sexual perverts but the adherents to the philosophy of *Sadisme*—have encouraged men to distrust experience (not your testimony about your experience, but my own experience in my own thoughts) and to deny community as a lying dream (not such and such an unjust nation in history, but the very idea of society, institutions, customs, laws). These radical distrusts are so devious and obscure that the vitiation they have caused cannot be demonstrated: all the same, I believe it has been far from negligible. An instance of the specific force of Sade's writing is the unbelievable inflation of the philosophical, scientific, and literary merit accorded his books by some who do not resist their power—his biographer Lely, Geoffrey Gorer, Simone de Beauvoir, among many. They compare him, seriously, to Nietzsche, Freud, and Shakespeare. They count the boredom of his books as a virtue, as being a part of his literary strategy. There are even those so chic they can say they enjoy his scourging fiction ("Epatez us again, Daddy-O, we love it")—which reduction, I think, would have enraged him yet more, for he intended his lashings to wound you morally, not titillate you fashionably. For other specific instances I must point to experience. I know a sophisticated literary critic of mature years, a professor at Yale opposed to censorship, who bought a copy of *The 120 Days* in English some years ago when he was in Italy and found himself, once he'd read it, uneasy at having it in the house.

He lent it to a friend, who tried to return it as soon as he found out what it was like, but the owner did not want it back. They wound up destroying the copy, they burned a book. Edmund Wilson, who likes to read at breakfast, has said *The 120 Days* is the only book he has been unable to read while eating, and he had to make himself finish it even in his study at night. For my own part, having spent a couple of hours reading around in it, I know that I *cannot* read that book.

For Sade knew how to spoil things in the reader's mind. He did not do it by violating narrative and syntax, making his books themselves confused in the manner of Burroughs; his prose is moderately elegant and his stories, though feeble, are shaped enough to provide occasions for the passages for whose sake they exist. It is in these many passages that his books accomplish their intention. Blasphemy, parody of moral structure as well as some straight literary parody, repetition, boredom in toxic but not quite lethal doses (Sade is the only writer who both bores and fascinates me), a slick gloss over mental blur, unresolvable paradox, dissolve of values from one end of the story to the other—all these are aids, they make their useful contributions, but they are not the main elements. The main things are confusion and defilement, that is, pseudo philosophy and massive pornography.

The philosophy, abstracted from the novels, is a sort of Humean parody of Rousseauism. Intellectually, Hume's skepticism is far better formulated and more devastating, but Sade's philosophizing, as it appears in the novels, hits harder imaginatively. (None of his ideas is original, only the way they are combined and used.) Philosophically, *Justine* is his central fiction, for not just the preaching author but the fable itself vilifies and ridicules and assaults the ideal of virtue in the person of the goody-goody heroine, who, abandoned by every lawful authority, is vilified, ridiculed, and assaulted by criminal force. As a character, Justine is as vapid as Pollyana, there's not enough to her to feel about one way or the other. But that very vapidity, though it is a reason the novel is without merit fictionally, helps one understand Sade because it makes Justine invulnerable to us emotionally; for the ideal which she incarnates could not be polluted by even Sade's hatred. Still, he knew it; he is at least that honest.

As I interpret the matter, it is his intention, in the name of unshackling us, setting us free, to undercut and confuse every hope of our ever knowing, much less attaining, the good—by assaulting religion and the religious, by sophistic reasoning, by the argument from comparative customs, by attributing to every action the lowest and most hypocritical motive. Of *Sadisme*'s entire arsenal of ideas, none is so damaging as its contempt for limits; it holds that to accept, much less to want, limits is mere atavism, a relic of our troglodyte ancestors who made taboos out of their fear and moral principles out of their taboos. We who are enlightened are beyond all that. But true *Sadistes* are not content with intellectual liberation alone; they want to be liberated morally as well, and, fired with apostolic zeal, they set about liberating others wholesale.

I hope this configuration of notions sounds familiar and current; for once an unchristianed Westerner grants, as very many do, that value comes only from one's own nature, *Sadisme* is hard to crack. In the ferocity with which it pushes toward its extremest statement, it is the most disquieting possible travesty of liberal, progressive attitudes. *If there are no moral limits, why not?* To this argument decent liberals have no adequate reply, only sentiments. *I don't want to. I wish you didn't want to. You must be sick.*

As for Sade's pornography, it is intentionally revolting. For him, love is a never-resting enemy that cannot be obliterated. Remember Genet: "I so need love from which to draw vigor enough to destroy it!" Sade knows that, if he is to impose himself sufficiently upon his reader, he must spoil love as best he can. The most intense form of love known to most of mankind is erotic communion, in which for a time things are what they seem and Another is not strange. Sexual intercourse can both make and be a symbol of making love; and love's perfection is what in more ceremonious days was called rapture or bliss (sexology teaches us to settle for simultaneous orgasm). It is this true dream of connection which Sade sets out to, and does, pollute—robbing love to pervert it. But his account of what he is up to is not, like Genet's, detached and lucid that we may understand, but steamy, blurred, turgid, that we may be uncoupled. A cartoon image that appears over and over in Sade's fiction in one form or another is of a hideous old man, rich, of high station, outside the law achieving a solitary sexual spasm while he is devouring the excrement of a beautiful young victim whom he watches being tortured to death by his brutal slaves. So put, such an image seems merely grotesque, but in the novels' detailed and exciting prose it has a certain force (and at least it is not death-sterile but full of filthy life). Still, that cartoon is nearly as far from my experience as an antineutrino in empty space. Pornography defeats philosophy: it is too ingenious, too pat.

I can more nearly reach the extremes of *Sadisme*, I can follow better the convolutions of its psychology, by remembering my little brother holding his breath. I imagine that the paroxysm bending his body taut as a strung bow ended in an obliteration more nearly total than orgasm even, that by annihilating his solipsist consciousness he annihilated all of us too and thereby imposed his will on his parents more cruelly than by any other act open to him—he was too young to know how to kill himself. In that little boy ashen with a fury the cause of which none of us understood but the potency of which was measured by its violation of our strongest taboo, hurting all he could, eyes rolled up till only the whites showed, froth at the corners of his mouth, I see Sade plain. That unappeasable baby is what a disappointed Christian absolutist had better have in him if he is to dedicate himself to taking vengeance on the world.

Genet, the whore's bastard, is luckier than Sade, the privileged nobleman. Because the world hurt Genet so cruelly when he was a child, because he was actually abandoned by his parents, he could hurt back at it with a free conscience, and out of simple fear that it, being so much stronger than he, would kill him, he dared try to please it by the very way he provoked it: his extremest fantasy is to be a saint—of evil. But Sade, who was not actually abandoned as a child, was unable to forgive the world for having pampered him; he interpreted every kindness as a sign of weakness, every mercy as a failure to stop him in time; and he dedicated his manhood to provoking the world to insult him relentlessly, that his fury might never dwindle into propitiatory gestures; almost nothing he wrote was meant to please the world, or did please it. By the common meaning of the word, the world has seen far worse sadists than the Marquis himself, but never a writer so devoted to polluting the wells of truth and love. Yet, since such malice exists in the world, and in myself, I am not sorry to have read a good deal of Sade's fiction: to confront an adversary as majestic as this is to learn something ultimately important about the nature of things and of oneself.

But I could never have confronted him by myself; to do that, I needed and got much help. At Christmastime when I was four or five, my father sang Herod in a nativity play at the Quaker church. I had not been to a play before, I did not know who Herod was, I sat beside my mother, the church was full of Friends. Father's robe and crown made him appear very tall, and the makeup, especially the heavy eyebrows, made him cruel and strong; everyone looked up to him, bowed before him. When the wise men told him what the bright star meant, he shouted that all the firstborn men-children in his kingdom must be killed. I was sheltered by my mother's arm, the room was full of tranquil-seeming people, that very afternoon he had kissed my elbow where I'd fallen on the ice and bumped it. But for these, I would surely have given way to the hysteria that swelled to bursting in me, for all that my emotions knew at that moment was that he wanted to kill me. For an hour that night he sat by my bed holding my hand till I dared to go to sleep.

Dante has helped me, too, even as I am sure he has helped unnumbered thousands of others, even as Virgil helped him. When the two of them had crossed that desolate lake, they came to Satan. Dante looked at him and understood what he saw—"if he were once as handsome as he is ugly now." But they did not stay long in that frigid "air of lost connections" (in Robert Lowell's phrase). Dante took hold of Virgil, who "caught hold of the shaggy sides," clinging to Satan for a while because there was no other way to go beyond him, and when they had passed through dead center in a kind of parody of birth, they turned around so that what had been down now became up, what left now right. Then, right side up, they went away, leaving that dark cave, which will always be there and which they could do nothing about, their ears no longer ringing with the howls of those whom

God had abandoned, of those travesty-babies in that dead womb, and they climbed back up to the world of light, where the sun and the other stars shine unobscured, where communion is possible.